A GRAMMAR OF THE PUKKHTO OR PUKSHTO LANGUAGE

A GRAMMAR OF THE PUKHTO OR PUKSHTO LANGUAGE

ON

A NEW AND IMPROVED SYSTEM

COMBINING BREVITY WITH PRACTICAL UTILITY, AND INCLUDING

EXERCISES AND DIALOGUES

INTENDED TO FACILITATE THE ACQUISITION OF THE COLLOQUIAL

HENRY WALTER BELLEW

GYAN

Published by

Gyan Publishing House
5, Ansari Road
Daryaganj, New Delhi-110002
Phone: 011-47034999, 9811692060
E-mail: books@gyanbooks.com

Distribution Network
gyanbooks.com
India, USA, Canada, UK, Australia, France

ISBN : 978-81-212-4399-5 (PB)
First Published, London, 1867

2nd Impression 2020

Printed at: Gyan Press, Delhi.

A
Grammar of the
Pukkhto or Pukshto Language
Author: Henry Walter Bellew

A

GRAMMAR

OF THE

PUKKHTO OR PUKSHTO LANGUAGE,

ON

A NEW AND IMPROVED SYSTEM,

COMBINING BREVITY WITH PRACTICAL UTILITY, AND INCLUDING

EXERCISES AND DIALOGUES,

INTENDED TO FACILITATE THE ACQUISITION OF THE COLLOQUIAL.

BY

HENRY WALTER BELLEW,

ASSISTANT SURGEON, BENGAL ARMY.

LONDON:

THACKER & CO., NEWGATE STREET;

TRÜBNER & CO., 60, PATERNOSTER ROW.

MDCCCLXVII.

STEPHEN AUSTIN,

PRINTER, HERTFORD.

DEDICATED

TO

BRIGADIER-GENERAL HARRY BURNETT LUMSDEN, C.B.,

COMMANDANT HYDERABAD CONTINGENT,

BY

HIS OBEDIENT HUMBLE SERVANT,

H. W. BELLEW.

PREFACE.

In submitting my Grammar of the Pukkhto or Pukshto language to the notice of the public, it is necessary that I should offer a few words of explanation as to the object of the Work, and the reasons that have induced me to publish it.

During ten years' service, more or less continuously on the Trans-Indus Frontier of British India, it has often occurred to me as a notable fact, that comparatively very few of the Frontier officials possessed any knowledge of the language of the people they ruled, or at all events, amongst whom they dwelt. And this the more so, as the Pukkhto Works of Vaughan and Raverty had already appeared, and for the past decade, at least, have been well known to Frontier officers.

But, notwithstanding the aid to be derived from these Works in the study of the language of the Afghans, the number of Pukkhto-speaking officers is, nevertheless, at the present time very small, though, in all probability, greater now than at any preceding period since our tenure of the Trans-Indus States.

This fact was exemplified in a remarkable manner, and their paucity no less severely felt, during the Ambela campaign at the close of 1863, at which time the officials with the British Force who could claim any acquaintance with the Afghan language were to be counted on the digits.

In January 1863, examinations in the Pukkhto language were

most instances, according to fixed laws of language, known to philologists, underwent alterations and modifications, more or less extensive or complete according to circumstances (varying, very possibly, with reference to their introduction in the first instance, colloquially or through the channel of written literature), so as to be adapted to the mould of the new dialect into which they became incorporated.

That the Pukkhto had already assumed its present form prior to the spread of the Arabs over Afghanistan, towards the close of the seventh century, when they first carried their arms towards India, would appear probable, since (although the Afghans have for many centuries adopted the religion and laws of their Muḥammadan conquerors) it has in no way materially been affected by contact with their language, for the numerous words and phrases borrowed from that source are very rarely found incorporated with the Pukkhto, as are words from the Hindī and Persian, but are always distinct, and in most instances used in an unaltered, or but very slightly modified, form.

Further, it would seem that the region represented by modern Afghanistan was in those times, and even for centuries preceding the Muḥammadan era, successively ruled by Persian and Indian sovereigns, as is evidenced by the coins of the Sassanian kings and Hindu Rājās, which are found in such abundance, together with the multiform relics of a Hindu people, in the numerous ruins scattered over this region at the present day. And such alternations of rule from Persian to Hindu and from Hindu to Persian, must, it seems probable, have continued for centuries subsequent to the time of the Saracen conquest, for we find that, even as late as the time of Maḥmūd of Ghazni, in the beginning of the eleventh century, a Hindu Rājā was ruling at Kabul. His subjects too, it is probable, were, as are the tribes of Afghanistan at this day, a mixture of aboriginal Indians and Persian colonists. Their descendants are probably represented by the Kafirs, Gujars, and other tribes of Hindu Kush and the Eastern provinces of Afghanistan (who at the present day speak dialects more or less Indian, and quite distinct from the Pukkhto), in the one case, just as in the other the ancient inhabitants of the provinces to the westward of Kabul are represented by the Tājiks and Hazārahs of this day, who speak modern Persian, or dialects but very slightly differing from it.

This persistence of the distinct and uncorrupted dialects, Persian on the one hand and Indian on the other, in the midst of a nation who speak a language manifestly consisting of a combination of both, is a noteworthy fact. More especially as the said nation, though it has for many centuries occupied its present ground at the point of junction between the Indian and Persian Empires—in the country known as Afghanistan to strangers, and as Pukkhtūnkhwā to the Afghans or Pukkhtūns—and more or less as the dominant race, since the tenth century, boast that they are a distinct nation, a peculiar people, separate from the tribes (whether Persian or Indian) amongst whom they are settled, and, claiming descent from the house of Jacob, declare that their ancestors were emigrants from the west.

But to enter here upon the question of the origin of the Afghan nation, an enquiry full of interest though it be, would be foreign to the subject of this work. It is hoped, however, that the preceding remarks will suffice as an indication to the student desirous of entering further into an analysis of the Pukkhto language, whilst by a reference to the Preface to my Pukkhto Dictionary will be found illustrations of the changes which words from the Persian and Hindī undergo on being transformed into Pukkhto.

With these brief indications as to the structure and family connection of the Pukkhto language, I trust that the details contained in the following pages, despite the many shortcomings, resulting from the hasty manner in which the whole has been put together, will in some measure facilitate its study.

H. W. B.

LONDON,
4TH JANUARY, 1867.

ERRATA.

Page 9,	line 16,	*for* "abolished e,"	*read* "abolished y."
〃 12,	〃 6,	〃 *mungal,*	〃 *mangul.*
〃 15,	〃 21,	〃 woman,	〃 wife.
〃 *ib.*	〃 31,	〃 wife,	〃 woman.
〃 27,	〃 6,	〃 ملا,	〃 مُلا.
〃 34,	〃 15,	〃 ٢٠,	〃 ٦٠
〃 43,	〃 8,	〃 *da dai,*	〃 *da de,*
〃 *ib.*	〃 32,	〃 *talali,*	〃 *tlali.*
〃 44,	〃 20,	〃 *tali,*	〃 *tili.*
〃 61,	〃 20,	〃 شِو يوُ *shiwi yū,*	〃 شِوي يوُ *shiwī yū.*
〃 62,	〃 1,	〃 We would,	〃 We will.
〃 63,	〃 13,	〃 شول *shwal,*	〃 شوه *shwah.*
〃 104,	〃 7,	〃 هيخري,	〃 هيچري.
〃 105,	〃 18,	〃 *lagkūtī,*	〃 *la-agkūtī.*
〃 115,	〃 5,	〃 Daghah,	〃 Dagha-ah.
〃 *ib.*	〃 19,	〃 dwāṛah,	〃 dwāṛa-ah.
〃 116,	〃 21,	〃 Gīdaṛl aka,	〃 Gīdaṛ laka.
〃 119,	〃 12,	〃 Māstah,	〃 Māsta-ah.
〃 120,	〃 16,	〃 ṭaga-ī,	〃 ṭagī.
〃 121,	〃 5,	〃 Haghah,	〃 Hagha-ah.
〃 136,	〃 40,	〃 wuwai,	〃 wu wai.
〃 137,	〃 11,	〃 haghah,	〃 hagha-ah.
〃 143,	〃 15,	〃 sakkht,	〃 sakht.

PUKKHTO OR PUKSHTO GRAMMAR.

SECTION I.

1. The Pukkhto or Pukshto in some respects resembles the Hindūstānī or Urdū. It has the same grammatical construction, and like it also is a mixed language, or, as the Afghans style it, a *gaḍa-wada-jiba*. Round a nucleus of original words it comprises a large number of foreign ones. These latter are mostly from the Arabic, Persian, and Turki on the one hand, and from the Sanskrit and Hindūstānī on the other.

a. The former, Persian especially, predominate in the dialects current in the western parts of the country, and the latter in those current in its eastern parts; the several nations from whom they have been derived bordering on those parts respectively.

b. Further, in the western parts of Afghanistan, and mixed with the general Afghan population, are numerous clans of Tajiks and Hazarahs, whose language is the Persian. And similarly, in its eastern parts, are the Gujars and Hindkis, whose language is a dialect of the Hindī.

c. Most of these foreign words are met with in Pukkhto in an unaltered form, and, except in the vicinity of the countries whence they have been derived, are for the most part used in composition only. The rest have undergone more or less modification, but the change is seldom so complete as to prevent ready recognition.

2. Pukkhto, as a written language, is seldom used otherwise than

in composition, as a vehicle for the literature and history of the nation. Epistolary correspondence and the general business of the country are conducted through means of the Persian, which is the court language, and used in preference to Pukkhto by the nobility and educated classes more or less generally throughout the country westward of Kabul. Again, the theological and judicial literature of the Afghans is almost wholly in the language of the nation whence they have derived their religion and laws, namely, the Arabic. This kind of learning, however, is entirely confined to the priesthood.

3. Owing to the restricted employment of Pukkhto as a written language, there is noticeable a considerable diversity in the modes of writing and spelling the same words, not only in different districts or provinces, but even in the same district, and often by the same author.

a. This difficulty, though at first a stumbling block to the beginner in the study of the language, is in fact more apparent than real. It is owing to the indiscriminate and seemingly capricious use of the modified forms of certain letters to represent sounds peculiar to Pukkhto, and varying in pronunciation as used by the different tribes composing the nation.

b. For the same reasons, the long and short vowels, as also a few consonants of cognate sound, are constantly met with changed the one for the other.

c. These remarks, if borne in mind, will, with the explanations hereafter given with the letters, in some degree simplify the study of the language to the beginner.

4. Pukkhto is written in the Naskh form of the Arabic character, and contains forty letters. With a few additions and modifications they are the same as those used in the Hindūstānī, with which the reader is supposed to be acquainted. The several letters used in the Pukkhto are shown in the subjoined table.

PUK̲K̲H̲TO ALPHABET, OR PAṬA-Ī (*Ḥurūfi-tahajjī*, A.)

FORM.	NAME. I.	NAME. II.	POWER.	FORM.	NAME. I.	NAME. II.	POWER.
ا	الف	*Alif*	*a*	س	سين	*Sīn*	*s*
ب	بي	*Be*	*b*	ش	شين	*S̲h̲īn*	*s̲h̲*
پ	پي	*Pe*	*p*	ښ	ښين	*K̲k̲h̲īn*, *K̲s̲h̲īn*	*k̲k̲h̲*, *k̲s̲h̲*
ت	تي	*Te*	*t*	ص	صاد	*Swād*	*ṣ*
ټ	ټي ټه	*Ṭe*, *Ṭa*	*ṭ*	ض	ضاد	*Dwād*	*ẓ*
ث	ثي	*S̤e*	*s̤*	ط	طوي	*T̤oe*	*t̤*
ځ	ځيم	*D̲z̲īm*	*d̲z̲*	ظ	ظوي	*Z̤oe*	*z̤*
ج	جيم	*Jīm*	*j*	ع	عين	*'Ain*	*'*
څ	څي	*T̲s̲e*	*t̲s̲*	غ	غين	*G̲h̲ain*	*g̲h̲*
چ	چي	*C̲h̲e*	*c̲h̲*	ف	في	*Fe*	*f*
ح	حي	*Ḥe*	*ḥ*	ق	قاف	*Qāf*	*q*
خ	خي	*K̲h̲e*	*k̲h̲*	ك	كاف	*Kāf*	*k*
د	دال دي	*Dāl*, *De*	*d*	ګ	ګاف	*Gāf*	*g*
ډ	ډال ډه	*Ḍāl*, *Ḍa*	*ḍ*	ل	لام	*Lām*	*l*
ذ	ذال	*Z̲āl*	*z̲*	م	ميم	*Mīm*	*m*
ر	ري	*Re*	*r*	ن	نون	*Nūn*	*n*
ړ	ړي	*Ṛe*	*ṛ*	ڼ	ړوڼ	*Ṛūn̲r̲*	*n̲r̲*
ز	زي	*Ze*	*z*	و	واو	*Wāw*	*w*
ژ	ژي	*Ĵe*	*ĵ*	ه	هي	*He*	*h*
ږ	ږي	*G̣e*	*g̣*	ي	يي	*Ye*	*y*

a. Of the above letters, ث, ح, ص, ض, ط, ظ, ع, and ق are purely Arabic, and for the most part only found in words from that language.

b. The letters خ, ذ, ز, and غ are found in words either from the Arabic or Persian, but, with the exception in a few instances of خ when it takes the place of ख *kh* of the Hindī, not in the words from the Hindī.

c. The letters پ, چ, ژ, and گ are found in words either purely Pu<u>kkh</u>to or introduced from the Persian and Hindī, but not from the Arabic.

d. The letters ټ, څ, ډ, ړ, ښ, and ڼ or ڼ are only found in words purely Pu<u>kkh</u>to. The rest of the letters are common to all the languages above named.

e. In composition, the letters of the Pu<u>kkh</u>to alphabet assume the same initial, medial, and final forms as those of the Hindūstānī.

5. All the letters of the Pu<u>kkh</u>to alphabet are considered to be, and are used as, consonants. The letters ا, و and ي are also used as vowels. Some of the letters require separate notice.

a. ب *be* is sometimes changed to و *wāw*. Ex. وار *wār* for بار *bār* (a turn), وند *wand* for بند *band* (a dike, bank). When preceded in a word by ن it takes the compound sound of *mb*. Ex. لنبه *lanba* (a flame), pronounced *lamba*.

b. پ *pe* is often substituted for ف *fe*. Ex. پتنه *patna* for فتنه *fitna* (strife), پقير *paqīr* for فقير *faqīr* (a beggar).

c. ت *te* is pronounced as a very soft dental. ټ *ṭa* is a very hard palatal, and in sound resembles the ٹ of the Hindūstānī or the ट of the Hindī, like which it is also called *ṭa*.

d. څ *<u>dz</u>īm* or *<u>dz</u>e* is an altered and softened form of ج *jīm*, for which it is frequently substituted. Ex. ځان *<u>dz</u>ān* for جان *jān* (life), ځاي *<u>dz</u>āe* for جاي *jāe* (place), ځگر *<u>dz</u>igar* for جگر *jigar* (liver), etc. The letter ج *jīm* itself is sometimes changed to ز *ze*.

e. څ *<u>ts</u>e* is an altered and softened form of چ *<u>ch</u>e*, for which it is substituted in such words as څادر *<u>ts</u>ādar* for چادر *<u>ch</u>ādar* (a sheet), څاره *<u>ts</u>āra* for چاره *<u>ch</u>āra* (remedy), څرخ *<u>ts</u>ar<u>kh</u>* for چرخ *<u>ch</u>ar<u>kh</u>* (a wheel), etc.

f. ح *he* is a hard aspirate. It is sometimes replaced by ه *he*.

g. د *dāl* or *de* is a very soft dental. ډ *ḍāl* or *ḍe* or *ḍa* is a very hard palatal, and has the sound of the Hindūstānī ڈ, or the Sanskrit ड.

h. ر *re* is a soft *r*, but always fully pronounced. ڕ *ṛe* or *ṛa* is a rough palatal rolled out of the mouth with emphasis. It has a sound very similar to that of the Hindūstānī ڑ, or the ड़ or ढ़ of the Sanskrit.

i. ز *ze* has the sound of *z* in *zeal*. It is sometimes interchanged with ځ *dze* and ج *jīm*. ژ *je* has the sound of the French *j* in *jour*, or of the English *z* in *azure*, or the *s* in *pleasure*. It is a Persian letter, and in Pukkhto is sometimes used in place of ج *jīm* by the Eastern Afghans, with whom it has the sound of that letter.

j. ږ *g* is an altered form of ج *jīm*, and like that letter, as pronounced by Arabs and others, has two sounds distinct from each other. By the Yusufzais and eastern Afghans generally it is pronounced hard, as the *g* in *gun*, and is often replaced by گ *gāf*, with which it has the same sound amongst them. By the Khataks and Western Afghans generally it is pronounced soft, as the English *g* in *gem*, or more frequently as the French *g* in *gens*, and is sometimes, though rarely, replaced by ژ *je*, with which it has the same sound amongst them. Ex. ږلۍ *gala-ī* (hail) pronounced and often written گلۍ *gala-ī* by the eastern Afghans is pronounced and occasionally written ژلۍ *jala-ī* by the western tribes. Similarly, خوږ *khog* (sweet), pronounced and often written خوګ *khog* by the Yusufzais, is pronounced and may be written خوژ *khoj* by the Khataks and western tribes. ږيره *gīra* (the beard), يږ *yag* (a he-bear), etc., are other instances.

k. ښ *kkhīn* or *kshīn*, called also *kshe* and *kkheshīn*, is a combined form of خ *khe* and ش *shīn*, and corresponds with the ष of the Sanskrit. This letter also has two distinct sounds. By the Yusufzais and eastern tribes it is pronounced hard, as *kkh*, and by the Khataks and western tribes soft, as *ksh*. Ex. ښه *kkhah* (good) with the Yusufzais is pronounced *kshah* by the Khataks. پښتو *pukkhto* or *pukshto*, ښادي *kkhādī* or *kshādī*, etc., are instances. ښ *kkhīn* is often used for ش *shīn* in words introduced from the Persian. Owing to the different sounds of this letter ښ *kkhīn* or *kshīn*, the following transformations are observed when it is combined with the letter ک *kāf* without the intervention of a vowel. By the Yusufzais and eastern Afghans the ښ *kkhīn*, when thus combined, is always made to *precede* the ک *kāf*, as in the words *kkhkenāstal* (to sit), *kkhkal* (to draw), *kkhkārah* (apparent), *kkhke* (in), *kkhkata* (under), etc. But by the Khataks and western tribes the ښ *kshīn*, under similar combinations, is always made to *follow* the ک *kāf*, as *kkshenāstal*, *kkshal*, *kkshārah*, *kkshe*, *kkshata*, etc.

l. گ *gāf* invariably has the sound of *g* hard, as in *go, gun.* When written ږ *ge,* with which it is sometimes changed, it may have either sound of that letter, as has been explained above (*i*).

m. ن *nūn* has always the full sound of *n* as in *none,* except when followed by ب *be,* when it takes the sound of *m.* Ex. لنبه *lanba* (flame) pronounced *lamba,* تنبه *tanba* (a shutter) pronounced *tamba,* ورنبي *wṛunbe* (firstly) pronounced *wṛumbe.* In such cases the ن *nūn* is frequently replaced by م *mīm,* as لمبه , تمبه , ورمبي, etc. When ن *nūn* is combined with ړ *ṛe* it forms the compound consonant *nr* (ڼ or ړ *ṛūnr*), in which the *n* is nasal. This letter is never found at the commencement of a word. Its sound is peculiar to the Pukkhto and difficult to acquire correctly.

n. و *wāw* used as a consonant has the sound of *w* in *was, wet.* By itself it is used as the conjunction *and* to connect words and sentences, and also as a prefix to the particles used as signs to the dative case. For its sounds as a vowel see Art. 8, *b.*

o. ه *he* is a mild aspirate like the *h* in *humble.* At the end of a word it is either sounded or perceptible, or else unsounded or imperceptible. In the former case it is called *hāe-ẓāhir,* and in the latter *hāe-khafī.* The ه *khafī* is the final letter of a large class of feminine nouns, and is added to masculine nouns and adjectives whose terminal letter is a consonant, for the formation of their feminines. In poetry this final ه is often dropped and replaced by the short vowel *zwar* or *zabar* (َـ). All nouns, adjectives, etc., ending in ه *ẓāhir* are of the masculine gender. When the letter ه occurs at the end of Arabic words introduced into Pukkhto it is written thus ة and sounded as ت, and generally this letter is substituted for it, as زكات for زكاة *zakāt* (alms).

6. In this work the ه *khafī* is represented by the letter *a* at the end of a word, and the ه *ẓāhir* by *h.* For the rest, Professor Forbes' system of Romanizing is here adopted, as shown in the table of the alphabet.

THE CONSONANTS. (*Ḥurūfi-ṣaḥīḥ.*)

7. According to the Arabian system, on which the Pukkhto, like other Oriental grammars, is based, all the letters of the alphabet are used as consonants.

a. The only letters requiring notice here are ا *alif* and ع *'ain*. These consonants at the commencement of a word or syllable are very weak aspirates. The former proceeds from the mouth alone, and the latter from the throat. In common with the other consonants, they depend for their sound upon the vowel by which they may be "moved."

b. A consonant when moved by a vowel to form a syllable is said to be *mutaharrik* or "moveable." When in the middle or end of a word and not so "moved," it is said to be *sākin* or "quiet," and is then marked with the sign ـْ *jazm*.

c. When a consonant is doubled the sign ـّ *tashdīd* is written over it and the letter is distinctly sounded twice.

THE VOWELS. (*Harakāt.*)

8. The letters ا *ā*, و *wāw*, and ي *ye*, when *sākin*, are used with the three short vowels *zwar* or *zabar* ـَ, *zer* ـِ, and *pesh* ـُ, or *fatha*, *kasra*, and *zamma*, as they are respectively styled in Arabic, to form the long vowels and diphthongs.

a. Thus ا *alif*, which is invariably preceded by ـَ *zwar*, unites with it and forms the long vowel represented by *ā* and sounded as in *yarn*, *barn*, etc. Ex. بَاد *bād* (air), لار *lār* (road), etc.

b. و *wāw sākin*, preceded by its corresponding short vowel ـُ *pesh*, unites with it and produces two distinct sounds, viz., as *ū* in *rule*, called *wāwi-m'arūf*, and as *o* in *pole*, called *wāwi-majhūl*. خُوږ *khūg* (hurt), کُوڼ *kūnr* (deaf), لُوند *lūnd* (wet), etc., are examples of the former. خوږ *khog* (sweet), خوب *khob* (sleep), کوڼ *konr* (a dog-louse), تور *tor* (black), etc., are examples of the latter.

When و *wāw* is preceded by the short vowel ـَ *zwar*, it sometimes unites with it and produces the diphthong *au*, sounded as the *ou* in *sound*, *house*, etc. ځَور *dzaur* (oppression), قَوم *qaum* (tribe), کَونتر *kauntar* (a pigeon), etc., are examples. In Pukkhto, however, it is more common for the و *wāw* to remain distinct as a consonant, retaining the sound of *w*. This is particularly the case at the end of words or syllables where the و *wāw* is preceded by ـَ *zwar*. Ex. رَوڼدل *rawdal* (to suck), لَوَدل *lawdal* (to say), پلَو *palaw* (side), گرَو *graw* (pledge), منډَو *mandaw* (a porch), etc.

When و *wāw* is preceded by the short vowel ـِ *zer*, it never unites with it, but remains separate, and is sounded as a consonant. Ex. سوِري *siwrai* (shade), زِوي *ziwe* (matter), لِوال *liwāl* (hungry), etc.

c. ي *ye sākin*, preceded by the short vowel ـَ *zwar*, unites with it and produces the diphthong *ai*, which is sounded like the *i* in *file* if in the middle of a word, and like the *ai* in *sail* if at the end of a word. سيل *sail* (a ramble), خيمه *khaima* (a tent), etc., are examples of the former sound; and سړي *saṛai* (a man), لرگي *largai* (a stick), etc., are examples of the latter.

When ي *ye* is preceded by the short vowel ـُ *pesh*, which is a rare occurrence in Pukkhto, no union takes place; it remains as a consonant with the sound of *y*, as in the word مُيَسّر *muyassar* (procurable).

When ي *ye* is preceded by the short vowel ـِ *zer* it unites with it, and produces two distinct sounds, viz., as ī (sounded like the double *e* in *feel*), called *yāe-m'arūf*, and as *e* (sounded like the *a* in *fate*), called *yāe-majhūl.* سپين *spīn* (white), شين *shīn* (green), ټيټ *ṭīṭ* (bowed), etc., are examples of the former; and بينش *bensh* (a rafter), ديرش *dersh* (thirty), تيل *tel* (oil), etc., of the latter.

d. When و *wāw* and ي *ye* are followed by the long vowel ا *ā*, they retain their sounds as consonants, *w* and *y* respectively, forming no union with the preceding vowel, as توان *tuwān* (power), بيان *bayān* (recital).

9. There are then, to recapitulate, ten vowel sounds in the Pukkhto, viz., the three short vowels, *zabar*, *zer*, and *pesh*, represented by *a*, *i*, and *u* respectively; the three long vowels, formed by their combinations with ا *alif*, ي *ye*, and و *wāw*, and represented by *ā*, *ī*, and *ū* respectively; the two diphthongs *au* and *ai*, formed by the union of و *wāw* and ي *ye* respectively with a preceding ـَ *zwar*; and the two *majhūl* sounds of و *wāw* and ي *ye*, formed by their combinations with ـُ *pesh* and ـِ *zer* respectively, as above explained.

10. The following table, taken from Forbes' Hindūstānī Grammar, shows the several vowel sounds above mentioned, as pronounced in English in column I., as written in the Naskh character in column II., and as represented in the Roman character in column III.

DESCRIPTION.	COL. I.	COL. II.	COL. III.
Short Vowels	fun	فَن	fan
	fin	فِن	fin
	foot	فُت	fut
Long Vowels	fall	فَال	fāl
	feel	فِيل	fīl
	fool	فُول	fūl
Diphthongs	fowl	فَول	faul
	file	فَيل	fail
Majhūl و and ي . . .	foal	فول	fol
	feil	فيل	fel

11. The following symbols are used with the vowel ا *alif.*

a. ٓ *madda,* which signifies prolongation, is written over ا *alif* commencing a word to prolong its sound or make it a long vowel, as آزاد *āzād* (free), instead of اازاد.

b. ٔ or ء or ئ *hamza,* called also *yāe-m'adūm,* or the "abolished e," is placed above and between two contiguous vowels of different syllables to indicate their separation from each other. Ex. نائي *nā-ī* (a barber), فائده *fā-ida* (benefit), etc. This symbol corresponds to and in this work is represented by the hyphen in English. In Pukkhto it is used with a large class of mostly monosyllabic words to indicate a separation or division of the short vowel composing such words. Ex. وړ *wa-aṛ* (winning), پڅ *pa-ats* (blunt), خټ *kha-aṭ* (a hillock), etc. By some tribes such words are pronounced as if the short vowel was ُ (*pesh*), as *wuṛ, puts, khuṭ,* etc.

c. ٱ *waṣla* signifies "union," and, written over the ال *al* commencing Arabic words, gives it the vowel sound of the last letter of the preceding word, and denotes union with it, as بيت ٱلمقدس *baitu-l-muqaddas* (the holy temple, Jerusalem).

d. The symbols ً, ٍ, and ٌ *tanwīn,* or "nunation," occur at the end of

Arabic words to denote their termination in *n*. It will be observed that these symbols are merely the doubling of the three vowel points, which then take the sounds of *-an*, *-in*, and *-un* respectively.

SECTION II.

THE PARTS OF SPEECH. (*Kalima.*)

12. In Pukkhto, as in the Arabic and Persian, the several parts of speech are classified under three heads, viz., the noun, the verb, and the particle.

THE NOUN. (*Ism.*)

13. The noun is a word which by itself expresses an independent meaning, but does not indicate time. It possesses gender, number, and case, and comprises all substantives, adjectives, pronouns, participles, and infinitives, as کاڼړي *kāṉrai*, s. (stone), سپک *spuk*, a. (light), هغه *haghah*, pr. (that), ويونکي *wayūnkai*, part. act. (speaker), وهلي *wahalai*, part. pass. (beaten), شاربل *shārbal*, v. a. (churning).

14. The Article.—In Pukkhto there is no word corresponding with the articles *a*, *an*, or *the*. The articles are inherent in the nouns, but when special distinction is required they are expressed by the numeral يو *yo* (one) for the indefinite article, and by the demonstrative pronouns دا *dā*, and دغه *daghah* (this) for the definite article.

15. Gender (*jins*).—The noun in Pukkhto has two genders, the masculine (*muẕakkar* or *nar*) and the feminine (*muwannas̱* or *kkhadza*). They affect also the terminations of the verb. When not explained by the word itself, the gender of substantives, adjectives, etc., is determined by the termination of the nominative case singular, according to the following rules.

16. All substantives, adjectives, participles, etc., of the masculine gender terminate in the nominative case singular in one or other of the following ways, viz:—

a. Rule 1.—All nouns ending in the diphthong ی *ai* are, without exception, masculine. Ex.—

سړی *saṛai*, a man.	لرګی *largai*, a stick.
کاڼړی *kāṉṟai*, a stone.	نمسی *nmasai*, a grandson.

b. Rule 2.—All nouns denoting profession or calling, and ending in ی *ī* (*yāe-m'arūf*), are, without exception, of the masculine gender. Ex.—

دوبي *dobī*, a dyer.	سپاهي *spāhī*, a soldier.
خوني *khūni*, a murderer.	نائي *nā-ī*, a barber.

c. Rule 3.—All nouns ending in the perceptible ه (*hāe-ẓāhir*) are, without exception, of the masculine gender. Ex.—

اوړه *oṛah*, flour.	ويښته *wekkhtah*, hair.
غوبه *ghobah*, a cowherd.	میړه *meṛah*, a master.
پريواته *prewātah*, a falling.	خاته *khātah*, a rising.

d. Rule 4.—Nouns terminating in any consonant, including و *wāw* and ي *ye*, when used as such, are, as a rule, of the masculine gender. Ex.—

کټ *kaṭ*, a cot.	لاس *lās*, a hand.
اوښ *ūkkh*, a camel.	چرګ *chirg*, a cock.
بيلهو *belho*, a hone.	منډو *manḍaw*, a shed.
ځوي *dzoe*, a son.	مرئي *mra-e*, a slave.

17. To the above rule 4 there are numerous exceptions. In several of them the gender is indicated by the sex, as will be seen in the annexed list, which includes most of the exceptions to the rule noted.

a. A list of feminine nouns with a masculine termination.

بجل *bujul*, ankle bone.	پمبيچو *pumbechū*, cotton stalk.
برخو *barkho*, the cheek.	ترښځ *tarkkhadz*, an adze.
بړستن *bṛastan*, a quilt.	ترور *tror*, aunt.
بڼ *ba-an*, rival wife.	تندار *tandār*, uncle's wife.
بورجل *borjal*, a resort (place).	ټبر *ṭabar*, a wife.
پلټن *paltan*, a regiment	څرمن *tsarman*, skin.

جن *ja-an*, a girl.
څنګل *tsangal*, elbow.
چنګل *changul*, a claw.
خارو *khāro*, a cock's spur.
خپر *khapar*, palm, sole.
خور *khor*, sister.
درشل *darshal*, door frame.
درکړ *drakar*, wheel tire.
رندار *rundār*, brother's wife.
زانګو *zāngo*, a swing.
ږمنز *gamanz*, a comb.
ستن *stan*, a needle.
سمڅ *smats*, a cave.
غوجل *ghojal*, a cow-shed.
غندل *ghandal*, a sprout.
غیږ *gheg*, the bosom.
ګاهر *gāhar*, herd of oxen.
لار *lār*, a road.
لانبو *lānbo*, swimming.
لمن *laman*, a skirt.
لنګور *langor*, a span.
لور *lūr*, daughter.
لویشت *lwesht*, a span.
مرز *mraz*, a quail.
منګل *mungal*, a paw.
مور *mor*, a mother.
میاشت *myāsht*, a month.
میچن *mechan*, hand-mill.
میرمن *merman*, mistress.
میږ *meg*, an ewe.
ناوي *nāwe*, a bride.
ندرور *ndror*, husband's sister.
نږور *ngor*, son's wife.
ورشو *warsho*, a lawn.
ورځ *wradz*, a day.
وریځ *waryadz*, a cloud.
وندر *wandar*, a tether.
یور *yor*, husband's brother's wife

b. Some nouns ending in و *wāw*, and denoting animate beings, are both masculine and feminine: Ex.—

باګو *bāgū*, a goblin.
بیزو *bīzo*, a monkey.
پیشو *pīsho*, a cat.
میلو *melū*, a bear.

18. All substantives, adjectives, participles, etc., of the feminine gender terminate in one or other of the following ways, viz.:—

a. Rule 1.—All purely Pukkhto nouns, etc., ending in the letter ا *alif* are of the feminine gender. Ex.—

ژړا *jaṛā*, crying.
شا *shā*, the back.
غلا *ghlā*, robbery.
غوا *ghwā*, a cow.
ملا *mlā*, the loin.
نیا *nyā*, grandmother.

b. Rule 2.—Nouns of foreign derivation adopted into the Pukkhto and ending in ا *alif* are of the masculine gender. Ex.—

برړوا *baṛwā*, a pimp.
بوړا *bauṛā*, a drone bee.
بيگا *begā*, evening.
تونبيا *tonbiyā*, cotton thread.
چوړا *chūṛā*, a bangle.
جولا *jolā*, a weaver.
زنا *zinā*, adultery.
سبا *sabā*, morning.
کاکا *kākā*, uncle paternal.
ماما *māmā*, uncle maternal.
ملا *mullā*, a priest.
ميا *miyā*, a friar.

Some nouns of this class, in Pukkhto, take the masculine termination ي *e*, used as a consonant. Ex.—

آشناي *āshnāe*, a friend.
خداي *khudāe*, God.
گداي *gadāe*, a beggar.
امراي *umrāe*, a noble.

c. Rule 3.—All nouns terminating in the imperceptible ه (*hāe-khafī*) are, without exception, of the feminine gender. Ex.—

اوبه *oba*, water.
بيله *bela*, an island.
توره *tūra*, a sword.
چاړه *chāṛa*, a knife.
کنده *kanda*, a ravine.
نښه *nakkha*, a banner.

d. Rule 4.—All nouns terminating in ئ *a-ī* (*yāe-m'arūf* preceded by *hamza*) are, without exception, of the feminine gender. Ex.—

پټئ *paṭa-ī*, a bandage.
څپلئ *tsapla-ī*, a sandal.
سپوږمئ *spogma-ī*, the moon.
شوشئ *shūsha-ī*, a firebrand.
شونټئ *shonṭa-ī*, a pine torch.
مرئ *mara-ī*, the throat.

e. Rule 5.—Nouns terminating in ي *ī* (*yāe-m'arūf* alone), and denoting condition or state, are of the feminine gender. Ex. (see Art. 16, *b*)—

بدي *badī*, evil.
خواري *khwārī*, poverty.
خوښي *khwakkhī*, pleasure.
ښادي *kkhādī*, joy.
گداي *gadā-ī*, beggary.
نيکي *nekī*, honesty.

f. Rule 6.—A few plural nouns, whose singular ending in ه *khafī* is obsolete, terminate in ي *e* (*yāe-majhūl*), and are, without exception, of the feminine gender. Ex.—

ايري *īre*, ashes.	غني *ghane*, thorns.
خولي *khwale*, sweat.	نيني *nīne*, parched grain.
دوري *dūṛe*, dust.	واوري *wāwre*, snow.
تروي *tarwe*, whey.	وريژي *wrīje*, rice grain.
شوملي *shomle*, buttermilk.	ويني *wīne*, blood.
زوي *ziwe*, matter.	اوربوشي *orbūshe*, barley.

19. Feminines are formed from masculines according to the following rules:—

a. Rule 1.—If the masculine end in the diphthong ی *ai*, the feminine is formed by changing it to ئ *a-ī* (*yāe-m'arūf* preceded by *hamza*). Ex.—

اوسی *osai*, a buck.	اپریدی *aprīdai*, Afridi male.
اوسئ *osa-ī*, a hind.	اپریدئ *aprīda-ī*, Afridi female.
سپی *spai*, a dog.	یوسپزی *yūsupzai*, Yusufzai, *m.*
سپئ *spa-ī*, a bitch.	یوسپزئ *yūsupza-ī*, Yusufzai, *f.*

b. Rule 2.—If the masculine end in ي *ī* (*yāe-m'arūf* alone) the feminine is formed by dropping the final ي *ī*, and adding ڼړه *anra*. Ex.—(Art. 16, *b.*)

دوبي *dobī*, a dyer.	نائي *nā-ī*, a barber.
دوبنړه *dobanra*, dyer's wife.	نايڼړه *nāyanra*, barber's wife.
موچي *mochī*, a cobbler.	هاتي *hātī*, elephant, *m.*
موچنړه *mochanra*, cobbler's wife.	هاتنړه *hātanra*, elephant, *f.*

c. Rule 3.—If the masculine ends in any consonant, excepting ا *alif*, و *wāw*, and ه *hāe ẓāhir*, it forms the feminine by adding ه *hāe khafī* to the last letter. Ex.—

اوښ *ūkkh*, a camel, *m.*	آشناي *āshnāe*, a friend, *m.*
اوښه *ūkkha*, a camel, *f.*	آشنايه *āshnāya*, a friend, *f.*
چرگ *chirg*, a cock.	سوي *soe*, buck hare.
چرگه *chirga*, a hen.	سويه *soya*, doe hare.

d. Rule 4.—Those masculine nouns ending in a consonant which are of one syllable, formed by the long vowel و *ū* (*wāwi-m'arūf*), or of more than one syllable, the last of which is formed by that vowel, form the feminine by replacing و by the short vowel *zabar* ـَ and adding ه *hāe khafī* to the last letter of the word. Ex. (Art. 22, *e*)—

شپون *shpūn*, a shepherd.	پښتون *pukkhtūn*, Pukkhtūn, *m.*
شپنه *shpana*, a shepherdess.	پښتنه *pukkhtana*, Pukkhtūn, *f.*
شکونړ *shkūnr*, porcupine, *m.*	گډون *gadūn*, Gadūn, *m.*
شکنړه *shkanra*, porcupine, *f.*	گډنه *gadana*, Gadūn, *f.*

e. Rule 5.—Nouns terminating in the perceptible ه (*hāe-zāhir*) form the feminine by inserting ن *nūn* before the final ه *he*, which then becomes imperceptible (*hāe-khafī*), as in the following examples:—

اوښبه *ūkkhbah*, camel-man.	کوربه *korbah*, a host.
اوښبنه *ūkkhbana*, camel-woman.	کوربنه *korbana*, a hostess.
غوبه *ghobah*, cowherd.	میلمه *melmah*, a guest, *m.*
غوبنه *ghobana*, cowherdess.	میلمنه *melmana*, a guest, *f.*

20. To the above rules (Art. 19) there are several exceptions in the case of animate objects that have entirely different words for the opposite sexes, just as in the English. The following list comprises the most common examples:—

آس *ās*, a horse.	څښتن *tsakkhtan*, husband.
آسپه *āspa*, a mare.	ښځه *kkhadza*, woman.
آوښي *āwkkhai*, wife's brother.	خورئي *khora-e*, nephew.
ښينه *kkhīna*, wife's sister.	خورځه *khordza*, niece.
پلار *plār*, father.	ځوي *dzoe*, son.
مور *mor*, mother.	لور *lūr*, daughter.
پلندر *plandar*, step-father.	زلمي *zalmai*, youth.
میره *maira*, step-mother.	پیغله *peghla*, maid.
تربور *tarbūr*, cousin, *m.*	سخر *skhar*, father-in-law.
ترله *tarla*, cousin, *f.*	خواښه *khwākkha*, mother-in-law.
تره *trah*, uncle.	سړي *sarai*, man.
ترور *tror*, aunt.	ارتینه *artīna*, wife.

سنډه *sanḍah*, buffalo, *m.*	نږور *ngor*, daughter-in-law.
میښه *mekkha*, buffalo, *f.*	ځوم *dzūm*, son-in-law.
غوئي *ghwa-e*, bull.	نیکه *nīkah*, grandfather.
غوا *ghwā*, cow.	نیا *nyā*, grandmother.
لیور *lewar*, husband's brother.	وراره *wrārah*, brother's son.
ندرور *ndror*, husband's sister.	وریره *wrera*, brother's daughter.
میړه *meṛah*, master.	ورور *wror*, brother.
میرمن *merman*, mistress.	خور *khor*, sister.
نارینه *nārīnah*, male.	هلک *halak*, boy.
ماندینه *māndīna*, female.	جنۍ *jina-ī*, girl.

21. Number (*'adad*).—There are two numbers in Pukkhto, the singular (*wāḥid*) and plural (*jama'*). The singular terminations of nouns have been described in the preceding articles, 16 to 20. It remains now to explain how the plurals are formed from them.

22. The plurals of masculine nouns are formed from the singulars according to the following rules:—

a. Rule 1.—All masculine nouns ending in the diphthong ي *ai* form the nominative plural by changing it to ي *ī*. To this rule there are no exceptions. Ex.—

سپَي *spai*, a dog.	کوونکَي *kawūnkai*, a doer.
سپي *spī*, dogs.	کوونکي *kawūnkī*, doers.
سړَي *saṛai*, a man.	ویونکَي *wayūnkai*, a speaker.
سړي *saṛī*, men.	ویونکي *wayūnkī*, speakers.

b. Rule 2.—All masculine nouns ending in ي *ī* (*yāe-m'arūf*) (Art. 16, *b*) form the plural by adding ان *ān* to the last letter of the nominative singular. Ex.—

دوبي *dobī*, a dyer.	سپاهي *spāhī*, a soldier.
دوبیان *dobiyān*, dyers.	سپاهیان *spāhiyān*, soldiers.
خوني *khūnī*, a murderer.	کسبي *kasbī*, an artificer.
خونیان *khūniyān*, murderers.	کسبیان *kasbiyān*, artificers.

c. Rule 3.—Nouns masculine ending in any consonant, including و *wāw* and ي *ye* when used as such, but excepting ه *ẓāhir*, form the plural by adding ونه *ūna* to the nominative singular, if they denote inanimate objects. Ex.—

پرهار *parhār*, a wound.
پرهارونه *parhārūna*, wounds.
گرو *graw*, a pledge.
گروونه *grawūna*, pledges.

ډنډ *ḍanḍ*, a pond.
ډنډونه *ḍanḍūna*, ponds.
سکوي *skoe*, a stitch.
سکويونه *skoyūna*, stitches.

d. RULE 4.—Nouns masculine ending in any consonant, and denoting animate objects, form the plural by adding ان *ān*, گان *gān*, or يان *yān* to the nominative singular. Ex.—

مار *mār*, serpent.
ماران *mārān*, serpents.
لړم *laṛam*, a scorpion.
لړمان *laṛamān*, scorpions.
ليوه *lewah*, a wolf.
ليوهگان *lewahgān*, wolves.
شادو *shādo*, a monkey.
شادوگان *shādogān*, monkeys.

ميړه *meṛah*, a master.
ميړهگان *meṛahgān*, masters.
ملا *mullā*, a priest.
ملايان *mullāyān*, priests.
آشناي *āshnāe*, a friend.
آشنايان *āshnāyān*, friends.
کاکا *kākā*, an uncle.
کاکاگان *kākāgān*, uncles.

e. RULE 5.—Nouns ending in a consonant, and of one syllable formed by the long vowel و *wāw*, or of more than one syllable, the last of which is formed by that vowel, form the plural by changing و *wāw* into ا *alif* and adding ه *ẕāhir* to the last letter of the nominative singular. Ex.—

سوور *swor*, a horseman.
سواره *swārah*, horsemen.
شپون *shpūn*, a shepherd.
شپانه *shpānah*, shepherds.
شپول *shpol*, a hedge.
شپاله *shpālah*, hedges.

بيلتون *biyaltūn*, separation.
بيلتانه *biyaltānah*, separations.
کنډتون *kunḍtūn*, widowhood.
کنډتانه *kunḍtānah*, widowhoods.
لړمون *laṛmūn*, a gut.
لړمانه *laṛmānah*, the bowels.

NOTE.—Some of these nouns use the plural form as a singular noun. Ex. لړمانه *laṛmānah* (belly), زنگانه *zangānah* (knee), as دَ لړمانه درد *da laṛmānah dard* (belly-ache), دَ زنگانه سترگه *da zangānah starga* (knee-cap).

f. RULE 6.—Nouns masculine ending in ه *ẕāhir*, and which form their feminines by the insertion of ن *nūn* before the final ه *h* (Art. 19, *e*), form the plural by inserting ان *ān* before the terminal ه *h* of the nominative singular which itself remains unaltered. Ex.—

غوبه *g͟hobah*, a cowherd.	میلمه *melmah*, a guest.
غوبانه *g͟hobānah*, cowherds.	میلمانه *melmānah*, guests.

g. Rule 7.—A class of masculine nouns which end in a consonant and denote sound alone, form the plural by adding هار *hār* to the nominative singular. Ex.—

پرچ *prac͟h*, a sneeze.	شرنگ *s͟hṛang*, a jingling.
پرچهار *prac͟hahār*, sneezes.	شرنگهار *s͟hṛangahār*, jinglings.
شر *s͟hir*, a pattering.	گړ *ga-ar*, a rumbling.
شرهار *s͟hirahār*, patterings.	گړهار *ga-arahār*, rumblings.

h. Rule 8.—Many nouns of the masculine gender, ending in any letter and for the most part denoting inanimate objects, have a plural signification, and are the same in the singular and plural. Ex.—

اوړه *oṛah*, flour.	مالوچ *mālūc͟h*, cotton.
رانجه *rānjah*, collyrium.	رابښه *rāk͟kh͟hah*, herbage.
کچ *kuc͟h*, butter.	ویښته *wek͟kh͟htah*, hair.

23. To the above rules there are a few exceptions. The following list comprises the most common examples.

پلار *plār*, a father.	خرشن *k͟hars͟han*, horse dung.
پلارونه *plārūna*, fathers.	خرشنه *k͟hars͟hana*, stable refuse.
ورور *wror*, a brother.	زړه *zṛah*, a heart.
وروڼړه *wrūn͟ra*, brothers.	زړونه *zṛūna*, hearts.
تره *trah*, an uncle.	غل *g͟hal*, a thief.
ترونه *trūna*, uncles.	غلهٔ *g͟hla-ah*, thieves.
ځوي *d͟zoe*, a son.	آس *ās*, a horse.
ځامن *d͟zāman*, sons.	آسونه *āsūna*, horses.
خر *k͟har*, an ass.	مل *mal*, a comrade.
خرهٔ *k͟hra-ah*, asses.	ملهٔ *mla-ah*, comrades.

Note.—Some nouns, the last syllable of which ending in a consonant is formed by the short vowel ـَ *zwar*, make the nominative plural by inserting ـٔ *hamza* above the last syllable. Ex. وزر *wazar* (a wing), وزرٙ *waza-ar* (wings), سخوندر *skhwandar* (a steer), سخوندرٙ *skhwanda-ar* (steers), etc.

24. The plurals of feminine nouns are formed from the singulars according to the following rules.

a. Rule 1.—Nouns of the feminine gender ending in ا *alif*, and denoting inanimate objects, undergo no change for the nominative plural with the eastern Afghans, but with the tribes of the west the plural of such words is formed by adding وي *we* or *wī* to the nominative singular. Ex.—

ژړا *jaṛā*, a crying.	وينا *wainā*, a dirge.
ژړاوي *jaṛāwe*, cryings.	يناوي *waināwe*, dirges.
ها *hā*, an egg.	بلا *balā*, a calamity.
هاوي *hāwe*, eggs.	بلاوي *balāwe*, calamities.

b. Rule 2.—Nouns feminine ending in ئ *a-ī* in the nominative singular make no change for the nominative plural. Ex.—

جنئ *jina-ī*, a girl, girls.	مرئ *mara-ī*, the throat, throats.
سپوږمئ *spogma-ī*, the moon, moons.	نوړئ *nwaṛa-ī*, a morsel, morsels.

c. Rule 3.—Feminine nouns ending in ي *ī* in the nominative singular form the nominative plural by changing it to ئ *a-ī*. Ex.—

بدي *badī*, evil.	خواري *khwārī*, distress.
بدئ *bada-ī*, evils.	خوارئ *khwāra-ī*, distresses.
تنگي *tangī*, strait.	نيکي *nekī*, virtue.
تنگئ *tanga-ī*, straits.	نيکئ *neka-ī*, virtues.

d. Rule 4.—Nouns feminine ending in the ه *khafī* form the plural by changing it to ي *e* (*yāe-majhūl*). Ex.—

خره *khara*, a she-ass.	ښځه *kkhadza*, a woman.
خري *khare*, she-asses.	ښځي *kkhadze*, women.
توره *tūra*, a sword.	ناله *nāla*, a canal.
توري *tūre*, swords.	نالي *nāle*, canals.

e. Rule 5.—Nouns feminine ending in a consonant form the plural by adding the short vowel *zer* ـِ *i* to the last letter of the nominative singular, or ي *e*, as in the preceding rule. Ex.—

برستن *bṛastan*, a coverlet.	لار *lār*, a road.
برستنِ *bṛastani*, coverlets.	لارِ *lāri*, roads.
پلټن *palṭan*, a regiment.	ميچن *me<u>ch</u>an*, a handmill.
پلټنِ *palṭani*, regiments.	ميچنِ *me<u>ch</u>ani*, handmills.

f. Rule 6.—But if the feminine noun end in و *wāw* in the singular, it forms the plural by adding گانِ *gāni*, or گاني *gāne*. Ex.—

پيشو *pī<u>sh</u>o*, a she-cat.	زانگو *zāngo*, a cradle.
پيشوگانِ *pī<u>sh</u>ogāni*, she-cats.	زانگوگانِ *zāngogāni*, cradles.
ميلو *melū*, a she-bear.	ورشو *war<u>sh</u>o*, a lawn.
ميلوگانِ *melūgāni*, she-bears.	ورشوگانِ *war<u>sh</u>ogāni*, lawns.

25. To the above rules there are a few exceptions, in the case of some feminine nouns which, denoting consanguinity or relationship, form their plurals irregularly. The following list comprises most of them. The final ي *e* is often replaced by ـِ *i*.

خور *<u>kh</u>or*, a sister.	ندرور *ndror*, husband's sister.
خويندي *<u>kh</u>wainde*, sisters.	ندرندي *ndrande*, husband's sisters.
مور *mor*, a mother.	نږور *ngor*, son's wife.
ميندي *mainde*, mothers.	نږيندي *ngende*, sons' wives.
لور *lūr*, a daughter.	ناوي *nāwe*, a bride.
لونړي *lū<u>nr</u>e*, daughters.	ناويانِ *nāwiyāni*, brides.
يور *yor*, a sister-in-law.	نيا *nyā*, a grandmother.
يونړي *yū<u>nr</u>e*, sisters-in-law.	نياگانِ *nyāgāni*, grandmothers.

26. Case (*ḥālat*).—Like the Arabic, the Pu<u>kkh</u>to recognizes only three states of the noun.

I. The actor or "agent" (*fā'il*), which includes the nominative and instrumental cases.

II. The adjunct or "oblique" (*iẓāfat*), which includes the genitive, dative, ablative, locative, and vocative cases.

III. The acted upon or "object" (*mafa'ūl*), which is represented by the accusative case.

a. Of these several cases, the nominative and accusative have one and the same form in all nouns and under all circumstances. The remaining cases, called oblique cases, are distinguished by the addition of certain particles to the nominative cases singular and plural, for each case separately except the instrumental, which has none.

27. In some classes of nouns the oblique cases of the singular are inflected, that is to say, the termination of the nominative case is changed. The following rules are observed:—

a. Rule 1.—Masculine nouns that end in any consonant, including ا *alif*, و *wāw*, and ه *zāhir*, as also such as end in the vowel ي *ī* (*yāe-m'arūf*), are, with rare exceptions, incapable of inflection in the singular. But those that end in the diphthong ئ *ai* inflect or change it to ي *ī* in the oblique cases of the singular.

b. Rule 2.—Feminine nouns that end in the letters ا *alif*, و *wāw*, or ي *ye*, as also such as end in the vowels ي *ī* and ئ *a-ī*, are incapable of inflection in the singular. But those that end in ه *khafī* change it in the oblique cases singular to ي *e* (*yāe-majhūl*), and those that end in a consonant inflect the oblique cases singular by adding the short vowel *zer* ـِ *i* to the last letter of the nominative.

28. All nouns of whatever kind, and of both genders, invariably inflect the oblique cases of the plural by the sign و *o* or ـُ *u* at the end of the nominative. The following rules are observed:—

a. Rule 1.—In the plural the oblique cases of all masculine nouns are inflected by the addition of و *o* to the last letter of the nominative case, if it end in ي *ī*, ان *ān*, گان *gān*, or يان *yān*. But if the nominative end in ونه *ūna*, then the final ه is dropped and replaced by و in the inflected cases. Sometimes the inflected terminations انو *āno*, گانو *gāno*, and ونو *ūno* are contracted to و *o* and گو *go*.

b. Rule 2.—In the plural of all feminine nouns the oblique cases are formed by dropping the ي *e*, ئ *a-ī*, or ـِ *i* of the nominative, and replacing them by و *o* or ـُ *u*. If the nominative end in ا *alif* the oblique cases are formed by adding و *wāw* to it.

29. The nominative case (*ḥālati-fā'il*) is the simple form of the noun, as سري *sarai* (a man), زمكه *zmaka* (the earth). In all nouns and in both numbers the nominative has the same form as the accusative case, from which it is distinguished by its position in a sentence. In those nouns that are not capable of inflection in the singular the instrumental case has the same form as the nominative and accusative. They are distinguished from each other by the following rules:—

a. Rule 1.—The nominative case precedes the accusative in all constructions with an intransitive verb, or the present and future tenses of a transitive verb. Ex. پلار خپل څوي پيژني *plār khpul dzoe pejanī* (the father recognises his own son), څوي خپل پلار پيژني *dzoe khpul plār pejanī* (the son recognises his own father), سري سري وهي *sarai sarai wahī* (man beats man), سري ښځه وهي *sarai kkhadza wahī* (man beats woman), ښځه سري وهي *kkhadza sarai wahī* (woman beats man).

b. Rule 2.—The nominative case follows the instrumental in all constructions with the imperfect and past tenses of transitive verbs. Ex. مار آس ؤ چيچه *mār ās wu chīchah* (the snake bit the horse), آس مار ؤ واژه *ās mār wu wājah* (the horse killed the snake).

30. The genitive case (*ḥālati-iẓāfat*) is distinguished by the particle دَ *da* (of), which invariably precedes its noun. Ex. دَ كور چت *da kor chat* (the roof of a house), دَ سري لاس *da sarī lās* (the man's hand), دَ ښځې دَ سر دَ ويښتو رنګ *da kkhadze da sar da wekkhto rang* (the colour of hair of head of woman).

31. The dative case (*ḥālati-mafa'ūliyat*) is distinguished by the particle ته *ta* or تَ *ta* (to, unto), which always follows its noun. Ex. ښهر ته تلي دي *kkhahr ta talai dai* (he has gone to the city), ما ته راكه *mā ta rāka* (give to me), سري ته وركړه *sarī ta warkṛah* (he gave to the man).

a. The particles له *la*, لره *lara*, وتَ *wata*, and وته *wata*, are commonly used in place of تَ or ته.

b. In composition و , وته *wa wata* is often used instead of the forms above noted, but the و *wa* precedes and the وته *wata* follows the noun.

32. The accusative case (*ḥālati-mafa'ūl*) has the same form as the

nominative, except in the personal pronouns. That is to say, it has no particle either prefixed or affixed, and is never inflected in the singular number. It is distinguished by its position in a sentence, which is after the nominative, as has been explained above. (Art. 29, *a.*)

33. The instrumental case (*ḥālati-fā'il*) is recognised by its simple inflection in nouns capable of inflection, and by its position at the commencement of a sentence in nouns incapable of inflection in the singular number. It is thus, in the latter case, distinguished from the nominative, which has the same form, but follows the instrumental and agrees with the verb in gender and number. The instrumental case can only be used with the imperfect and past tenses of transitive verbs.

a. The instrumental case in Pukkhto is analogous to the instrumental case with ني *ne* of the Hindūstānī, when the particle كو *ko* of that language is not used with the noun which represents the object. That is to say, the instrumental case in Pukkhto represents the "agent" or actor, and precedes the "acted upon" or object, which is placed in the nominative case, the verb agreeing with it in gender and number. Ex.—

Hindūstānī, آدمي ني عورت ماري *ādmī ne 'aurat mārī* (the man beat the woman).
Pukkhto, سري ښځه وُ وهله *sarī kkhadza wu wahala* (the man beat the woman).
Hindūstānī, عورت ني آدمي مارا *'aurat ne ādmī mārā* (the woman beat the man).
Pukkhto, ښځي سړي وُ واهه *kkhadze sarai wu wāhah* (the woman beat the man).

34. The ablative case (*ḥālati-jarrī*) is distinguished by the particle له *la* or ده *da* placed before the noun, and the particle نه *na* after it. Ex. له كور نه *la kor na* (from the house), له وني نه *la wane na* (from the tree).

a. Sometimes the complement نه *na* is rejected and replaced by the short vowel *zabar* ـَ *a* or ه *khafī* added to the last letter of such nouns as end in a consonant and are uninflected in the singular. Ex. له كورَ *la kora* (from the house), له ځايه *la dzāya* (from the place).

35. The locative case (*ḥālati-nisbatī*) is distinguished by the preposition په *pa* (on, by, with, etc.). Ex. په سر *pa sar* (on the head),

پہ سترگو *pa stargo* (with the eyes), پہ زرونو *pa zarūno* (by thousands), پہ دورو ډک *pa dūṛo ḍak* (filled with dust).

a. This preposition is sometimes written پ *pa.* It is also coupled with the adverb کښي *kkshe* or کښِ *kkshi*, which follows the noun as a complement, to denote in, at, with, etc. Ex. پہ کور کښي څوک شته *pa kor kkshe tsok shta* (is any body in the house?), پہ کال ښکي *pa kāl kkhke* (in the year).

36. The vocative case (*ḥālati-nidā*) is distinguished by the interjection اي *ai* or او *o* preceding the noun. The former is properly a Persian word, but it is in common use, and perhaps as frequently heard as the proper Pukkhto word او. In words and phrases from the Arabic the interjection يا *yā* of that language is used.

a. In nouns of the masculine gender, and denoting animate objects, the letter ہ *khafī*, or the short vowel ـَ is added to the last letter of the vocative case in the singular, whether the noun be inflected or not. Ex. اي پلارَ *ai plāra* (oh father!), اي سريہ *ai saṛiya* (oh man!).

b. In nouns of the feminine gender, and denoting animate objects, the short vowel ـِ *i* is added to the last letter of the vocative singular, if the noun end in a consonant. In other feminine nouns the vocative case singular, whether inflected or not, has no sign besides the prefixed interjection. Ex. اي خورِ *ai khori* (oh sister!), اي جنۍ *ai jina-ī* (oh girl!), اي ښادي *ai kkhādī* (oh joy!).

c. In the plural of all nouns, both masculine and feminine, the vocative case has no other sign than the interjection prefixed to the inflected form of the noun. Ex. اي سپاهيانو *ai spāhiyāno* (oh soldiers!), اي ميندو *ai maindo* (oh, mothers!).

37. In conformity with the preceding rules all nouns in the Pukkhto language may be classed under eight declensions. Of these four are for nouns of the masculine gender, and four for nouns of the feminine gender.

DECLENSIONS OF NOUNS OF THE MASCULINE GENDER.

38. DECLENSION I.—In this declension are comprised all nouns of the masculine gender that end in the diphthong ي *ai.* They inflect the

oblique cases in the singular, and are declined according to the subjoined form.

سړي *saṛai*, a man.

	SINGULAR.	PLURAL.
N.	سړي *saṛai*, a man.	سړي *saṛī*, men.
G.	دَ سړي *da saṛī*, of a man.	دَ سړيو *da saṛiyo*, of men.
D.	سړي ته *saṛī ta*, to a man.	سړيو ته *saṛiyo ta*, to men.
Ac.	سړي *saṛai*, a man.	سړي *saṛī*, men.
In.	سړي *saṛī*, by a man.	سړيو *saṛiyo*, by men.
L.	په سړي *pa saṛī*, on a man.	په سړيو *pa saṛiyo*, on men.
Ab.	له سړي نه *la saṛī na*, from a man.	له سړيو نه *la saṛiyo na*, from men.
V.	اي سړيه *ai saṛiya*, oh man!	اي سړيو *ai saṛiyo*, oh, men!

a. The oblique form of the plural is sometimes contracted by elision of the final letter of the nominative. Ex. دَ سړو *da saṛo*, for دَ سړيو *da saṛiyo*, etc.

b. Examples of nouns of the first declension.

اوسَي *osai*, deer.	غاښَي *ghākkhai*, peak.
پټَي *paṭai*, field.	کانړَي *kāṉrai*, stone.
ژمَي *jamai*, winter.	لرګي *largai*, stick.
ستورَي *storai*, star.	ميږَي *megai*, ant.

39. Declension II.—In this declension are included those nouns of the masculine gender that end in any consonant, and denote inanimate objects. As a rule they do not inflect the oblique cases in the singular, and are declined according to the subjoined form.

کور *kor*, a house.

	SINGULAR.	PLURAL.
N.	کور *kor*, a house.	کورونه *korūna*, houses
G.	دَ کور *da kor*, of a house.	دَ کورونو *da korūno*, of houses.
D.	کور ته *kor ta*, to a house.	کورونو ته *korūno ta*, to houses.
Ac.	کور *kor*, a house.	کورونه *korūna*, houses.
In.	کور *kor*, by a house.	کورونو *korūno*, by houses.
L.	په کور *pa kor*, on a house.	په کورونو *pa korūno*, on houses.
Ab.	له کور نه *la kor na*, from a house.	له کورونو نه *la korūno na*, from houses.
V.	اي کور *ai kor*, oh house!	اي کورونو *ai korūno*, oh houses!

a. Sometimes the oblique cases of the plural are contracted by rejection of the final نو *no.* Ex. دَ كورو *da koro,* for دَ كورونو *da korūno,* etc.

b. A few nouns of this declension inflect the oblique cases in the singular. They are of rare occurrence, of only one syllable, and effect the change by transposing the short vowel from the centre to the end of the word. Ex. غر *ghar* (a mountain), دَ غرَ *da ghra* (of a mountain), etc.

c. Examples of nouns of the second declension.

برج *bruj,* tower.	كمر *kamar,* cliff.
پرهار *parhār,* wound.	گرو *graw,* pledge.
ډنډ *dand,* pool.	لوړ *lawar,* club.
سکوي *skoe,* stitch.	مرګ *marg,* death.

40. Declension III.—This declension includes those nouns of the masculine gender that end in a consonant, or in the long vowel ي *ī* (*yāe-m'arūf*), and denote animate objects. They do not inflect the oblique cases in the singular, and are declined according to the subjoined form.

مار *mār,* a snake.

	SINGULAR.	PLURAL.
N.	مار *mār,* a snake.	ماران *mārān,* snakes.
G.	دَ مار *da mār,* of a snake.	دَ مارانو *da mārāno,* of snakes.
D.	مار ته *mār ta,* to a snake.	مارانو ته *mārāno ta,* to snakes.
Ac.	مار *mār,* a snake.	ماران *mārān,* snakes.
In.	مار *mār,* by a snake.	مارانو *mārāno,* by snakes.
L.	په مار *pa mār,* on a snake.	په مارانو *pa mārāno,* on snakes.
Ab.	له مار نه *la mār na,* from a snake.	له مارانو نه *la mārāno na,* from snakes.
V.	اي مارَ *ai māra,* oh snake!	اي مارانو *aī mārāno,* oh snakes!

a. This declension also includes one or two nouns which, ending in the long vowel و *ū* (*wāwi-m'arūf*), denote inanimate objects. Ex. کندُو *kandū* (a corn-bin), pl. کندوان *kandūān* (corn-bins).

b. As in the preceding declensions, the oblique cases of the plural are sometimes contracted. Ex. دَ مارو *da māro,* for دَ مارانو *da mārāno,* etc.

c. Many nouns of this declension are often declined in the same way as those of the second declension. Ex. آس *ās*, pl. آسونه *āsūna;* پلار *plār*, pl. پلارونه *plārūna*, etc.

d. Examples of nouns of the third declension.

اوښ *ūkkh*, camel.	لړم *laṛam*, scorpion.
چرګ *chirg*, cock.	ملک *malik*, chief.
سوي *soe*, hare.	ملا *mullā*, priest.
ګډ *ga-aḍ*, ram.	يار *yār*, friend.

41. Declension IV.—In this declension are comprised only those nouns, ending in a consonant, that denote actual sound. They do not inflect the oblique cases in the singular, and are thus declined:—

کرپ *krap*, a crunch.

	Singular.	Plural.
N.	کرپ *krap*, a crunch.	کرپهار *krapahār*, crunches.
G.	دَ کرپ *da krap*, of a crunch.	دَ کرپهارو *da krapahāro*, of crunches.
D.	کرپ ته *krap ta*, to a crunch.	کرپهارو ته *krapahāro ta*, to crunches.
Ac.	کرپ *krap*, a crunch.	کرپهار *krapahār*, crunches.
In.	کرپ *krap*, by a crunch.	کرپهارو *krapahāro*, by crunches.
L.	په کرپ *pa krap*, on a crunch.	په کرپهارو *pa krapahāro*, on crunches.
Ab.	له کرپ نه *la krap na*, from a crunch.	له کرپهارو نه *la krapahāro na*, from crunches.
V.	اي کرپَ *ai krapa*, oh crunch!	اي کرپهارو *ai krapahāro*, oh crunches!

a. Examples of nouns of the fourth declension.

ترنګ *trang*, twang.	شر *shir*, patter.
چر *char*, chirp.	شرنګ *shṛang*, ring.
خر *khuṛ*, retch.	کرچ *krach*, squash.
ډز *ḍaz*, bang.	ګرنګ *gṛang*, smash.

DECLENSIONS OF NOUNS OF THE FEMININE GENDER.

42. All nouns of the feminine gender in Pukkhto are comprised in the four following declensions.

43. Declension V.—Comprises all feminine nouns that end in ۍ *a-ī* or ي *ī*. They do not inflect the oblique cases in the singular, and are declined according to the subjoined form. (Art. 24, *c.*)

جنۍ *jina-ī*, a girl.

	SINGULAR	PLURAL.
N.	جنۍ *jina-ī*, a girl.	جنۍ *jina-ī*, girls.
G.	د جنۍ *da jina-ī*, of a girl.	دَ جنو *da jino*, of girls.
D.	جنۍ ته *jina-ī ta*, to a girl.	جنو ته *jino ta*, to girls.
Ac.	جنۍ *jina-ī*, a girl.	جنۍ *jina-ī*, girls.
In.	جنۍ *jina-ī*, by a girl.	جنو *jino*, by girls.
L.	په جنۍ *pa jina-ī*, on a girl.	په جنو *pa jino*, on girls.
Ab.	له جنۍ نه *la jina-ī na*, from a girl.	له جنو نه *la jino na*, from girls.
V.	اي جنۍ *ai jina-ī*, oh girl!	اي جنو *ai jino*, oh girls!

a. Examples of nouns of the fifth declension.

اوسۍ *osa-ī*, hind.	خواري *khwārī*, poverty.
څپلۍ *tsapla-ī*, sandal.	ښادي *kkhādī*, delight.
سپۍ *spa-ī*, bitch.	نيکي *nekī*, honesty.
شوشۍ *shūsha-ī*, firebrand.	ياري *yārī*, friendship.

44. Declension VI.—Comprises all nouns of the feminine gender that end in ة *khafī*. They inflect the oblique cases in the singular, and are declined according to the subjoined form.

ښځه *kkhadza*, a woman.

	SINGULAR.	PLURAL.
N.	ښځه *kkhadza*, a woman.	ښځي *kkhadze*, women.
G.	دَ ښځي *da kkhadze*, of a woman.	دَ ښځو *da kkhadzo*, of women.
D.	ښځي ته *kkhadze ta*, to a woman.	ښځو ته *kkhadzo ta*, to women.
Ac.	ښځه *kkhadza*, a woman.	ښځي *kkhadze*, women.
In.	ښځي *kkhadze*, by a woman.	ښځو *kkhadzo*, by women.
L.	په ښځي *pa kkhadze*, on a woman.	په ښځو *pa kkhadzo*, on women.
Ab.	له ښځي نه *la kkhadze na*, from a woman.	له ښځو نه *la kkhadzo na*, from women.
V.	اي ښځي *ai kkhadze*, oh woman!	اي ښځو *ai kkhadzo*, oh women!

a. Examples of nouns of the sixth declension.

توره *tūra*, sword	کوڅه *kūtsa*, lane.
چرگه *chirga*, hen.	لينده *līnda*, bow.
سويه *soya*, hare.	مالگه *mālga*, salt.
شپه *shpa*, night.	ونه *wana*, tree.

45. Declension VII.—Comprises those nouns of the feminine gender that end in ا *alif.* For the most part they denote inanimate objects. They do not inflect the oblique cases of the singular, and are declined according to the subjoined form.

بلا *balā*, a calamity.

	SINGULAR.	PLURAL.
N.	بلا *balā*, a calamity.	بلاوي *balāwe*, calamities.
G.	دَ بلا *da balā*, of a calamity.	دَ بلاو *da balāo*, of calamities.
D.	بلا ته *balā ta*, to a calamity	بلاو ته *balāo ta*, to calamities.
Ac.	بلا *balā*, a calamity.	بلاوي *balāwe*, calamities.
In.	بلا *balā*, by a calamity.	بلاو *balāo*, by calamities.
L.	په بلا *pa balā*, on a calamity.	په بلاو *pa balāo*, on calamities.
Ab.	له بلا نه *la balā na*, from a calamity.	له بلاو نه *la balāo na*, from calamities.
V.	اي بلا *ai balā*, oh calamity!	اي بلاو *ai balāo*, oh calamities!

a. In the oblique cases plural بلاوو *balāwo* is sometimes used instead of the form above given.

b. Examples of nouns of the seventh declension.

پرنا *parnā*, doze.	غلا *ghlā*, theft.
دعا *d'uā*, prayer.	خوا *khwā*, side.
دنيا *duniyā*, world.	ملا *mlā*, loin.
شا *shā*, back.	وينا *wainā*, dirge.

46. Declension VIII.—Comprises those feminine nouns that end in a consonant. They inflect the oblique cases of the singular by adding the short vowel *zer* ـِ *i* to the nominative, and are declined according to the subjoined form.

لار *lār*, a road.

	SINGULAR.	PLURAL.
N.	لار *lār*, a road.	لارِ *lāri*, roads.
G.	دَ لارِ *da lāri*, of a road.	دَ لارو *da lāro*, of roads.
D.	لارِ ته *lāri ta*, to a road.	لارو ته *lāro ta*, to roads.
Ac.	لار *lār*, a road.	لارِ *lāri*, roads.
In.	لارِ *lāri*, by a road.	لارو *lāro*, by roads.
L.	په لارِ *pa lāri*, on a road.	په لارو *pa lāro*, on roads.
Ab.	له لارِ نه *la lāri na*, from a road.	له لارو نه *la lāro na*, from roads.
V.	اي لارِ *ai lāri*, oh road!	اي لارو *ai lāro*, oh roads!

a. Examples of nouns of the eighth declension.

برستن *bṛastan*, coverlet.	ستن *stan*, needle.
پلټن *palṭan*, battalion.	سمڅ *smats̲*, cave.
څرمن *t̲sarman*, skin.	مرز *mṛaz*, quail.
ږمنز *g̲amanz*, comb.	ميچن *mec̲h̲an*, handmill.

THE ADJECTIVE. (*Ismi-ṣifat.*)

47. The adjective is a noun of quality, denoting the property or attribute of the noun with which it is coupled.

a. An adjective, when used purely as such, must always precede its noun, and agree with it in gender, number, and case. Ex. ګډ آس *guḍ ās* (a lame horse), ګډه آسپه *guḍa āspa* (a lame mare), کوږ لرګي *kog̲ largai* (a crooked stick), کږه کوڅه *kag̲a kūt̲sa* (a crooked lane), دَ ګډ آس *da guḍ ās* (of a lame horse), ګډې آسپې ته *guḍe āspe ta* (to a lame mare), په کوږو لرګو *pā kog̲o largo* (on crooked sticks), له کږو کوڅو نه *la kag̲o kūt̲so na* (from crooked lanes).

b. An adjective, when used as a noun, follows the substantive it qualifies, and agrees with it in gender, number, and case. Ex. آس ګډ دي *ās guḍ dai* (the horse is lame), آسپه ګډه ده *āspa guḍa da*.(the mare is lame), توره تيره ده *tūra tera da* (the sword is sharp), سړي تکړه دي *saṛai takṛah dai* (the man is strong).

c. If an adjective qualify more than one noun, and they be of different genders, then it is used in the masculine pl. Ex. آس او آسپه دواړه ګډ دي *ās o āspa dwāṛa-ah guḍ dī* (the horse and mare are both lame), سړي او ښځه او وينځه دري واړه ناجوړ دي *saṛai o k̲k̲h̲ad̲za o wind̲za dre wāṛa-aḥ nājoṛ dī* (the man and woman and slave girl are all three ill), دَ ناجوړو سړو او ښځو زړوکي *da nājoṛo saṛo o k̲k̲h̲ad̲zo zaṛūkī* (the clothes of sick men and women).

48. Adjectives follow precisely the same rules as the nouns in regard to gender, number, and case.

a. Rule 1.—Adjectives ending in the diphthong ىَ *ai* are of the masculine gender, and declined like nouns of the first declension. They form their feminines like nouns of the same class by changing the diphthong ىَ *ai* to the vowel ئ *a-ī* (Art. 19, *a*), and are then declined like nouns of the fifth declension. Frequently the feminine termination يٍ *a-ī* is dropped, and replaced by the short vowel *zer* ـِ *i*, as ترِ *tagi* for تريٍ *taga-ī*. Ex.—

پردي *pradai*, strange.	گړندي *garandai*, silent.
تري *tagai*, thirsty.	گنجي *ganjai*, bald.
خوشي *khūshai*, empty.	ليوني *lewanai*, mad.
غلي *ghalai*, silent.	نري *narai*, slender.

b. RULE 2.—Adjectives ending in any consonant are of the masculine gender and declined like nouns of the second declension, with this difference only, that they generally make no change for the nominative plural, which remains the same as the nominative singular. In the oblique cases of the plural the و *o* of inflection is added direct to the nominative. Such adjectives form their feminines in the same way as nouns that end in a consonant (Art. 19, *c.*), by adding ه *khafī* to the last letter of the masculine form, and are then declined like feminine nouns of the sixth declension. Ex.—

اورد *ūgd*, long.	کلک *klak*, hard.
پلن *plan*, wide.	گډ *gad*, mixed.
خور *khūg*, hurt.	لږ *la-ag*, little.
سپک *spuk*, light.	نيغ *negh*, straight.

c. RULE 3.—Adjectives that end in ه *zāhir* are masculine, and declined like nouns of the second declension. They form the nominative plural masculine by adding *hamza* over the last syllable of the nominative singular masculine. Ex. خپه *khapah*, pl. خپهٔ *khapa-ah* (angry). In the oblique cases of the plural the و of inflection takes the place of the terminal ه of the nominative, that letter being rejected in those cases. They form the feminine by changing the terminal ه *zāhir* of the masculine to ه *khafī*, and are then declined like feminine nouns of the sixth declension. Ex.—

تيره *terah*, sharp.	غوره *ghwarah*, chosen.
خپه *khapah*, angry.	ناکاره *nākārah*, useless.
سوچه *sūchah*, genuine.	يله *yalah*, free.
ښکاره *kkhkārah*, evident.	ښه *kkhah*, good.

d. RULE 4.—A small class of adjectives that end in a consonant, and generally consist of only one syllable formed by the long vowel و *ū* (*wāwi-m'arūf*) or و *o* (*wāwi-majhul*), form the feminine by dropping the و, replacing it by the short vowel *zabar* ـَ *a*, and adding ه *khafī* to the last letter of the masculine form (Art. 19, *d*). Such adjectives are declined according to the second declension in the masculine, and according to the sixth declension in the feminine. Ex. پروت *prot*, پرته *prata* (prostrate). (Art. 22, *e*.)

روند *ṛūnd*, ړنده *ṛanda*,	blind.	کونړ *kūnṛ*, کنړه *kanṛa*,	deaf.
کوږ *kog*, کږه *kaga*,	crooked.	موړ *moṛ*, مړه *maṛa*,	satiated.

e. There are some exceptions to the last rule, in the case of adjectives that form their feminines irregularly. Ex.—

تود *tod*, تَوده *tauda*,	hot.	شين *shīn*, شنه *shna*,	green.
دروند *drūnd*, درنه *drana*,	heavy.	تور *tor*, توره *tora*,	black.
تريخ *trīkh*, ترخه *tarkha*,	bitter.	خوږ *khog*, خوَږه *khwaga*,	sweet.
تريو *trīw*, تروه *tarwa*,	sour.	خور *khor*, خوَره *khwara*,	scattered.

f. A few adjectives in the masculine form the nominative plural in the same way as the nouns خر *khar*, غل *ghal*, مل *mal* (Art. 23), by adding ه *ẓāhir* to the nominative singular and dropping its terminal long or short vowel. Ex. شين *shīn*, pl. شنَه *shnah* (green); سور *sūr*, pl. سرَه *srah* (red); مړ *muṛ*, pl. مړَه *mṛah* (dead), etc.

49. Comparison.—Adjectives in Pukkhto have no regular degrees of comparison expressed by one word.

a. The comparative is expressed by using the positive with the ablative case of the noun to which it refers, itself agreeing in gender, number, and case with the noun it qualifies. Ex. سړي له ښځي نه دنګ دي *saṛai la kkhadze na dang dai* (the man is taller than the woman), ښځه له هلک نه دنګه ده *kkhadza la halak na danga da* (the woman is taller than the boy), دَ جنّت لار له ويښته نه نرئ ده *da jannat lār la wekkhtah na nara-ī da* (the road of paradise is finer than a hair), کانړي له لرګو نه درانه دي *kānṛī la largo na drānah dī* (stones are heavier than sticks), ښځي له سړو نه کمزوري دي *kkhadze la saṛo na kamzore dī* (women are weaker than men).

b. The superlative is expressed by using a noun of multitude or quantity with the positive, the noun and adjective agreeing in gender, number, and case. The words commonly used are the following:—

تک *tak*, perfectly.	زيات *ziyāt*, more.
ټول *ṭol*, all.	حد *ḥadd*, limit.
ډير *ḍer*, much.	واړه *wāṛah*, whole.

ژوندون ډير خوږ دي *jwandūn ḍer khog dai* (life is most sweet), له ټولو نه دا ډير ښه دي *la ṭolo na dā ḍer kkhah dai* (this is the best of all), ټول ملک په واورو تک سپين وُه *ṭol mulk pa wāwro tak spīn wuh* (the whole country was perfectly white with snow), تکه توره شپه وه *taka tora shpa wa* (it was a pitch dark night), له حدّ ډير ناکاره سړي دي *la ḥadda ḍer nākārah saṛai dai* (he is a most worthless man), تر حدّ ډير قهرجن دي *tar ḥadda ḍer qahrjan dai* (he is most wrathful).

THE NUMERALS. (*'Adād.*)

50. The numerals are used as adjective nouns, and are subject to the same rules for gender, number, and case as the nouns generally. They are cardinal and ordinal.

51. Cardinal Numbers.—Of the cardinals, the first, يو *yo*, has only the singular. It is subject to change for gender like a noun with the same termination; that is to say, the feminine is formed by the addition of ه *khafī*. The masculine form is declined like a noun of the second declension, and the feminine form like a noun of the sixth. Ex. دَ يو سړي *da yo saṛī* (of one man), دَ يوي ښځي *da yawe kkhadze* (of one woman).

a. All the other cardinals have only the plural. They make no change for gender, except دوه *dwah* (two), which becomes دوي *dwe* in the feminine, and form the oblique cases by adding the و of inflection to the nominative. In those that end in ه, this letter suffers elision in the oblique cases. Ex. دوه *dwah* (two), دَ دوو *da dwo* (of two); پنځه *pindzah* (five), پنځو ته *pindzo ta* (to five).

b. The cardinal numbers are as follows:—

يو *yo*	. . . . .	1	١
دوه *dwah*	. . . .	2	٢
دري *dre*	. . . . .	3	٣
څلور *tsalor*	. . . .	4	۴
پنځه *pindzah.*	. . .	5	٥
شپږ *shpag*	. . . .	6	٦
اوه *awah*	. . . .	7	٧
اته *atah.*	. . . .	8	٨
نه *nah*	. . . . .	9	٩
لس *las*	. . . . .	10	١٠
يو لس *yo las*	. . . .	11	١١
دوه لس *dwah las*	. . .	12	١٢
ديار لس *dyār las*	. . .	13	١٣
څوار لس *tswār las*	. . .	14	١۴
پنځه لس *pindzah las*	. .	15	١٥
شپاړس *shpāras*	. . .	16	١٦
اوه لس *awah las*	. . .	17	١٧
اته لس *atah las*	. . .	18	١٨
نه لس *nah las*	. . . .	19	١٩
شل *shil*	. . . . .	20	٢٠
يو ويشت *yo wīsht*	. . .	21	٢١
دوه ويشت *dwah wīsht*	.	22	٢٢
دريويشت *dre wīsht*	. .	23	٢٣
څلور ويشت *tsalor wīsht*	.	24	٢۴
پنځه ويشت *pindzah wīsht*	.	25	٢٥
شپږ ويشت *shpag wīsht*	.	26	٢٦
اوه ويشت *awah wīsht*	.	27	٢٧
اته ويشت *atah wīsht*	. .	28	٢٨
نه ويشت *nah wīsht*	. .	29	٢٩
ديرش *dersh*	. . .	30	٣٠
څلويښت *tsalwekkht*	. .	40	۴٠
پنځوس *pindzos*	. . .	50	٥٠
شپيته *shpetah*	. . .	60	٢٠
اويا *awiyā*	. . .	70	٧٠
اتيا *atiyā*	. . .	80	٨٠
نوي *nawe*	. . .	90	٩٠
سل *sil*	. . . .	100	١٠٠
دوه صو *dwah ṣawa*	.	200	٢٠٠
زر *zar*	. . .	1,000	١٠٠٠
دوه زره *dwah zara*	.	2,000	٢٠٠٠
لک *lak*	. .	100,000	١٠٠٠٠٠
دوه لکه *dwah laka*		200,000	٢٠٠٠٠٠

52. Ordinal Numbers.—These are formed from the cardinals by adding م *am* to their final letters. Ex. څلور *tsalor* (four), څلورم *tsaloram*; شپږ *shpag*, شپږم *shpagam*, etc. If the cardinal end in ه it is dropped before the ordinal termination. Ex. پنځه *pindzah* (five), پنځم *pindzam*; اوه *awah*, اوَم *awam*, etc. If the cardinal end in ا or ي then يم *yam* is added instead of م *am* for the ordinal. Ex. دري *dre* (three), دريم *dreyam* (third); اتيا *atiyā* (eighty), اتيايم *atiyāyam*, etc.

a. The first and second ordinals are formed differently from the rest. The first cardinal یو *yo* (one) is never formed into an ordinal. اول *awwal*, or وړومبي *wṛūnbai* (first) is used to express the first ordinal. The second cardinal دوه *dwah* (two) is changed into an ordinal by replacing the last letter with یم *yam*, as دویم *dwayam* (second).

b. The ordinals form their feminines according to the general rule by adding ه *khafī* to the last letter of the masculine form. Ex. دریم سړي *dreyam saṛai* (the third man), دریمه ورځ *dreyama wradz* (the third day).

53. Some of the cardinals are used as nouns of number. Ex. شل *shil* (a score), سل *sil* (a hundred or centum, but only used in the singular), زر *zar* (a thousand or mille), لک *lak* (a hundred thousand or lac).

a. Distribution is expressed by doubling the cardinals, as یو یو *yo yo* (one by one), شپږ شپږ *shpag shpag* (by sixes), etc. Ex. مزدورانو له دري دري پیسي ورکړ *mazdūṛāno la dre dre paise warka* (give the labourers three pice a-piece).

b. Precision is expressed by repeating the cardinal with the particle په *pa* interposed, as دوه په دوه *dwah pa dwah* (exactly two). Ex. لس په لس سړي دي *las pa las saṛī dī* (there are precisely ten men).

c. Duplication is expressed by adding the word برغ *bragh* (a fold) to the cardinal, as دري برغ *dre bragh* (three-fold), where the meaning to be conveyed is with reference to layers, or strata, or multiples. Ex. دا سپۍ پنځه برغ زوزات زېږیدلِ ده *dā spa-ī pindzah bragh zawzāt zegedali da* (this bitch has produced a litter of five). With reference to crops, the particle په *pa* is used interposed between the cardinals. Ex. دا زمکه زوراوره ده لس په یو دَ دانو به راوړي *dā zmaka zorāwara da las pa yo da dāno ba rāwṛī* (this land is strong, it will yield ten-fold in grain).

d. Multitude is expressed by using the particle په *pa* with the oblique plurals of the cardinals, as په لکونو *pa lakūno* (in lacs). Ex. په زرګونو را مات شوي دي *pa zargūno rā māt shawī dī* (they have broken in on us by thousands).

e. Universality is expressed by coupling the word واړه *wāṛah* (the whole) with the cardinals, as اته واړه *atah wāṛah* (all eight). Ex. شپږ تنَ سړي دي او شپږ واړه کاڼړه دي *shpag tana saṛī dī o shpag wāṛah kāṇrah dī* (there are eight men, and they are all deaf), دوه آسونه لرم او دواړه ګډ دي *dwah āsūna laram o dwāṛah guḍ dī* (I have two horses, and they are both lame). (N.B. دواړه is a contraction of دوه واړه *dwah wāṛah*.)

f. Fractional numbers are expressed as follows:—پاو *pāo* (a quarter), نيم *nīm* (a half), درې پاوَ *dre pāwa* (three-quarters), پنځه پاوَ *pindzah pāwa*, or پاو باندې يو *pāo bānde yo*, or پاو دَ پاسَ يو *pāo da pāsa yo* (one and a quarter), يو نيم *yo nīm* (one and a half), پاو کم دوه *pāo kam dwah* (one and three-quarters), پاو باندِ دوه *pāo bāndi dwah* (two and a quarter).

THE PRONOUN. (*Ẓamīr.*)

54. In Pukkhto there are six different classes of pronouns. They are the personal, the demonstrative, the possessive, the interrogative, the relative, and the indefinite pronouns.

55. Personal Pronoun (*ẓamīri-munfaṣila*).—There are three personal pronouns, corresponding to the first, second, and third persons. They are زه *zah*, I; ته *tah*, thou; and دې *de* (proximate), هغه *haghah* (remote), he, she, it.

56. First personal pronoun (*mutakallim*) makes no change for gender, and is thus declined:—

زه *zah*, I.

SINGULAR.

N.		زه *zah*		I.
G.	مي – مِ	ځما *dzamā*	*me, mi*	of me.
D.	راته – لاله	ماته *māta*	*rā ta, lā la*	to me.
Ac.		ما *mā*		me.
In.	مي – مِ	ما *mā*	*me, mi*	by me.
L.		په ما *pa mā*		on me.
Ab.		له ما نه *la mā na*		from me.
V.		اي ما *ai mā*		oh me!

PLURAL.

N.	موږ	مونږ *mūng*	*mūg*	we.
G.	ځموږَ – مو – مُه	ځمونږه *dzamūnga*	*dzamūga, mū, muh*	of us.
D.	موږَ ته	مونږه ته *mūnga ta*	*mūga ta*	to us.
Ac.	موږ	مونږ *mūng*	*mūg*	us.
In.	موږَ – مو – مُه	مونږه *mūnga*	*mūga, mū, muh*	by us.
L.	په موږَ	په مونږه *pa mūnga*	*pa mūga*	on us.
Ab.	له موږَ نه	له مونږه نه *la mūnga na*	*la mūga na*	from us.
V.	اي موږَ	اي مونږه *ai munga*	*ai mūga*	oh us!

a. The Genitive Case.—Of the two different forms of this case in the singular, the first or ځما *dzamā* is used when emphasis, particularity, or contradistinction is meant to be expressed. Ex. ځما ځوي دي *dzamā dzoe dai* (he is my son), دا ځما كور دي *dā dzamā kor dai* (this is my house), ځما توره له ستا نه تيره ده *dzamā tūra la stā na tera da* (my sword is sharper than yours), آس ځما دي *ās dzamā dai* (the horse is mine). When no particularity or emphasis is meant to be expressed, the second form مِ *mi* or مي *me* is used, and it always follows its noun. Ex. ځوي مِ ناجوړ دي *dzoe mi nājoṛ dai* (my son is sick), كور مي خوشي دي *kor me khūshai dai* (my house is empty), سر مي خوږيږي *sar me khūgegī* (my head aches).

This second form of the genitive case must be carefully distinguished from the same form of the instrumental case. It can be used with intransitive verbs in all tenses, but with transitives only in the present and future tenses.

b. The Dative Case.—The particle ته *ta*, both in the singular and plural, may be changed for any of the affixes mentioned as signs of the dative case in Art. 31, *a*, *b*. The second form of the dative را *rā*, though mostly used in the singular, may also be used in the plural. It is commonly employed in ordinary conversation where no emphasis or distinction is intended. Ex. را ته وايه *rā ta wāya* (tell me, or any one else present). It is also prefixed to verbs and adverbs to indicate the dative of the first personal pronoun, as راكول *rākawul* (to give me) راباندي *rābānde* (upon me). It is sometimes changed to لا *lā*. Ex. لا له راكه *lā la rāka* for را ته راكه *rā ta rāka* (give to me), ډوډۍ ما ته راكړِ ده *ḍoḍa-ī mā ta rākiṛi da* (has given me the bread), ملك تاوان راباندي ښكيښود *malik tāwān rābānde kkhkekkhod* (the chief put the loss upon me).

c. The Instrumental Case.—This case, in both its forms, is only used with the imperfect and past tenses of transitive verbs. The first form, ما *mā*, always precedes the verb, and is used when special emphasis or distinction is meant to be expressed. Ex. ما دا كار كړي دي *mā dā kār kaṛai dai* (I have done this deed), ما وړونبي صاحب خبراوه *mā wṛūnbe ṣāḥib khabarāwah* (I first informed the master), ما دا هسي هيڅري نه دي ويلي *mā dā hase hechare na dai wayalai* (I never said so). The second form of the instrumental case, مي *me* or مِ *mi*, is employed when no special emphasis or distinction is meant. It may precede or intervene between parts of the verb. Ex. ورته مي وي *warta me wai* or ورته مِ وِ *warta mi wi* (I said to him), وركړي مي دي *warkaṛai me dai* (I have given it to him, or her, or it), ډوډۍ مي خوړلِ ده *doḍa-i me khwuṛali da* (I have eaten the bread).

d. The second form of the genitive and instrumental cases in the plural, مو *mū* or مُه *muh*, is used precisely in the same manner *mutatis mutandis* as the مي *me* or مِ *mi* of the singular to which it corresponds. Ex. ملك مو زيږ دي *mulk mū zīg dai* (our country is rugged), خبري ور سره مو کړِ دي *khabare war sara mu kiṛi dī* (we have conversed with him), زمكه مو كرلِ ده *zmaka mū karali da* (we have tilled the earth).

57. Rule.—Whenever the second forms of the first, second, and third personal pronoun are used in construction with a transitive verb in the imperfect or past tenses, they denote the agent in the sentence. In any other construction with intransitive verbs, or the present and future tenses of transitive verbs, they indicate the possessive or genitive case.

58. Second personal pronoun (*mukhāṭib* or *ḥāẓir*) makes no change for gender, and is declined as follows:—

تهٔ *tah*, thou.

SINGULAR.

N.		تهٔ *tah*		thou.
G.	دي ـ دِ	ستا ـ دَ ستا *stā, da stā*	*de, di*	of thee.
D.	درته ـ درله	تا ته ـ تا له *tā ta, tā la*	*darta, darla*	to thee.
Ac.		تا *tā*		thee.
In.	دي ـ دِ	تا *tā*	*de, di*	by thee.
L.		په تا *pa tā*		on thee.
Ab.		له تا نه *la tā na*		from thee
V.		اي تا *ai tā*		oh thou!

PLURAL.

N.		تاسو ـ تاسُ *tāsū, tāsu*		you.
G.	مو ـ مُه	ستاسو ـ دَ ستاسو *stāsū, da stāsū*	*mo, mah*	of you.
D.		تاسو ته *tāsū ta*		to you.
Ac.		تاسو *tāsū*		you.

In.	مو ـ مه	تاسو *tāsū*	*mo, mah*	by you.
L.		په تاسو *pa tāsū*		on you.
Ab.		له تاسو نه *la tāsū na*		from you.
V.		اي تاسو *ai tāsū*		oh you!

a. THE GENITIVE CASE.—The two forms ستا *stā* and دي *de* or دِ *di* are used under precisely the same conditions as the corresponding forms of the first personal pronoun (Art. 56, *a*). Ex. ستا كور كوم دي *stā kor kūm dai* (which is thine house?). دا ستا توره ده يا څما *dā stā tūra da yā dzamā* (is this thy sword or mine?), دا ده ستا کړه دي *dā da stā kṛah dai* (this is thy doing), ځوي دي چرته دي *dzoe de charta dai* (where is your son?), توره دي څه شه *tūra de tsa sha* (what is become of your sword?).

b. THE DATIVE CASE.—The second form of this case is used in the same way as the corresponding form of the first personal pronoun (Art. 56, *b*). Ex. درته گوري *darta gorī* (he is looking at thee), ناري درته وهي *nāre darta wahī* (he is shouting to thee), تا ته وايي *tā ta wāyī* (he is speaking to thee). Emphatic, تا ته درکړي مِ دي *tā ta darkaṛai mi dai* (I have given it to thee). The form در *dar* of this pronoun, like the corresponding dative form of the first personal pronoun (را *rā*), is used as a pronominal dative prefix with verbs and adverbs, to indicate their relation to the dative of the second personal pronoun, as درتلل *dartlal* (to go to thee), درپسي *darpase* (after thee). Ex. درځم *dardzam* (I am coming to thee), درپسي يم *darpase yam* (I am after thee).

c. THE INSTRUMENTAL CASE.—The two forms are used in precisely the same manner as the corresponding forms of the first personal pronoun (Art. 56, *c*). Ex.—تا هغه سړي وژلي دي *tā haghah saṛai wajalai dai* (thou hast killed that man), تا ولي ما خبر کړي نه دي *tā wale mā khabar kaṛai na dai* (why hast not thou informed me?), or better تا ولي خبر نه کړلم *tā wale khabar na kṛalam* (why did you not tell me?), خوږ دي کړم *khūg de kṛam* (thou hast hurt me), وُ دي ليده *wu de līdah* (didst thou see it?), ورکه شِو غوا دِ بيا موندلِ ده *wruka shiwi ghwā di biyā mūndali da* (hast thou found the strayed cow?)

59. Third personal pronoun (*ghā-ib*). There are two pronouns to

represent the third person, viz., a proximate and a remote. They are thus declined :—

(Proximate.) دي *de*, he, she, it.

SINGULAR.

N.	دي ـ دا ـ ده	*de, dā, dah*	he, she, it.
G.	دَ دي ـ دَ ده ـ دَ دِ	*da de, da dah, da di*	of him, her, it.
D.	دي ته ـ ده ته ـ دِ ته	*de ta, dah ta, di ta*	to him, her, it.
Ac.	دي ـ ده ـ دِ	*de, dah, di*	him, her, it.
In.	دي ـ ده ـ دِ	*de, dah, di*	by him, her, it.
L.	په دي ـ په ده ـ په دِ	*pa de, pa dah, pa di*	on him, her, it.
Ab.	له دي نه ـ له ده نه etc.	*la de na, la dah na*, etc.	from him, her, it.
V.	اي دي	*ai de*	oh him! etc.

PLURAL.

N.	دوي ـ دي	*dwī, de*	they.
G.	دَ دويو ـ دَ دئُو	*da dwīo, da deo*	of them.
D.	دويو ته ـ دئُو ته	*dwīo ta, deo ta*	to them.
Ac.	دوي ـ دي	*dwī, de*	them.
In.	دويو ـ دئُو	*dwīo, deo*	by them.
L.	په دويو ـ په دئُو	*pa dwīo, pa deo*	on them.
Ab.	له دويو نه ـ له دئُو نه	*la dwīo na, la deo na*	from them.
V.	اي دويو ـ اي دئُو	*ai dwīo, ai deo*	oh them!

a. This pronoun is used to designate the third person when present before the speaker, or to point out the proximate of two or more third persons mentioned together. It undergoes no change for gender, and of the different forms that first given is the one most commonly used in conversation. The others are chiefly met with in books. Ex. دي هوښيار سړي دي *de hokkhyār saṛai dai* (he is a clever man), هغه برستن دي ته ورکه *hagha bṛastan de ta warka* (give that quilt to him or her), دي ډيره عجزه ده *de ḍera 'ajaza da* (she is very humble), دوي زوراوُر دي *dwī zorāwa-ar dī* (they are powerful), دَ دويو کار تول ښه دي دَ هغو هيڅ ندي *da dwīo kār ṭol kkhah dai da hagho hets na dai* (their work is all good, theirs is nothing), هغه توپک دي (or ده or دِ) ته ورکه *haghah ṭopak de* (or *dah* or *di*) *ta warka*, give the gun to him (out of many).

(Remote.) هغه *haghah*, he, it.

SINGULAR.

N.		هغه *haghah*		he, it.
G.	ئي	دَ هغه *da haghah*	*e*	of him, it.
D.	ورته	هغه ته *haghah ta*	*warta*	to him, it.
Ac.		هغه *haghah*		him, it.
In.	ئي	هغه *haghah*	*e*	by him, it.
L.		په هغه *pa haghah*		on him, it.
Ab.		له هغه نه *la haghah na*		from him, it.
V.		اي هغه *ai haghah*		oh him! it!

PLURAL.

N.		هغهٔ *hagha-ah*		they.
G.		دَ هغو *da hagho*		of them.
D.		هغو ته *hagho ta*		to them.
Ac.		هغهٔ *hagha-ah*		them.
In.	ئي	هغو *hagho*	*e*	by them.
L.		په هغو *pa hagho*		on them.
Ab.		له هغو نه *la hagho na*		from them.
V.		اي هغو *ai hagho*		oh them!

a. This pronoun is subject to change for gender, and in the feminine becomes هِغِه *highi* or *hagha* (she), and is declined like a noun of the sixth declension. Ex. دَ هغي ښځي *da haghe* (or *highe*) *kkhadze* (of that woman), هغو ښځو ته *hagho* (or *higho*) *kkhadzo ta* (to those women).

b. The second forms of the genitive, dative, and instrumental cases of the remote third personal pronoun, هغه *haghah*, are used under the same rules precisely as the corresponding forms of the first and second personal pronouns. Ex. پښه ئي ماته ده *pkkha e māta da* (his leg is broken), کور ئي وران شه *kor e wrān sha* (ruined be his house), ورته مي وُ وِ *warta me wu wi* (I said to him), ورته نژدي شه *warta nijde sha* (get close to him), خپله ښځه ئي وُ وهله *khpula kkhadza e wu wahala* (he beat his own wife), کندول ئي مات کړ *kandol e māt kaṛ* (he broke the cup).

c. The second form of the dative case, ور *war*, like the corresponding forms of the first and second personal pronouns (را *rā* and در *dar*), is used as a pronominal dative prefix with verbs and adverbs to denote their relation to the dative of third personal pronouns, as ورکول *warkawul* (to give him, her, it), ورځخه *wartsakha* (with him, her, it). Ex. فقير ته يو روپئ دي ورکړِ ده *faqīr ta yo rūpa-ī de warkiṛi da* (hast thou given one rupee to the beggar?), ور ي کړ *war e kaṛ* (he has given (it) to him), ورځخه څه دولت شته *wartsakha tsa daulat shta* (has he any wealth?) ورځخه کښيناست *wartsakha kkshenāst* (he sat down with him), etc.

d. These pronominal dative prefixes را *rā*, در *dar*, ور *war*, when used as simple pronouns are often subject to change, as لا له *lā la* for را له *rā la*, دَ له *da la* for در له *dar la*, وَ له *wa la* for ور له *war la*, etc.

60. Demonstrative Pronouns (*ẓamīri-ishārat*).—There are two kinds of demonstrative pronoun, viz., the proximate and the remote.

a. Proximate.—The proximate demonstrative pronouns are three in number, viz., دغه *daghah*, دا *dā*, and هايه *hāyah* (this). They are declined as follows :—

دغه *daghah*, this.

SINGULAR.

	f.	*m.*			
N.	دَغه	دغه *daghah*		*dagha*	this.
G.	دَ دِغي	دَ دغه *da daghah*		*da dighe*	of this.
D.	دِغي ته	دغه ته *daghah ta*		*dighe ta*	to this.
Ac.	دَغه	دغه *daghah*		*dagha*	this.
In.	دِغي	دغه *daghah*		*dighe*	by this.
L.	په دِغي	په دغه *pa daghah*		*pa dighe*	on this.
Ab.	له دِغي نه	له دغه نه *la daghah na*		*la dighe na*	from this.
V.	اي دِغي	اي دغه *ai daghah*		*ai dighe*	oh this!

PLURAL.

	f.	*m.*			
N.	دغي	دغهٔ *dagha-ah*		*daghe*	these.
G.	دَ دِغو	دَ دغو *da dagho*		*da digho*	of these.
D.	دِغو ته	دغو ته *dagho ta*		*digho ta*	to these.
Ac.	دغي	دغهٔ *dagha-ah*		*daghe*	these.
In.	دِغو	دغو *dagho*		*digho*	by these.
L.	په دِغو	په دغو *pa dagho*		*pa digho*	on these.
Ab.	له دِغو نه	له دغو نه *la dagho na*		*la digho na*	from these.
V.	اي دِغو	اي دغو *ai dagho*		*ai digho*	oh these!

Ex. دغه سړي غل دي *daghah saṛai ghal dai* (this man is a thief), دغي توري تولي پڅي دي *daghe tūre ṭole pa-atse dī* (these swords are all blunt), دَ دغو سړو په مطلب باندي پوه نشوم *da dagho saṛo pa matlab bānde poh nashwam* (I don't understand the meaning of these men).

b. دا *dā*, this.

	SINGULAR.	PLURAL.
N.	دا *dā.*	دي *de.*
G.	دَ دي ـ دَ ده *da dai, da dah.*	دَ ديو *da deo.*
D.	دي ته ـ ده ته *de ta, dah ta.*	ديو ته *deo ta.*
Ac.	دا *dā.*	دي *de.*
In.	دي ـ ده *de, dah.*	ديو *deo.*
L.	په دي ـ په ده *pa de, pa dah.*	په ديو *pa deo.*
Ab.	له دي نه ـ له ده نه *la de na, la dah na.*	له ديو نه *la deo na.*
V.	اي دي ـ اي ده *ai de, ai dah.*	اي ديو *ai deo.*

Ex. دَ دي وني ميوي په څه شان وي *da de wane mewe pa tsa shān wī* (what like may be the fruit of this tree?), دي ته مونګ کاڼړي وايو *de ta mūng kāṇrai wāyū* (we call this a stone), دا څه شي دي *dā tsa shai dai* (what thing is this?)

c. The third form of proximate demonstrative pronoun, هايه *hāyah* (this), makes no change for gender or number, but in the oblique cases is inflected to هاي *hās* by the rejection of the final ه. It is a very emphatic form of the demonstrative pronoun, and is only used with reference to an object actually present. Ex. امسا مِ چړته ده *amsā mi charta da* (where is my stick?), هايه ده *hāya da* (this is it).

d. Remote.—The remote demonstrative pronouns are two in number, viz., هغه *haghah* and دي *de* (that). They are the proximate and remote third personal pronouns (Art. 59).

61. Possessive Pronoun (*ẓamīri-mushtarak*).—Pukkhto has no separate word for the possessive pronoun; but it is expressed by the adjective خپل *khpul* (own) used with the several personal pronouns respectively. It is declined regularly, like a masculine adjective (Art. 48, *b*), and forms its feminine according to the general rule. Ex. پلار مِ خپل راته ويلي دي *plār mi khpul rāta wayalai dai* (my father himself has told me), ښځه خپله تللي ده *kkhadza khpula talali da* (the woman herself has gone), زه خپل تلي يم

zah khpul talai yam (I myself have gone), خپل پلار وهلي يم *khpul plār wahalai yam* (my own father has beaten me).

a. More frequently the oblique form in the locative case is used. Ex. زه پلار په خپلَ وهلي يم *zah plār pa khpula wahalai yam* (father himself beat me), هغه په خپلَ ليدلي دي *haghah pa khpula līdalai dai* (he himself has seen).

62. Interrogative Pronoun (*ẓamīri-istifhām*).—There are five interrogative pronouns commonly used in Pukkhto. They are څوک *tsok* (who?), کوم *kūm* or کُم *kum* (which?), څه *tsa* (what?), څو *tso* (how many?), and څومره *tsomra* (how much?).

a. څوک *tsok* (who?) is only used with reference to animate objects, and in practice is applied only to human beings. It undergoes no change for gender or number, but in the oblique cases becomes چا *chā*. Ex. څوک يي *tsok ye* (who art thou?), دَ چا آس دي *da chā ās dai* (whose horse is it?), له چا نه دِ آخستي دي *la chā na di ākhistai dai* (from whom have you taken it?), چا ته ورکوم *chā ta warkawam* (to whom shall I give it?).

b. کوم *kūm* or کُم *kum* (which?) is applied to both animate and inanimate objects. It is declined regularly like a masculine adjective, and forms the feminine according to the general rule (Art. 48, *b*). Ex. کوم دي *kūm dai* (which is it?), دَ کوم کَلي يي *da kūm kilī ye* (of which village are you?), په کومي لارِ تلِ ده *pa kūme lāri tali da* (on which road has she gone?), دَ کومو سړو توپک ورک شوي دي *da kūmo saṛo ṭopa-ak wruk shawī dī* (which men's muskets have been lost?).

c. څه *tsa* (what?) can only be applied to inanimate objects. It makes no change for gender, number, or case, that is to say, is indeclinable. Ex. څه وايي *tsa wāyī* (what does he say?), دلته څه کار لري *dalta tsa kār lare* (what business hast thou here?), دا څه څيز دي *dā tsa tsīz dai* (what thing is this?).

d. څو *tso* (how many?) and څومره *tsomra* (how much) are both indeclinable, and used only in the plural. The former is applied to both animate and inanimate objects, and the latter to inanimate only. Ex. څو تنَ سړي دي *tso tana saṛī dī* (how many men are there?), په کندو کښي به څومره غنم وي *pa kandū kkhe ba tsomra ghanum wī* (how much wheat may there be in the bin?).

63. Relative Pronoun (*ismi-mauṣul*).—The relative pronouns are

formed by combining the interrogatives with the conjunction چه chi (that). Thus څوک چه tsok chi (whoever) applied only to animate objects; کوم چه kūm chi (whichever) applied to both animate and inanimate objects; and څه چه tsa chi (whatever) applied only to inanimate objects.

a. The relative pronouns must always precede the conjunction چه chi or commence the sentence. The correlative pronoun (*jawābi-mauṣūl*) always follows the conjunction or completes the sentence.

b. The remote third personal pronoun هغه *haghah* (he, she, it) is used as the correlative to the relative pronouns. Ex. څوک چه نیکي کوي هغه به ثواب گټي *tsok chi nekī kawī haghah ba ṣawāb gaṭi* (whoever does rightly he shall reap the future reward), کومه غوا چه گډه ده هغه زیارت لره بیایه *kūma ghwā chi guḍa da hagha ziyārat lara biyāya* (whichever cow is lame, her take to the sanctuary or asylum, *i.e.*, take the lame cow to the asylum), هر څه چه درته وایي ته هغه و منه *har tsa chi darta wāyī tah haghah wu mana* (whatever he says to thee, that thou believe, *i.e.*, believe whatever he says), کومي وني چه دَ میوو ندي هغي پریکه *kūme wane chi da mewo nadī haghe preka* (whichever trees are not of fruit, them cut down, *i.e.*, cut down those that are not fruit trees), کومو سړو چه دا کار کړي دي هغو ته سخته سزا پکاره ده *kūmo saṛo chi dā kār kaṛai dai hagho ta sakhta sazā pakāra da* (whichever men have done this deed, for them a severe punishment is necessary, *i.e.*, a severe punishment is necessary for the men who have done this deed).

64. INDEFINITE PRONOUN (*ismi-tankīr*).—The following are commonly used as indefinite pronouns, viz., څوک *tsok* (any one), ځني *dzane* (some), څه *tsa* (anything), and يو *yo* (one).

a. څوک *tsok* (any one) is the same word as the interrogative pronoun (Art. 62, *a*), and is only used in reference to human beings. Ex. په کور ښکي څوک شته *pa kor kkhke tsok shta* (is any one in the house?), هیڅ څوک نشته *hets tsok nishta* (there is no one), چا ته زیان مه رسوه *chā ta ziyān ma rasawa* (bring not injury to any one, *i.e.*, do injury to no one), دَ چا پردي سړي په مال باندي لاس مه وا چوه *da chā pradī saṛī pa māl bānde lās ma wā chawa* (lay not your hands on the property of any strange man).

b. ځني *dzane* or ځني *dzini* (some) is only used in the plural and for both genders. In the oblique cases it is inflected in the regular way. It is used with reference to both animate and inanimate objects. Ex. ځني ښه دي ځني بد *dzane kkhah dī dzane bad* (some are good, some bad), دَ ځنو خبرو تپهوس مناسب نګنړي *da dzano khabaro tapahūs munāsib naganṛī* (enquiry of some matters he does not consider fitting).

c. څه *tsa* (anything) is used with reference both to animate and inanimate objects. It is indeclinable (Art. 62, *c*). Ex. څه شته په کښې *tsa shta pa kkshe* (is there anything in it?), په کلي ښکي څه چرګان دي *pa kilī kkhke tsa chirgān dī* (are there any fowls in the village?), څه دي آوريدلي دي *tsa de āwredalai dai* (have you heard anything?).

d. يو *yo* (one or a) is used mostly with reference to animate objects. It is declined regularly, but has only the singular (Art. 51). Ex. يو سړي وهلي يم *yo saṛī wahalai yam* (a man has beaten me), يو لږ شان خو لا له راکه *yo la-ag shān kho lā la rāka* (give me at least a somewhat?).

e. The following adjectives are also in common use as indefinite pronouns:—

بل *bul*, another.	نور *nor*, more.
ډير *ḍer*, many.	هر *har*, every.

f. The following compound indefinite pronouns are in common use.

m.	بل يو *bul yo,*	other one.	نور ټول *nor ṭol,*	all the rest.
f.	بله يوه *bula yawa,*		نوره ټوله *nora ṭola,*	
m.	کوم يو *kūm yo,*	which one.	نور ډير *nor ḍer,*	many more.
f.	کومه يوه *kūma yawa,*		نوره ډيره *nora ḍera,*	
m.	هر يو *har yo,*	every one.	ډير بل *ḍer bul,*	many another.
f.	هره يوه *hara yawa,*		ډيره بله *ḍera bula,*	

g. The following make no change for gender or number, and only those combinations with څوک *tsok* are subject to inflection.

بل څوک *bul tsok*, other person.	هر څوک *har tsok*, every body.
بل څه *bul tsa*, other thing.	هر څه *har tsa*, every thing.
نور څوک *nor tsok*, who else.	هيڅ څوک *hets tsok*, nobody.
نور څه *nor tsa*, what else.	هر څو *har tso*, however many.

INFINITIVES. (*Muṣādir.*)

65. Under this head are included simple infinitives, and the verbal nouns derived from them, as well as the participles.

a. THE INFINITIVE MOOD (*maṣdar*) of both transitive and intransitive verbs is used as a masculine noun, and as such is subject to inflection in the oblique cases plural, like a noun of the second declension. Ex. ستا ويل په ځاي دي *stā wayal pa dzāe dai* (thy speech is appropriate), څما دَ تللُ په وخت راغي *dzamā da tlalu pa wakht rāghai* (he arrived at the time of my departure), له ډيرو وهلو نه ټپ شوي دي *la ḍero wahalo na ṭap shawai dai* (he has become exhausted (or haggard) by many beatings).

b. THE GERUND OR VERBAL NOUN (*ismi-maṣdar*) is only used as an abstract noun, and is formed from the infinitive, whether of active or neuter verbs, by rejecting the final لَ and substituting ون *ūn* for the masculine and نه *na* for the feminine. Ex.—

ترل *taṛal*, to bind.	ترون *taṛūn*,	ترنه *taṛana*, binding.
ساتل *sātal*, to keep.	ساتون *sātūn*,	ساتنه *sātana*, keeping.
پريکول *prekawul*, to cut off.	پريکوون *prekawūn*,	پريکوونه *prekawuna*, lopping.
منل *manal*, to obey.	منون *manūn*,	منىه *manana*, obeying.
ريژيدل *rejedal*, to be shed.	ريژيدون *rejedūn*	ريژيدنه *rejedana*, shedding.
پيژندل *pejandal*, to recognize.	پيژندون *pejandūn*,	پيژندنه *pejandana*, recognising.
آوريدل *āwredal*, to hear.	آوريدون *āwredūn*,	آوريدنه *āwredana*, hearing.
ګډيدل *gaḍedal*, to be mixed.	ګډيدون *gaḍedūn*,	ګډيدنه *gaḍedana*, mixing.

NOTE.—The masculine affix ون *ūn*, as above shown, appears to be the true one for forming the gerund from all verbs, and thus assimilating it with the class of nouns having the same termination (Art. 19, *d*). In practice, however, the feminine form is generally used, the masculine seldom. Ex. ريژيدنه دَ پانړو نښه دَ ژمي ده *rejedana da pāṇro nakkha da jimī da* (the falling of leaves is a sign of winter), په ترون دَ خپل سوګند پروا نلري *pa taṛūn da khpul saugand parwā nalari* (he has no care for the binding of his own oath).

c. THE PRESENT PARTICIPLE (*ismi-ḥāliya*), which is the same as the third person singular of the imperfect tense of verbs, denotes indefinite present action, and is only used as a noun. It is formed from the infinitive by rejecting the final ل and substituting the ۀ *zahir* for the masculine form. In those verbs, whose penultimate or antepenultimate syllable is formed by the short vowel *zabar* ـَ *a*, this is prolonged to the long vowel ا *ā* previous to the change for the present participle. The former class form their feminines by changing the final ه *h* to نه *na*. Ex. بليده *baledah, m.* بليدنه *baledana, f.* (igniting); ژووه *ǰowah, m.* ژوونه *ǰowana, f.* (chewing). In those of the latter class the lengthened vowel ا *ā* reverts to the short one ـَ *a*, and the final ه *h* is replaced by نه *na*. Ex. خاته *k͟hātah, m.* ختنه *k͟hatana, f.* (rising); پيژانده *peǰāndah, m.* پيژندنه *peǰandana, f.* (recognition).

d. The Active Participle (*ismi-fā'il*) is formed from the infinitive, whether of active or neuter verbs, by rejecting the final ل and substituting ونکي *ūnkai* or وني *ūnai* for the masculine, and ونکِ *ūnki* or ونِ *ūni* for the feminine. Ex. اوسيدل *osedal* (to abide), اوسيدونکي *osedūnkai* or اوسيدوني *osedūnai* (a resident); ويل *wayal* (to speak), ويونکي *wayūnkai* or ويوني *wayūnai* (a speaker).

e. The Passive Participle (*ismi-mafa'ūl*) is formed direct from the infinitive by adding the diphthong ي *ai* to the final ل of that mood for the masculine, and the short vowel *kasra* ـِ *i* for the feminine (Art. 48, *a*). Ex. وهل *wahal* (to beat), وهلي *wahalai, m.* وهلِ *wahali, f.* (beaten); سوليدل *sūledal* (to be abraded), سوليدلي *sūledalai, m.* سوليدلِ *sūledali, f.* (abraded).

f. In some verbs the passive or past participle is contracted by the elision of the final ل of the infinitive. Ex. آخستل *āk͟histal* (to take), آخستي *āk͟histai* (taken), for آخستلي *āk͟histalai*; کښيناستل *kks͟henāstal* (to sit), کښيناستي *kks͟henāstai* (seated), for کښيناستلي *kks͟henāstalai*.

g. The present and past participles are commonly used as adjectives. Ex. دنيا تيريدونِ ده *duniyā teredūni da* (the world is fleeting), نښتِ ژبه لري *nk͟khati ǰiba larī* (he has an obstructed speech).

SECTION III.

THE VERB. (*Fi'al.*)

66. The verb is a word that expresses being, doing, or suffering in reference to time, either present, future, or past. It is of two kinds, viz., active or transitive, and neuter or intransitive, and possesses mood, tense, number, and person.

67. MOOD (*ṣīgha*) indicates the kind or character of the action. There are five moods, viz., the infinitive, the indicative, the imperative, the subjunctive, and the potential.

68. THE INFINITIVE MOOD (*maṣdar*) is the simple form of the verb, and for the most part is only used as a verbal noun (Art. 65, *a*). All infinitives end in one of three terminations, viz., ل *al*, ول *wul*, and یدل *edal*. The two last of these infinitive terminations are added to nouns and adjectives in converting them to verbs. Ex.—

تود *tod*, hot	تودول *todawul*, to heat, تودیدل *todedal*, to become hot.
سپین *spīn*, white	سپینول *spīnawul*, to make white. سپینیدل *spīnedal*, to become white.
خوږ *khūg*, hurt	خوږول *khūgawul*, to hurt. خوږیدل *khūgedal*, to ache.
لنډ *lanḍ*, short	لنډول *lanḍawul*, to shorten. لنډیدل *lanḍedal*, to grow short.

a. Verbs whose infinitives end in ل *al* alone may be either transitive or intransitive. Ex.—

ښبل *bakkhal*, to give.	ختل *khatal*, to rise.
شاربل *shārbal*, to churn.	زنگل *zangal*, to swing.
کتل *katal*, to look.	نښتل *nkkhatal*, to stick.
موندل *mūndal*, to find.	وتل *watal*, to issue.

b. Verbs whose infinitives end in ول *wul* are, without exception, transitives. Ex.—

برندول *brandawul*, to frown.	لمسول *lamsawul*, to incite.
پاڅول *pātsawul*, to raise.	ماتول *mātawul*, to break.

c. Verbs whose infinitives end in يدل *edal* are, with only two or three exceptions, such as آوريدل *āwredal* (to hear), پښتيدل *pukkhtedal* (to ask) etc., all intransitives. Ex.—

پړسيدل *parsedal*, to swell.	رپيدل *rapedal*, to shiver.
خوئيدل *khwa-edal*, to slip.	شليدل *shledal*, to tear.

69. The Indicative Mood (*mushīr*) denotes simple being or doing, as پوهيږم *pohegam* (I understand), اور تود دي *or tod dai* (fire is hot), سپي غاپي *spai ghāpī* (the dog barks), ستړي يم *starai yam* (I am tired).

a. The Indicative Mood has nine tenses, viz., three of present time formed from the verbal root, and six of past time formed from the infinitive mood (Art. 73).

70. The Imperative Mood (*amr*) properly has only a second person in both numbers, but a third also is commonly used. The imperative mood is always formed from the present tense, both in transitive and intransitive verbs, by substituting the ه *khafī* for the pronominal affix of the second person singular, and prefixing the particle و *wu* for both singular and plural.

a. In derivative verbs formed from nouns and adjectives the imperative is formed by using the imperative mood of the auxiliary کول *kawul* (to do), in combination with the noun or adjective, if transitive, and with the imperative of the auxiliary شول *shwal* (to be), if intransitive. Ex.—

سپينول *spīnawul*, to whiten or make white.	سپين که *spīn ka*, make white.
سپينيدل *spīnedal*, to become white.	سپين شه *spīn sha*, be white.

71. The Subjunctive Mood (*shartiya*) implies doubt or condition, and generally requires another verb to complete the sentence. Ex. که واک ځما وي دا کار به هيڅري نه وه شوي *ki wāk dzamā wai dā kār ba hechare na wuh shawai* (were the power mine that deed would never have occurred), که زه جوړ وي *ki zah jor wai* (if I were well).

a. The Subjunctive Mood has three tenses preceded by the conjunction كه *ki* (if). They are the present, past, and future. The first is the same as the present indicative with the conjunction prefixed. The past and future tenses are formed from the past participle of the verb, coupled with the corresponding tenses of the auxiliary يم *yam* (I am).

72. THE POTENTIAL MOOD (*imkānī*) implies possibility or obligation, and also has three tenses, a present, past, and future. They are formed by coupling the past participle of the verb with the corresponding tenses of the auxiliary شول *shwal* (to become or be able). Ex. دروغ نه شم ويلي *darogh na sham wayalai* (I cannot tell a lie), نوكري كول شي *nokrī kawuli she* (canst thou do duty ?), پښه ي خوږه شه به تلي نشي *pkkha e khūga sha ba tilai na shī* (his foot is hurt, he will not be able to go).

73. TENSE (*zamān*) denotes time. There are nine different tenses. Three of them relate to present time, and the other six to past time.

74. PRESENT TENSES.—The tenses of present time are the present, the aorist, and the future. They are always formed from the root of the verb in all regular transitives and intransitives; and the root of the verb is obtained by rejecting the infinitive terminations ل *al*, ول *wul*, يدل *edal.*

a. The Present Tense (*hāl*) is formed in three different ways, in accordance with the three different terminations of the verb. Thus—

1. Those verbs, whether active or neuter, whose infinitives end in ل *al*, form the present tense by adding the pronominal affixes (Art. 76, *a*) direct to the root of the verb for each person in both numbers.

2. Those verbs whose infinitives end in ول *wul*, which is merely the transitive auxiliary كول *kawul* (to do) deprived of its initial letter, form the present tense by adding that of the auxiliary, deprived of its initial letter, to the root of the verb for the several persons in both numbers.

3. And similarly those verbs whose infinitives end in يدل *edal*, which is the intransitive auxiliary كيدل *kedal* (to become) deprived of its initial letter, form the present tense by adding that of the auxiliary, thus deprived of its initial letter, to the root of the verb for the several persons in both numbers.

The formation of the present tenses from the verbal root is shown in the subjoined table :—

	INFINITIVE.	PRESENT.	AORIST.	FUTURE.
Active	تړل to bind	تړم	وُ تړم	وُ به تړم
	کرزول to turn	کرزوم	وُکرزوم	وُ به کرزوم
Neuter	زنګل to swing	زانګم	وُ زانګم	وُ به زانګم
	پوهيدل to understand	پوهيږم	وُ پوهيږم	وُ به پوهيږم

In Pukkhto, as in the Hindūstānī, the present tense is constantly used to represent past action, the speaker adopting the *dramatic* instead of the *narrative* style, when relating past occurrences. Ex. ما وُليده چه سړي ناجوړ دي *mā wulīdah chi saṛai nājoṛ dai* (I saw that the man was sick), زه خبر نه وُم چه مکر کوي *zah khabar na wum chi makar kawī* (I was not aware that he was shamming), هغه وُويل چه زه به دا خبري هيچري نه منم *haghah wu wayal chi zah ba dā khabare hechare na manam* (he said that he would never believe that news).

b. The Aorist or Indefinite Future Tense (*muẓār'ī*) is formed from the present simply by prefixing the particle وُه or وُ *wu*, which corresponds with the Persian prefix مي *me* or *mī*, to each person in both numbers. In some verbs (generally those commencing with two consonants without an intervening vowel, such as پريږدل *pregdal*, ښکينول *kkhkenawul*, etc., with which the prefix could not be euphonious) this particle is altogether rejected. In such cases there is no difference between the aorist and the present tense, except in meaning, which is decided by the context. Ex. ستړي وګړي په خوب کښي آرام مومي *staṛai wagaṛai pa khob kkshe ārām mūmī* (the tired mortal finds rest in sleep), اُميد لرم چه له خپلو وبالونو نه بښنه مومم *umed laram chi la khpulo wabālūno na bakkhana mūmam* (I hope I shall or may obtain forgiveness for my sins).

c. The Future Tense (*mustaqbil*) is formed from the aorist simply by adding the particle به *ba*, the characteristic sign of the future, to its several persons in both numbers. This sign may precede or follow the particle وُ *wu*, when that sign of the aorist exists; and when it does not, the future sign may intervene between the syllables of the verb, as پري به ږدم *pre ba gdam* for به پريږدم *ba pregdam*, ښکي به نم *kkhke ba nam* for به ښکينم *ba kkhkenam*, ښکي به نه ني *kkhke ba na nī* for به نه ښکيني *ba na kkhkenī*.

1. If the personal pronouns (emphatic form, Art. 56) be expressed in their

emphatic forms, the future sign به *ba* always precedes the particle وُ *wu*, and may even be separated from it by the intervention of other words of the sentence. Ex. مونګ به سبا هغه کار وُ کړو *mūng ba sabā haghah kār wu kawū* (we will do that work in the morning or to-morrow).

2. If the personal pronouns be expressed in their non-emphatic forms, then the sign of the future always follows the particle وُ *wu*, and may either intervene between it and the verb, or follow the verb itself. Ex. ګوره مار دي وُ به دِ چيچي *gora mār dai wu ba di chīchī* (see! it is a snake, it will bite thee), اوس پوه شه وُ وهم به دِ که بيا دا هسي کوي *os poh sha wu waham ba di ki biyā dā hase kawe* (now mark, I will beat you if you do so again).

75. Past Tenses.—The tenses of past time are six in number, viz., the imperfect, the past, the continuative past, the perfect, the pluperfect, and the doubtful past. They are formed directly from the infinitive as regards the three first, and directly from the past participle as regards the three last, both in active and neuter verbs, as is shown in the subjoined form.

	Infinitive.	Imperfect.	Past.	Cont. Past.
Active	ترل to bind.	ترل-تاړه	وُ ترل-وُ تاړه	ترل به-تاړه به
	ګرزول to turn.	ګرزول-ګرزاوه	وُ ګرزول-وُ ګرزاوه	ګرزول به-ګرزاوه به
Neuter	زنګل to swing.	زنګل-زانګه	وُ زنګل-وُ زانګه	زنګل به-زانګه به
	پوهيدل to understand.	پوهيدل-پوهيده	وُ پوهيدل-وُ پوهيده	پوهيدل به-پوهيده به

	Past Participle.	Perfect.	Pluperfect.	Doubt. Past.
Active	ترلي bound.	ترلي دي	ترلي وُه	ترلي به وُه
	ګرزولي turned.	ګرزولي دي	ګرزولي وُه	ګرزولي به وُه
Neuter	زنګلي swung.	زنګلي دي	زنګلي وُه	زنګلي به وُه
	پوهيدلي understood.	پوهيدلي دي	پوهيدلي وُه	پوهيدلي به وُه

a. The Imperfect Tense (*māẓī istimrārī*) implies continuity of past action not yet complete.

1. In active or transitive verbs the imperfect, like all other past tenses, is only used in the third person with the pronoun or other *agent* of the verb in the *instrumental* case, and is subject to change for gender and number to agree with the *object* in the *nominative* case, if other than the first or second personal pronouns. In the

singular it has two forms for the masculine: either the infinitive is used in its unaltered form, or it is altered by substituting ه *ẓāhir* for its final ل *l* and prolonging the penultimate short vowel *zabar* — *a* to its corresponding long vowel ا *ā*, as ترل *taṛal*, تاړه *tāṛah*; گرزول *girzawul*, گرزاوه *girzāwah*. The feminine is formed by merely adding ه *khafī* to the unaltered infinitive, as ترل *taṛal*, ترله *taṛala*; گرزول *girzawul*, گرزوله *girzawula*. In the plural the masculine is formed from the unaltered infinitive, and the feminine by adding to it the long vowel ي *e*, or more commonly its corresponding short vowel *kasra* — *i*. But if the object of the verb be either the first or second personal pronoun, then the infinitive alone is used with the proper pronominal affix attached, and the corresponding pronoun itself may be expressed or understood in the nominative case, as ترل *taṛal*, ترلم *taṛalam*, etc. Ex. ما سپي تاړه *mā spai tāṛah* (I was tying the dog), هغو ښځه ترله *hagho kkhadza taṛala* (they were tying the woman), زه هغو سړو ترلم *zah hagho saṛo taṛalam* (those men were tying me), تاسو چا ترلي *tāsū chā taṛala-ī* (who were tying you?).

2. In regular neuter or intransitive verbs whose infinitives end in يدل *edal* the imperfect tense is formed direct from the infinitive by attaching the proper pronominal affixes for the first and second persons, which are not subject to change for gender. But for the third person the following changes occur. In the singular the masculine is formed by substituting ه *ẓāhir* for the final ل *l* of the infinitive, and the feminine by simply adding ه *khafī* to it, as پوهيدل *pohedal*, *m.* پوهيده *pohedah*, *f.* پوهيدله *pohedala*. In the plural the masculine is formed from the unaltered infinitive, and the feminine by adding ي *e* or — *i* to it.

b. The Past Tense (*māẓī muṭlaq*) denotes an indefinite perfect action. It is formed from the imperfect tense merely by the prefix of the particle و *wu* for both active and neuter verbs. In some verbs this particle is altogether rejected as redundant or inharmonious, as explained with respect to the aorist tense. Ex. ما سپي و تاړه *mā spai wu tāṛah* (I tied the dog), هغو ښځه و ترله *hagho kkhadza wu taṛala* (they tied the woman), etc.

c. The Continuative Past Tense (*māẓī mudāmī*) denotes continuous past action, habit, or usage, and is formed from the imperfect by the addition simply of the particle به *ba*, which may follow or precede the verb. Ex. سپي م تاړه به *spai mi tāṛah ba*, or سپي به م تاړه *spai ba mi tāṛah* (I used to tie the dog), هغه به راته به ما سره ښکيناسته او به خبري کول *haghah ba rātah ba mā sara kkkkenāstah aw va khabare kawuli* (he used to come to me, sit with me and talk), هغه كله به خپله ښځه نازوله كله به وهله *haghah kala ba khpula kkhadza nāzawula kala ba wahala* (he used sometimes to pet his wife, sometimes to beat her).

d. The Perfect Tense (*māẓī qarīb*) implies the recent or perfect completion of an act. It is formed from the past participle of the verb coupled with the third person present tense of the auxiliary يم *yam* (I am) for transitives, the agent being in the instrumental case as previously explained. For intransitives no such change is observed, and the past participle is conjugated regularly with the present tense of the auxiliary in number and person. But in verbs, transitive and intransitive, the participle suffers inflection for gender and number in all the persons, but the auxiliary only in the third person singular. This rule applies to all compound tenses. Ex. كتاب دِ لوستي دي *kitāb di lwustai dai* (have you read the book?) ما ډوډئ خوړلِ ده *mā doḍa-ī khwuṛali da* (I have eaten the bread), روپئ دِ وركړي دي *rūpa-ī di warkiṛī dī* (have you given him the rupees?), غلو ځمونګه څلور اوښان نيولي دي *ghlo dzamūnga tsalor ūkkhān nīwulī dī* (thieves have seized four of our camels).

e. The Pluperfect Tense (*māẓī ba'īd*) denotes action long since completed or past. It is formed according to the same rules for transitives and intransitives as the preceding tense, by coupling the past participle of the verb with the past tense of the auxiliary يم *yam* (I am).

f. The Doubtful Past Tense (*māẓī tashkīk*) is formed from the past participle of the verb, coupled with the future tense of the auxiliary يم *yam* (I am) according to the rules above given, both for verbs transitive and intransitive.

76. Person and Number (*ẓamā-ir wa 'idād*).—Each tense has three persons, corresponding with the first, second, and third personal pronouns, and two numbers, the singular and plural. In all tenses and both numbers the third person is subject to inflection for gender, and in compound tenses the first and second persons also.

a. In all present tenses of transitive verbs, and in tenses present and past of intransitive verbs, the different persons in the singular and plural, are distinguished by the affix of certain pronominal particles that are inseparable from the verbs. They are styled "affixed personal pronouns" (*ẓamā-iri muttaṣila*) and are as follows, viz.—

First person	م *am*			ؤ *ū*	
Second person	ې *e*	singular.		ئ *a-ī*	plural.
Third person	ي *ī*			ي *ī*	

The first and second of these pronominal affixes in both numbers are also used with the imperfect and past tenses of transitive verbs, when their corresponding personal pronouns happen to be the *object* in a sentence governed by such a verb, which, as has been previously explained, requires that the *agent* or subject should be in the *instrumental* case, and the *object* in the *nominative* case, and to agree with the verb in gender, number, and person. Ex. زه هغه سړي ؤ وهلم *zah hag͟hah saṛī wu wuhalam* (that man beat me), ته چا بللي *tah c͟hā balale* (who called thee?), صاحب مونږ بللو *ṣāḥib mūng balalū* (the master called us).

b. The regular personal pronoun, styled, in contradistinction to the pronominal affixes above-mentioned, "detached personal pronouns" (*ẓamā-iri munfaṣila*), are also used in the nominative case as the agent in a sentence, with the present tenses of transitive verbs, and with all tenses, present and past, of intransitives. They are not always expressed with the verbs, but must be always understood when not so. Generally their expression denotes emphasis or distinction. They are as follows, viz.—

SINGULAR.	PLURAL.
زه *zah*, I.	مونږ ـ موږ *mūng*, *mūg*, we.
ته *tah*, thou.	تاسو *tāsū*, you.
هغه *hag͟hah*, he, it.	*هغه *hag͟hah*, they.
هغه *hag͟ha*, *f.*, she.	هغي *hag͟he*, *f.*, they.

As the *agent* in construction with the past tenses of transitive verbs, these pronouns are conjugated in the instrumental case with the third person of the verb, both in the singular and plural. They always precede the verb, and are as follows, viz.—

SINGULAR.	PLURAL.
ما ـ مي ـ م *mā*, *me*, *mi*, by me.	مونږه ـ مُه ـ مو *mūnga*, *muh*, *mū*, by us.
تا ـ دي ـ دِ *tā*, *de*, *di*, by thee.	تاسو ـ مَه ـ مو *tāsū*, *mah*, *mo*, by you.
هغه ـ ئ *hag͟hah*, *e*, by him, etc.	هغو ـ ئ *hag͟ho*, *e*, by them, *m.* and *f.*
هغي ـ ئ *hag͟he*, *e*, *f.*, by her.	

77. Besides the moods and tenses before-mentioned, the verb has a

* The nominative plural of the third personal pronoun is usually met with as above given, but the correct form is هغهٔ *hag͟ha-ah*.

gerund or verbal noun, a present participle, an active participle, and a passive or past participle, as has been explained in Art. 65.

78. In Pukkhto the verbs may be divided into three classes, viz., the active or transitive verb, the neuter or intransitive verb, and the derivative or compound verb, which may be either active or neuter in signification. Each of these classes of verbs is here described separately, as they present numerous variations in the modes of forming their paradigms.

79. But before proceeding to the description of the several classes of verbs, it is necessary first to show the conjugation of certain verbs that are used as auxiliaries in the formation of several of the tenses of both active and neuter verbs. The auxiliaries are يم *yam* (I am), infinitive wanting; كيدل *kedal* (to become); and شول *shwal* (to be).

80. The verb يم *yam* (I am) is very defective and irregular. It has no infinitive nor imperative mood, and is thus conjugated.

INDICATIVE MOOD.

	PRESENT TENSE. I am, thou art, etc.	We are, you are, etc.
	SINGULAR.	PLURAL.
	زه يم *zah yam.*	مونگ يو *mūng yū.*
	ته يي *tah ye.*	تاسو ييئ *tāsū ya-ī.*
m.	هغه دي - شته *haghah dai, shta.*	هغه دي - شته *haghah dī, shta.*
f.	هغه ده - شته *hagha da, shta.*	هغي دي - شته *haghe dī, shta.*

	PAST TENSE. I was, thou wast, etc.	We were, you were, etc.
	SINGULAR.	PLURAL.
	زه وُم *zah wum.*	مونگ وُو *mūng wū.*
	ته وي *tah we.*	تاسو وئ *tāsū wa-ī.*
m.	هغه وُه *haghah wuh.*	هغه وُو *haghah wū.*
f.	هغه وَه - وَ *hagha wa.*	هغي وي - وِ *haghe we, wi.*

	FUTURE TENSE. I shall or will be, etc.	We shall or will be, etc.
	SINGULAR.	PLURAL.
	زه به يم *zah ba yam.*	مونگ به يو *mūng ba yū.*
	ته به يي *tah ba ye.*	تاسو به ييئ *tāsū ba ya-ī.*
m.	هغه به وي *haghah ba wī.*	هغه به وي *haghah ba wī.*
f.	هغه به وي *hagha ba wī.*	هغي به وي *haghe ba wī.*

SUBJUNCTIVE MOOD

Present Tense. If I were, etc. — If we were, etc.

	SINGULAR.	PLURAL.
	كه زه وُم *ki zah wum.*	كه مونګ وُو *ki mūng wū.*
	كه ته وي *ki tah we.*	كه تاسو وئِ *ki tāsū wa-ī.*
m.	كه هغه وي *ki haghah wī.*	كه هغه وي *ki haghah wī.*
f.	كه هغه وي *ki hagha wī.*	كه هغي وي *ki haghe wī.*

Past Tense. If I had been, etc. — If we had been, etc.

	SINGULAR.	PLURAL.
	كه زه وي ـ واي *ki zah wai, wāe.*	كه مونګ وي ـ واي *ki mūng wai, wāe.*
	كه ته وي ـ واي *ki tah wai, wāe.*	كه تاسو وي ـ واي *ki tāsū wai, wāe.*
m.	كه هغه وي ـ واي *ki haghah wai, wāe.*	كه هغه وي ـ واي *ki haghah wai, wāe.*
f.	كه هغه وي ـ واي *ki hagha wai, wāe.*	كه هغي وي ـ واي *ki haghe wai, wāe.*

Future Tense. If I would have been, etc. — If we would have been, etc.

	SINGULAR.	PLURAL.
	كه زه به وُم *ki zah ba wum.*	كه مونګ به وُو *ki mūng ba wū.*
	كه ته به وي *ki tah ba we.*	كه تاسو به وئِ *ki tāsū ba wa-ī.*
m.	كه هغه به وُه *ki haghah ba wuh.*	كه هغه به وُو *ki haghah ba wu.*
f.	كه هغه به وَه ـ وَ *ki hagha ba wa.*	كه هغي به وي ـ وِ *ki haghe ba we, wi.*

a. The Present Tense. Indicative Mood.—The form شته *shta* of the third person singular and plural, is both masculine and feminine. It is used instead of the form دي *dai*, when affirmation, interrogation, or emphasis is intended with reference to objects absent or remote. دي *dai*, on the other hand, is used under the same circumstances with reference to objects actually present or proximate. Ex. څوي دِ شته *dzoe di shta* (have you a son?), هو څوي مِ شته *ho dzoe mi shta* (yes, I have a son), نه څوي مِ نشته *na dzoe mi nishta* (no, I have not a son), ستا په وطن ښكي څه آسونه شته *stā pa waṭan kkhke tsa āsūna shta* (are there any horses in your country?), هو شته *ho shta* (yes, there are), ستا په كلي ښكي وني شته *stā pa kilī kkhke wane shta* (are there trees in your village?), شته *shta* (there are), دا ستا څوي دي *dā stā dzoe dai* (is this your son?), هو څما څوي دي *ho dzamā dzoe dai* (yes, he is my son), هغه څوك ده *hagha tsok da* (who is that person?), لور مِ ده *lūr mi da* (she is my daughter), څو آسونه دي *tso āsūna dī* (how many horses are there?), شپږ دي

shpag dī (there are six), دَ پلانکي توره ده *da palānkī tūra da* (it is so-and-so's sword). In cases where special emphasis is required, both forms are used together. Ex. يو تکي دَ اوبو نشته دي *yo ṭakai da obo nishta dai* (there is not a drop of water), ما کتلي دي کندو تش دي غله په کښې نشته ده *mā katalai dai kandū ta-ash dai ghala pa kkshe nishta da* (I have looked, the bin is empty, there is no corn in it), بيا وُ کوره شته ده درته زه وايم *biyā wugora shta da darta zah wāyam* (look again; there is, I tell you).

b. PRESENT TENSE. SUBJUNCTIVE MOOD.—There is another form of the third person, singular and plural, of this tense, formed by the addition of the (*nūn-i-tākīd* of Arabian grammarians) نَ *na* to the form above given, as وي *wī*, وين *wīna*. Its use implies probability or belief, and it is often added to the third person of the future and aorist tenses of verbs to denote certainty, belief, or obligation. It is seldom used in conversation, but is common in books.

81. The intransitive auxiliary verb کيدل *kedal* (to become) is very defective, but regular in its formation. It has only three tenses of the indicative mood, and these are used in forming the present and past tenses of intransitive verbs. It is conjugated as follows:—

INFINITIVE MOOD. کيدل *kedal* (to become).

INDICATIVE MOOD.

PRESENT TENSE. I become or am becoming, etc. We are becoming or become.

SINGULAR.	PLURAL.
کيږم - کيگم *kegam, kegam.*	کيږو - کيگو *kegū, kegū.*
کيږي - کيگي *kege, kege.*	کيږئ - کيگئ *kega-ī, kega-ī.*
کيږي - کيگي *kegī, kegī.*	کيږي - کيگي *kegī, kegī.*

FUTURE TENSE. I shall or will become, etc. We shall or will become, etc.

SINGULAR.	PLURAL.
به کيږم or کيگم *ba kegam* or *kegam.*	به کيږو or کيگو *ba kegū* or *kegū.*
به کيږي *ba kege.*	به کيږئ *ba kega-ī.*
به کيږي *ba kegī.*	به کيږي *ba kegī.*

Past Tense. I was becoming, etc.	We were becoming, etc.
SINGULAR.	PLURAL.
کیدلم - کیدم *kedalam, kedam.*	کیدلو - کیدو *kedalū, kedū.*
کیدلي - کیدي *kedale, kede.*	کیدلئ - کیدئ *kedala-ī, keda-ī.*
m. کیدل - کیده *kedal, kedah.*	کیدل *kedal.*
f. کیدله *kedala.*	کیدلي - کیدلِ *kedale, kedali.*

Gerund.—*m.* کیدون *kedūn*, *f.* کیدنه *kedana* (being, becoming).

Present Participle.—*m.* کیده *kedah*, *f.* کیدله *kedala* (been, become).

Active Participle.—کیدونکي *kedūnkai* (becomer).

Passive Participle.—کیدلي *kedalai* (having become).

a. For the sake of convenience, the personal pronouns have been omitted from the above conjugation. They may be expressed, as in the conjugation of یم *yam*, or understood with equal propriety in general, but they must always be expressed when emphasis or distinction is intended.

82. The auxiliary verb شول *shwal* (to be or become) differs from the preceding, inasmuch as it indicates change or transition from one state to another, whilst کیدل *kedal* merely indicates simple being or existence. It is perfect and regular in its form, and is thus conjugated.

INFINITIVE MOOD. شول *shwal* (to be or become).

INDICATIVE MOOD.

Present Tense. I become, etc.	We become, etc.
SINGULAR.	PLURAL.
شم *sham.*	شو *shū.*
شي *she.*	شئ *sha-ī.*
شي *shī.*	شي *shī.*

Aorist Tense. I may be or become, etc.	We may be or become, etc.
SINGULAR.	PLURAL.
و شم *wu sham.*	و شو *wu shū.*
و شي *wu she.*	و شئ *wu sha-ī.*
و شي *wu shī.*	و شي *wu shī.*

FUTURE TENSE. I shall or will be, etc. — We shall or will be, etc.

	SINGULAR.			PLURAL.	
	وُ به شم	*wu ba sham.*		وُ به شوُ	*wu ba shū.*
	وُ به شي	*wu ba she.*		وُ به شئ	*wu ba sha-ī.*
	وُ به شي	*wu ba shī.*		وُ به شي	*wu ba shī.*

IMPERFECT TENSE. I was being, etc. — We were being, etc.

	SINGULAR.			PLURAL.	
	شولم - شوم	*shwalam, shwam.*		شولوُ - شوُ	*shwalū, shwū.*
	شولي - شوي	*shwale, shwe.*		شولئ - شوئ	*shwala-ī, shwa-ī.*
m.	شوه - شه	*shwah, shah.*		شول - شوُ	*shwal, shwū.*
f.	شوله - شوَ - شَ	*shwala, shwa, sha.*		شولي - شوي	*shwale, shwe.*

PAST TENSE. I became, etc. — We became, etc.

	SINGULAR.			PLURAL.	
	وُ شولم - وُ شوم	*wu shwalam, wu shwam.*		وُ شولوُ - وُ شوُ	*wu shwalū, wu shwū.*
	وُ شولي - وُ شوي	*wu shwale, wu shwe.*		وُ شولئ - وُ شوئ	*wu shwala-ī, wu shwa-ī.*
m.	وُ شوه - وُ شه	*wu shwah, wu shah.*		وُ شول - وُ شوُ	*wu shwal, wu shwū.*
f.	وُ شوله - وُ شوَ	*wu shwala, wu shwa.*		وُشولي - وُ شوي	*wu shwale, wu shwe.*

PERFECT TENSE. I have become, etc. — We have become, etc.

	SINGULAR.			PLURAL.	
	شَوَی یم - شِوِ یم	*shawai yam, f. shiwi yam,*	f.	شَوِي يوُ - شِوِيوُ	*shawī yu, shiwi yū,*
	شَوَی يي	*shawai ye.* etc.		شَوِي يئ	*shawī ya-ī.* etc.
m.	شَوَی دي	*shawai dai.*		شَوِي دي	*shawī dī.*
f.	شِوِ ده	*shiwi da.*		شِوِي دي	*shiwī dī.*

PLUPERFECT TENSE. I had become, etc. — We had become, etc.

	SINGULAR.			PLURAL.	
	شَوَی وُم	*shawai wum.*		شَوِي وُو	*shawī wū.*
	شَوَی وي	*shawai we.*		شَوِي وئ	*shawī wa-ī.*
m.	شَوَی وُه	*shawai wuh.*		شَوِي وُو	*shawī wū.*
f.	شِوِ وَه - وَ	*shiwi wa.*		شِوِي وي - وِ	*shiwī we, wi.*

Doubtful Past Tense. I will have become, etc. We would have become, etc.

	SINGULAR.		PLURAL.	
	شَوَي بہ وُم	*shawai ba wum.*	شَوِي بہ وُو	*shawī ba wū.*
	شَوَي بہ وې	*shawai ba we.*	شَوِي بہ وئِ	*shawī ba wa-ī.*
m.	شَوَي بہ وُه	*shawai ba wuh.*	شَوِي بہ وُو	*shawī ba wū.*
f.	شِوِ بہ وَه ـ وَ	*shiwi ba wa.*	شِوِي بہ وې ـ وِ	*shiwī ba we, wi.*

SUBJUNCTIVE MOOD.

Present Tense. If I become, etc. If we become, etc.

SINGULAR.		PLURAL.	
کہ شم	*ki sham.*	کہ شُو	*ki shū.*
کہ شې	*ki she.*	کہ شئِ	*ki sha-ī.*
کہ شي	*ki shī.*	کہ شي	*ki shī.*

Aorist Tense. If I may become, etc. If we may become, etc.

SINGULAR.		PLURAL.	
کہ وُ شم	*ki wu sham.*	کہ وُ شُو	*ki wu shū.*
کہ وُ شې	*hi wu she.*	کہ وُ شئِ	*ki wu sha-ī.*
کہ وُ شي	*ki wu shī.*	کہ وُ شي	*ki wu shī.*

Past Tense. If I became or were, etc. If we became or were, etc.

SINGULAR.

شواي or شوَي (کہ زہ *ki zah* / کہ تہ *ki tah* / کہ هغہ *ki haghah* / هغہ *hagha, f.*) *shwāe* or *shwai.*

PLURAL.

شواي or شوي (کہ مونگ *ki mūng* / کہ تاسو *ki tāsū* / کہ هغہ *ki haghah* / هغي *haghe, f.*) *shwāe* or *shwai.*

Pluperfect Tense. If I had been, etc. If we had been, etc.

SINGULAR.

m. شَوَي وَي / *f.* شِوِ وَي (کہ زہ *ki zah* / کہ تہ *ki tah* / کہ هغہ *ki haghah* / هغہ *hagha, f.*) *shawai wai.* / *shiwi wai.*

PLURAL.

شَوِي وَي / شوِي وَي (کہ مونگ *ki mūng* / کہ تاسو *ki tāsū* / کہ هغہ *ki haghah* / هغي *haghe, f.*) *shawī wai.* / *shiwī wai.*

DOUBTFUL PAST TENSE. I will have been, etc. We will have been, etc.

	SINGULAR.			PLURAL.		
m.	به يم	شَوَئ shawai	ba yam.	به يو	شَوِي shawī	ba yū.
	به يې		ba ye.	به يئ		ba ya-ī.
f.	به وِي	شِوِ shiwi	ba wī.	به وِي	شِوِي shiwī	ba wī.

IMPERATIVE MOOD.

Become thou, let him become.	Become ye, let them become.
SINGULAR.	PLURAL.
وُ شه - شه wu sha, sha.	وُ شئ - شئ wu sha-ī, sha-ī.
or هغه دِ شي hagẖah di shī, or	or هغه دِ شي hagẖah di shī, or
وُ دِ شي wu di shī.	وُ دِ شي wu di shī.

GERUND.—*m.* شوون *shwūn*, *f.* شوونه *shwūna* (becoming, being).
PRESENT PARTICIPLE.—شول *shwal*, *f.* شوله *shwala* (been, become).
ACTIVE PARTICIPLE.—شوونکي *shwūnkai* or شووني *shwūnai* (becomer).
PASSIVE PARTICIPLE.—شولي *shwalai* or شوي *shawai* (having become).

a. In all the compound tenses the participle undergoes inflection for gender with each person in both numbers, as shown above.

83. THE TRANSITIVE VERB (*fi'ali-mut'addī*).—The active or transitive verb denotes action passing from an agent to an object. It has an active and a passive voice, and is distinguished by the *instrumental* construction of its past tenses in the active voice, and by the termination of the infinitive mood in ل *al* or ول *wul.*

a. Simple transitive verbs, in the tenses of present time, govern the accusative case, but causals, verbs of giving, telling, etc., govern the dative case.

b. The passive voice is formed by conjugating the past participle with the several tenses of the auxiliaries كيدل *kedal* and شول *shwal.*

c. Transitive verbs include all causals and derivatives, whose infinitive mood ends in ول *wul.* And they are formed from intransitives, whether primitive or derivative, by changing the terminal ل *al* or يدل *edal* of the infinitive into ول *wul.* Ex.—

خندل *khandal,* to laugh.	خندول *khandawul,* to make laugh.
زنگل *zangal,* to swing.	زنگول *zangawul,* to make swing.
ژرل *ǰaṛal,* to cry.	ژړول *ǰaṛawul,* to make cry.
خوئيدل *khwa-edal,* to slip.	خويول *khwayawul,* to make slip.
شليدل *shledal,* to tear.	شلول *shlawul,* to rend, tear.
كړيدل *kaṛedal,* to parch.	كړول *kaṛawul,* to scorch, dry.

84. The active voice (*faṣli-m'arūf*) of transitive verbs is conjugated according to the general rules explained in the preceding pages, and as shown in the following paradigm of the regular transitive verb وهل *wahal* (to strike).

INFINITIVE MOOD. وهل *wahal* (to strike).

INDICATIVE MOOD.

PRESENT TENSE. I strike, etc.	We strike, etc.
SINGULAR.	PLURAL.
وهم *waham.*	وهو *wahū.*
وهي *wahe.*	وهئي *waha-ī.*
وهي *wahī.*	وهي *wahī.*

AORIST TENSE. I may strike, etc.	We may strike, etc.
SINGULAR.	PLURAL.
وُ وهم *wu waham.*	وُ وهو *wu wahū.*
وُ وهي *wu wahe.*	وُ وهئي *wu waha-ī.*
وُ وهي *wu wahī.*	وُ وهي *wu wahī.*

FUTURE TENSE. I will or shall strike, etc.	We will or shall strike, etc.
SINGULAR.	PLURAL.
وُ به وهم *wu ba waham.*	وُ به وهو *wu ba wahū.*
وُ به وهي *wu ba wahe.*	وُ به وهئي *wu ba waha-ī.*
وُ به وهي *wu ba wahī.*	وُ به وهي *wu ba wahī.*

Imperfect Tense. Form I.—I, etc., was striking him, etc. I, etc., was striking them.

	Singular			Plural		
m.	واهه	ما *mā*	*wāhah*	وهل	ما *mā*	*wahal*
	وهل	تا *tā*	*wahal*		تا *tā*	
		هغه *hag̲h̲ah*			هغه *hag̲h̲ah*	
		هغي *hag̲h̲e* f.			هغي *hag̲h̲e*	
		مونگه *mūnga*			مونگه *mūnga*	
		تاسو *tāsū*			تاسو *tāsū*	
f.	وهله	هغو *hag̲h̲o*	*wahala*	وهلي	هغو *hag̲h̲o*	*wahale*

Imperfect Tense. Form II.—He, she, it was striking me, thee, etc. us, you, etc.

	Singular	Plural
	زه وهلم *zah wahalam*	مونگ وهلو *mūng wahalū*
	ته وهلي *tah wahale*	تاسو وهلئ *tāsū wahala-ī*
m.	هغه واهه - وهل *hag̲h̲ah wāhah, wahal*	هغه وهل *hag̲h̲ah wahal*
f.	هغه وهله *hag̲h̲a wahala*	هغي وهلي - وهلِ *hag̲h̲e wahale, wahali*

Past Tense. Form I.—I, etc., did strike him, etc. I, etc., did strike them.

	Singular			Plural		
m.	وُ واهه	ما *mā*	*wu wāhah*	وُ وهل	ما *mā*	*wu wahal*
	وُ وهل	تا *tā*	*wu wahal*		تا *tā*	
		هغه *hag̲h̲ah*			هغه *hag̲h̲ah*	
		هغي *hag̲h̲e*			هغي *hag̲h̲e*	
		مونگه *mūnga*			مونگه *mūnga*	
		تاسو *tāsū*			تاسو *tāsū*	
f.	وُ وهله	هغو *hag̲h̲o*	*wu wahala*	وُ وهلي	هغو *hag̲h̲o*	*wu wahale*

Past Tense. Form II.—He, etc., did strike or struck me, etc. us, etc.

	Singular	Plural
	زه وُ وهلم *zah wu wahalam*	مونگ وُ وهلو *mūng wu wahalū*
	ته وُ وهلي *tah wu wahale*	تاسو وُ وهلئ *tāsū wu wahala-ī*
m.	هغه وُ واهه *hag̲h̲ah wu wāhah*	هغه وُ وهل *hag̲h̲ah wu wahal*
f.	هغه وُ وهله *hag̲h̲a wu wahala*	هغي وُ وهلي *hag̲h̲e wu wahale*

Continuative Past. Form I.—I, etc., used to strike him, etc. them.

	SINGULAR.			PLURAL.		
m.	واهه به / وهل به	ما *mā*	*wāhah ba* / *wahal ba*	وهل به	ما *mā*	*wahal ba*
		تا *tā*			تا *tā*	
		هغه *haghah*			هغه *haghah*	
		etc.			etc.	
		مونگه *mūnga*			مونگه *mungā*	
		تاسو *tāṣū*			تاسو *tāsū*	
f.	وهله به	هغو *hagho*	*wahala ba*	وهلي به	هغو *hagho*	*wahale ba*

Continuative Past. Form II.—He, etc., used to strike me, etc. us, etc.

	SINGULAR.		PLURAL.	
	زه وهلم به	*zah wahalam ba*	مونگ وهلو به	*mūng wahalū ba*
	ته وهلي به	*tah wahale ba*	تاسو وهلئ به	*tāsū wahala-ī ba*
m.	هغه واهه به	*haghah wāhah ba*	هغه وهل به	*haghah wahal ba*
f.	هغه وهله به	*hagha wahala ba*	هغي وهلي به	*haghe wahale ba*

Perfect Tense. Form I.—I, etc., have struck him, etc. them.

	SINGULAR.			PLURAL.		
m.	وهلَي دَي	ما *mā*	*wahalai dai*	وهلي دي	ما *mā*	*wahalī dī*
		تا *tā*			تا *tā*	
		هغه *haghah*			هغه *haghah*	
		etc.			etc.	
		مونگه *mūnga*			مونگه *mūnga*	
		تاسو *tāsū*			تاسو *tāsū*	
f.	وهلِ ده	هغو *hagho*	*wahali da*	وهلِ دي	هغو *hagho*	*wahali dī*

Perfect Tense. Form II.—He, etc., has struck me, etc. us, etc.

	SINGULAR.		PLURAL.	
	زه وهلَي يم	*zah wahalai yam*	مونگ وهلي يو	*mūng wahalī yū*
	ته وهلَي يي	*tah wahalai ye*	تاسو وهلي يئ	*tāsū wahalī ya-ī*
m.	هغه وهلَي دي	*haghah wahalai dai*	هغه وهلي دي	*haghah wahalī dī*
f.	هغه وهلِ ده	*hagha wahali da*	هغي وهلِ دي	*haghe wahali dī*

Pluperfect Tense. Form I.—I, etc., had struck him, etc. them.

	SINGULAR.			PLURAL.	
m. وهلي وُه	ما *mā*	*wahalai wuh*	وهلي وُو	ما *mā*	*wahalī wū*
	تا *tā*			تا *tā*	
	هغه *ha<u>gh</u>ah*			هغه *ha<u>gh</u>ah*	
	etc.			etc.	
	مونگه *mūnga*			مونگه *mūnga*	
	تاسو *tāsū*			تاسو *tāsū*	
f. وهلِ وَه	هغو *ha<u>gh</u>o*	*wahali wa*	وهلِ وي	هغو *ha<u>gh</u>o*	*wahali we*

Pluperfect Tense. Form II.—He, etc., had struck me, etc. us, etc.

	SINGULAR.	PLURAL.
	زه وهلي وُم *zah wahalai wum*	مونگ وهلي وُو *mūng wahalī wū*
	ته وهلي وي *tah wahalai we*	تاسو وهلي وئِ *tāsū wahalī wa-ī*
m.	هغه وهلي وُه *ha<u>gh</u>ah wahalai wuh*	هغه وهلي وُو *ha<u>gh</u>ah wahalī wū*
f.	هغه وهلِ وَه *ha<u>gh</u>a wahali wa*	هغي وهلِ وي *ha<u>gh</u>e wahali we*

Doubtful Past Tense. Form I.—I, etc., would have struck him, etc. them.

	SINGULAR.			PLURAL.	
m. به وهلي وي	ما *mā*	*ba wahalai wī*	به وهلي وي	ما *mā*	*ba wahalī wī*
	تا *tā*			تا *tā*	
	هغه *ha<u>gh</u>ah*			هغه *ha<u>gh</u>ah*	
	etc.			etc.	
	مونگه *mūnga*			مونگه *mūnga*	
	تاسو *tāsū*			تاسو *tāsū*	
f. به وهلِ وي	هغو *ha<u>gh</u>o*	*ba wahali wī*	به وهلِ وي	هغو *ha<u>gh</u>o*	*ba wahali wī*

Doubtful Past Tense. Form II.—He, etc., would have struck me, etc. them.

SINGULAR.	PLURAL.
زه به وهلي يم *zah ba wahalai yam*	مونگ به وهلي يو *mūng ba wahalī yū*
ته به وهلي يي *tah ba wahalai ye*	تاسو به وهلي يئِ *tāsū ba wahalī ya-ī*
هغه به وهلي وي *ha<u>gh</u>ah ba wahalai wī*	هغه به وهلي وي *ha<u>gh</u>ah ba wahalī wī*
هغه به وهلِ وي *ha<u>gh</u>a ba wahali wī*	هغي به وهلِ وي *ha<u>gh</u>e ba wahali wī*

IMPERATIVE MOOD.

Strike thou; let him strike.	Strike ye; let them strike.
SINGULAR.	PLURAL.
وهه - وُ وهه *waha, wu waha*	وهئ - وُ وهئ *waha-ī, wu waha-ī*
or هغه دِ وهي *haghah di wahī* or	or هغه دِ وهي *haghah di wahī* or
وُ دِ وهي *wu di wahī*	وُ دِ وهي *wu di wahī*

SUBJUNCTIVE MOOD.

PRESENT TENSE. If I strike, etc.	If we strike, etc.
SINGULAR.	PLURAL.
که وهم *ki waham*	که وهو *ki wahū*
که وهې *ki wahe*	که وهئ *ki waha-ī*
که وهي *ki wahī*	که وهي *ki wahī*

PAST TENSE. Form I.—If I, etc., had struck him, etc. them.

	SINGULAR.			PLURAL.	
m. وهلی	که ما *ki ma*	*wahalai*	وهلي	که ما *ki mā*	*wahalī*
وی	که تا *ki tā*	*wai*	وی	که تا *ki tā*	*wai*
	که هغه *ki haghah*			که هغه *ki haghah*	
	که هغې *ki haghe*			که هغې *ki haghe*	
	که مونږه *ki mūnga*			که مونږه *ki mūnga*	
f. وهلې	که تاسو *ki tāsū*	*wahalī*	وهلې	که تاسو *ki tāsū*	*wahali*
وی	که هغو *ki hagho*	*wai*	وی	که هغو *ki hagho*	*wai*

PAST TENSE. Form II.—If he, etc., had struck me, etc. us, etc.

	SINGULAR.	PLURAL.
	که زه وهلی وی *ki zah wahalai wai*	که مونږ وهلي وی *ki mūng wahalī wai*
	که ته وهلی وی *ki tah wahalai wai*	که تاسو وهلي وی *ki tāsū wahalī wai*
m.	که هغه وهلی وی *ki haghah wahalai wai*	که هغه وهلي وی *ki haghah wahalī wai*
f.	که هغه وهلې وی *ki hagha wahali wai*	که هغې وهلې وی *ki haghe wahali wai*

Future Tense. Form I.—If I, etc., would have struck him, etc. them.

	SINGULAR.			PLURAL.	
m. به وهلي وُه	که ما *ki mā*	*ba waha-lai wūh*	به وهلي وُو	که ما *ki mā*	*ba waha-lī nū*
	که تا *ki tā*			که تا *ki tā*	
	که هغه *ki haghah*			که هغه *ki haghah*	
	که هغي *ki haghe*			که هغي *ki haghe*	
	که مونګه *ki mūnga*			که مونګه *ki mūnga*	
f. به وهلِ وَه	که تاسو *ki tāsū*	*ba waha-li wa*	به وهلِ وي	که تاسو *ki tāsū*	*ba waha-li ne*
	که هغو *ki hagho*			که هغو *ki hagho*	

Future Tense. Form II.—If he, etc., would have struck me, etc. us, etc.

SINGULAR.	PLURAL.
که زه به وهلي وُم *ki zah ba wahalai wum*	که مونګ به وهلي وُو *ki mūng ba wahalī we*
که ته به وهلي وي *ki tah ba wahalai we*	که تاسو به وهلي وئي *ki tāsū ba wahalī wa-ī*
m. که هغه به وهلي وُه *ki haghah ba wahalai wuh*	که هغه به وهلي وُو *ki haghah ba wahalī nū*
f. که هغه به وهلِ وَه *ki hagha ba wahali wa*	که هغي به وهلِ وي *ki hāghe ba wahali we*

POTENTIAL MOOD.

Present Tense. I can strike, etc. We can strike, etc.

	SINGULAR.			PLURAL.	
m. شم	وهلي *wahalai*	*sham*	شو	وهلي *wahalī*	*shū*
شي		*she*	شئي		*sha-ī*
f. شي	وهلِ *wahali*	*shī*	شي	وهلِ *wahali*	*shī*

Past Tense. Form I.—I, etc., could have struck him, etc. them.

	SINGULAR.			PLURAL.	
m. وهلي شه	ما *mā*	*wahalai shah*	وهلي شوُو	ما *mā*	*wahalī shwa*
	تا *tā*			تا *tā*	
	هغه *haghah*			هغه *haghah*	
	هغي *haghe*			هغي *haghe*	
	مونګه *mūnga*			مونګه *mūnga*	
	تاسو *tāsū*			تاسو *tāsū*	
f. وهلِ شَه	هغو *hagho*	*wahali sha*	وهلِ شوي	هغو *hagho*	*wahali shwe*

PAST TENSE. Form II.—He, etc., could have struck me, etc. us, etc.

SINGULAR.		PLURAL.	
زه وهلې شوم	*zah wahalai shwam*	مونږ وهلي شوُو	*mūng wahalī shwū*
ته وهلې شوي	*tah wahalai shwe*	تاسو وهلي شوئ	*tāsū wahalī shwa-ī*
هغه وهلې شه	*haghah wahalai shah*	هغه وهلي شوُو	*haghah wahalī shwū*
هغه وهلِ شَ	*hagha wahali sha*	هغي وهلِ شوي	*haghe wahali shwe*

FUTURE TENSE. Form I.—I, etc., would have struck him, etc. them.

		SINGULAR.			PLURAL.	
m.	به وهلې شه	ما *mā*	*ba wahalai shah*	به وهلي شوُو	ما *mā*	*ba wahalī shwū*
		تا *tā*			تا *tā*	
		هغه *haghah*			هغه *haghah*	
		هغي *haghe*			هغي *haghe*	
		مونګه *mūnga*			مونګه *mūnga*	
f.	به وهلِ شَ	تاسو *tāsū*	*ba wahali sha*	به وهلِ شوي	تاسو *tāsū*	*ba wahali shwe*
		هغو *hagho*			هغو *hagho*	

FUTURE TENSE. Form II.—He, etc., would have struck me, etc. us, etc.

	SINGULAR.		PLURAL.	
	زه به وهلې شوم	*zah ba wahalai shwam*	مونږ به وهلي شوُو	*mūng ba wahalī shwū*
	ته به وهلې شوي	*tah ba wahalai shwe*	تاسو به وهلي شوئ	*tāsū ba wahalī shwa-ī*
m.	هغه به وهلې شه	*haghah ba wahalai shah*	هغه به وهلي شوُو	*haghah ba wahalī shwū*
f.	هغه به وهلِ شَ	*hagha ba wahali sha*	هغي به وهلِ شوي	*haghe ba wahali shwe*

GERUND.—*m.* وهون *wahūn*, *f.* وهنه *wahana*, a striking.

PRESENT PARTICIPLE.—*m.* واهه *wāhah*, *f.* وهله *wahala*, striking.

ACTIVE PARTICIPLE.—وهونکي *wahūnkai* or وهوني *wahūnai*, a striker.

PAST PARTICIPLE.—*m.* وهلې *wahalai*, *f.* وهلِ *wahali*, struck.

a. In the Imperfect, Past, and other Tenses that have two forms, the first form shows the pronouns in the instrumental case as the agents in the sentence, and the verb in the third person, in both genders and numbers, to agree with the object (which is understood) in the nominative case. Ex. ما سري واهه *mā saṛai wāhah* (I was beating a man), تا سري واهه *tā saṛai wāhah* (thou wast beating a man), and so on. ما ښځه وهله *mā kkhadza wahala* (I was beating a woman), تا *tā*—, etc., thou wast—, and so on. ما سړي وهل *mā saṛī wahal* (I was beating men), etc. ما ښځي وهلي *mā kkhadze wahale* (I was beating women), etc. And so on for all the tenses.

The second form shows the pronouns as the object in the nominative case, the agent in the instrumental case being understood. Ex. زه سړي وهلم *zah saṛī wahalam* (a man beat me), etc. The first and second persons make no change for gender either in the singular or the plural. The third person is the same as is used in the first form.

b. The Imperfect and other past tenses of transitive verbs have really a passive construction, which is necessary for the government of the instrumental case with which such tenses alone are used. Ex. ما سړي وهلي دي *mā saṛai wahalai dai*, literally, a man is beaten by me; that is, I have beaten a man. And so on *mutatis mutandis* for all past tenses.

85. The Passive Voice (*faṣli-majhūl*) of transitive verbs is formed by conjugating the past participle with the auxiliaries کيدل *kedal*, and شول *shwal*, as shown in the following paradigm of the passive voice of the regular transitive verb وهل *wahal* (to strike).

INFINITIVE MOOD. وهلي کيدل *wahalai kedal* (to be struck).

INDICATIVE MOOD.

PRESENT TENSE. I am being struck, etc. We are being struck.

	SINGULAR.				PLURAL.			
m.	کيږم	وهلي	*wahalai*	*kegam*	کيږو	وهلي	*wahalī*	*kegū*
	کيږي			*kege*	کيږئ			*kega-ī*
f.	کيږي	وهلِ	*wahali*	*kegī*	کيږي	وهلِ	*wahali*	*kegī*

AORIST TENSE. I may be struck, etc. We may be struck, etc.

	SINGULAR.				PLURAL.			
m.	کيږم	وُ وهلي	*wu wahalai*	*kegam*	کيږو	وُ وهلي	*wu wahalī*	*kegū*
	کيږي			*kege*	کيږئ			*kega-ī*
f.	کيږي	وُ وهلِ	*wu wahali*	*keyī*	کيږي	وُ وهلِ	*wu wuhali*	*kegī*

Future Tense. I shall or will be struck, etc. — We shall or will be struck, etc.

	SINGULAR		PLURAL	
m.	وهلَي به كيږم	wahalai ba kegam	وهلي به كيږو	wahalī ba kegū
	كيږې	kege	كيږئ	kega-ī
f.	وهلِ به كيږي	wahali ba kegī	وهلِ به كيږي	wahali ba kegī

Imperfect Tense. I was being struck, etc. — We were being struck, etc.

	SINGULAR		PLURAL	
m.	وهلَي كيدم	wahalai kedam	وهلي كيدو	wahalī kedū
	كيدې	kede	كيدئ	keda-ī
	كيده	kedah	كيدل	kedal
f.	وهلِ كيدله	wahali kedala	وهلِ كيدلې	wahali kedale

Past Tense. I was struck, etc. — We were struck, etc.

	SINGULAR		PLURAL	
m.	وُ وهلَي كيدم	wu wahalai kedam	وُ وهلي كيدو	wu wahalī kedū
	كيدې	kede	كيدئ	keda-ī
	كيده	kedah	كيدل	kedal
f.	وُ وهلِ كيدله	wu wuhali kedala	وُ وهلِ كيدلې	wu wahali kedale

Continuative Past Tense. I used to be struck, etc. — We used to be struck, etc.

	SINGULAR		PLURAL	
m.	وهلَي به كيدم	wahalai ba kedam	وهلي به كيدو	wahalī bà kedū
	كيدې	kede	كيدئ	keda-ī
	كيده	kedah	كيدل	kedal
f.	وهلِ به كيدله	wahali ba kedala	وهلِ به كيدلې	wahali ba kedale

Perfect Tense. I have been struck, etc. — We have been struck, etc.

	SINGULAR		PLURAL	
m.	وهلَي شوَي يم	wahalai shawai yam	وهلي شوي يو	wahalī shawī yū
	يې	ye	يئ	ya-ī
	دَي	dai	دي	dī
f.	وهلِ شِوِ ده	wahali shiwi da	وهلِ شِوِي دي	wahali shiwī dī.

Pluperfect Tense. I had been struck, etc. — We had been struck, etc.

	SINGULAR		PLURAL	
m.	وهلَي شوَي وُم	wahalai shawai wum	وهلي شوي وُو	wahalī shawī wū
	وې	we	وئ	wa-ī
	وُه	wuh	وُو	wū
f.	وهلِ شِوِ وَه - وَ	wahali shiwi wa	وهلِ شِوِي وې - وِ	wahali shiwī we, wi

Doubtful Past. I would have been struck, etc. We would have been struck, etc.

SINGULAR.			PLURAL.		
m. وُم ، وي ، وُهٔ	وهلَي شَوَيَ به *wahalai shawai ba*	*wum*, *we*, *wuh*	وُو ، وئ ، وُو	وهلي شَوِي به *wahalī shawī ba*	*wū*, *wa-ī*, *wū*
f. وَ - وَهٔ	وهلِ شِوِ به *wahali shiwi ba wa*		وِ - وي	وهلِ شِوِي به *wahali shiwī ba we, wi*	

IMPERATIVE MOOD.

Be thou struck, let him be struck. Be ye struck, let them be struck.

SINGULAR.	PLURAL.
وهلَي شه *wahalai sha*	وهلي شئ *wahalī sha-ī*
m. or هغه دِ وهلَي شي *haghah di wahalai shī*, or	or هغه دِ وهلي شي *haghah di wahalī shī*, or
وهلَي دِ شي *wahalai di shī*	وهلي دِ شي *wahalī di shī*

SUBJUNCTIVE MOOD.

Present Tense. If I were struck, etc. If we were struck, etc.

SINGULAR.			PLURAL.		
m.	که وهلَي *ki wahalai*	شم *sham*		که وهلي *ki wahalī*	شو *shū*
		شي *she*			شئ *sha-ī*
f.	که وهلِ *ki wahali*	شي *shī*		که وهلِ *ki wahali*	شي *shī*

Past Tense. If I had been struck, etc. If we had been struck, etc.

SINGULAR.		PLURAL.	
m. که وهلَي شَوَيَ *ki wahalai shawai*	وَيَ *wai*	که وهلي شَوِي *ki wahalī shawī*	وَيَ *wai*
f. که وهلِ شِوِ *ki wahali shiwi*		که وهلِ شِوِي *ki wahali shiwī*	

Future Tense. If I would have been struck, etc. If we would have been struck, etc.

SINGULAR.			PLURAL.		
m. وُم ، وي ، وُهٔ	که وهلَي شَوَيَ به *ki wahalai shawai ba*	*wum*, *we*, *wuh*	وُو ، وئ ، وُو	که وهلي شوِي به *ki wahalī shawī ba*	*wū*, *wa-ī*, *wū*
f. وَ - وَهٔ	که وهلِ شِوِ به *ki wahali shiwi ba wa*		وِ - وي	که وهلِ شِوِي به *ki wahali shiwī ba we, wi*	

Gerund.—*m.* وهلَي کيدهٔ *wahalai kedah*, *f.* وهلِ کيدله *wahali kedala*, being struck.

Passive Participle.—*m.* وهلَي شَوَيَ *wahalai shawai*, *f.* وهلِ شِوِ *wahali shiwi*, having been struck.

86. Transitive verbs, whether they end in ل *al* or ول *wul* in the infinitive mood, are all conjugated on the model of the verb وهل *wahal* (to strike).

a. But they are not all of the same uniform construction throughout their conjugations. On the contrary, they comprise a number of irregular and defective verbs, whose present and past tenses are formed from separate verbal roots in order to complete the paradigm.

87. All transitive verbs, however, exclusive of causals and derivatives (which are noticed hereafter separately in Art. 101), may be reduced to three classes, according to the methods of forming their present and past tenses in the active voice.

88. CLASS I. comprises all regular primitive transitive verbs. They are conjugated regularly according to the model previously given (see وهل *wahal*, to strike). That is to say, they form the tenses of present time direct from the verbal root (derived by rejecting the final ل *al* of the infinitive mood), and those of past time from the infinitive itself, as shown in the subjoined examples, and as previously explained in Art. 74 and 75.

INFINITIVES.		PRESENT.			PAST.		
		PRESENT.	AORIST.	FUTURE.	IMPERFECT.	PAST.	PERFECT.
آچول *āchawul*	to cast	آچوم *āchawum*	واچوم *wāchawum*	وا به چوم *wā ba chawum*	آچول *āchawul*	واچول *wāchawul*	آچولي دي *āchawulai dai*
چُرلول *churlawul*	to twirl	چُرلوم *churlawum*	وُ چُرلوم *wu churlawum*	وُ به جُرلوم *wu ba churlawum*	چُرلول *churlawul*	وُ چُرلول *wu churlawul*	چُرلولي دي *churlawulai dai*
ساتل *sātal*	to keep	ساتم *sātam*	وُ ساتم *wu sātam*	وُ به ساتم *wu ba sātam*	ساتل *sātal*	وُ ساتل *wu sātal*	ساتلي دي *sātalai dai*
شړل *sharal*	to expel	شړم *sharam*	وُ شړم *wu sharam*	وُ به شړم *wu ba sharam*	شړل *sharal*	وُ شړل *wu sharal*	شړلي دي *sharalai dai*
لړل *laral*	to stir	لړم *laram*	وُ لړم *wu laram*	وُ به لړم *wu ba laram*	لړل *laral*	وُ لړل *wu larai*	لړلي دي *laralai dai*
لل *lal*	to utter	لم *lam*	وُ لم *wu lam*	وُ به لم *wu ba lam*	لل *lal*	وُ لل *wu lal*	للي دي *lalai dai*

89. CLASS II. comprises those transitive verbs that form the tenses of present time by altering the terminal letters of the verbal root, but retain the root or the infinitive itself unchanged for the tenses of past time. This class contains many verbs, but they may all be included in six orders, according to their changes of the root for the present tenses. The examples given with each order respectively include most of the verbs belonging to it, or at least such as are commonly used.

a. Order I.—In transitive verbs of this order the terminal ست *st*, or شت *sht* of the verbal root is rejected and replaced by ل *al* in the present tenses, and if preceded by a long vowel it also suffers elision, as is shown in the following examples. The verbs آغوستل *āghostal* (to wear) and لوَستل *lawastal* (to scatter) are exceptions to this rule. The first, following its original in the Persian, replaces the terminal letters of the root by ند *nd*, and the second by ن *n*.

INFINITIVE.		PRESENT.			PAST.		
		PRESENT.	AORIST.	FUTURE.	IMPERFECT.	PAST.	PERFECT.
آخستل *ākhistal*	to take	آخلم *ākhlam*	واخلم *wākhlam*	وا به خلم *wā ba khlam*	آخست *ākhist*	وا خست *wākhist*	آخستي دي *ākhistai dai*
راوستل *rāwustal*	to send	راولم *rāwulam*	راولم *rāwulam*	را به ولم *rā ba wulam*	راوست *rāwust*	را وُ وست *rā wu wust*	را وستي دي *rāwustai dai*
سکستل *skastal*	to shear	سکلم *skalam*	وُ سکلم *wu skalam*	وُ به سکلم *wu ba skalam*	سکست *skast*	وُ سکست *wu skast*	سکستلي دي *skastalai dai*
لوُستل *lwustal*	to read	لوُلم *lwulam*	وُ لوُلم *wu lwulam*	وُ به لوُلم *wu ba lwulam*	لوُست *lwust*	وُ لوُست *wu lwust*	لوُستي دي *lwustai dai*
ويشتل *wīshtal*	to throw	وُلم *wulam*	وُ وُلم *wu wulam*	وُ به وُلم *wu ba wulam*	ويشت *wīsht*	وُ ويشت *wu wīsht*	ويشتلي دي *wīshtalai dai*
آغوستل *āghostal*	to wear	آغندم *āghundam*	واغندم *wāghun-dam*	وا به غندم *wā ba ghundam*	آغوست *āghost*	وا غوست *wā ghost*	آغوستي دي *āghostai dai*
لوَستل *lawastal*	to scatter	لوَنم *lawanam*	وُ لوَنم *wu lawa-nam*	وُ به لوَنم *wu ba lawanam*	لوَست *lawast*	وُ لوَست *wu lawast*	لوَستي دي *lawastai dai*

b. Order II.—In transitive verbs of this order the terminal ښت *kkht* of the verbal root is rejected and replaced by ړ *ṛ* in the present tenses. The verb سکښتل *skakkhtal* (to cut out, as a dress, pattern, etc), takes نړ *nṛ*, and غوښتل *ghokkhtal* (to want), inserts an ا *ā* before the ړ *ṛ* in the present tenses. Examples:

INFINITIVE.		PRESENT.			PAST.		
		PRESENT.	AORIST.	FUTURE.	IMPERFECT.	PAST.	PERFECT.
آوُښتل *āwukkhtal*	to change	آورم *āwṛam*	واورم *wāwṛam*	وا به ورم *wā ba wṛam*	آوُښت *āwukkht*	وا وُښت *wā wukkht*	آوُښتي دي *āwukkhtai dai*
سکښتل *skakkhtal*	to clip out	سکنړم *skanṛam*	وُ سکنړم *wu skanṛam*	وُ به سکنړم *wu ba skanṛam*	سکښت *skakkht*	وُ سکښت *wu skakkht*	سکښتي دي *skakkhtai dai*
غوښتل *ghokkhtal*	to want	غوارم *ghwāṛam*	وُ غوارم *wu ghwāṛam*	وُ به غوارم *wu ba ghwāṛam*	غوښت *ghokkht*	وُ غوښت *wu ghokkht*	غوښتلي دي *ghokkhtalai dai*
نغښتل *nghakkhtal*	to roll up	نغړم *nghaṛam*	وُ نغړم *wu nghaṛam*	وُ به نغړم *wu ba nghaṛam*	نغښت *nghakkht*	وُ نغښت *wu nghakkht*	نغښتي دي *nghakkhtai dai*

c. Order III. includes those transitive verbs ending in ل *al* in the infinitive, whose last radical letter is د *d*. In the present tenses this letter is simply dropped, and if it be preceded by a long vowel it also is rejected. Examples:

INFINITIVE.		PRESENT.			PAST.		
		PRESENT.	AORIST.	FUTURE.	IMPERFECT.	PAST.	PERFECT.
اُودل *ūdal*	to weave	اُوم *ūwam*	وُ اُوم *wu ūwam*	وُ به اُوم *wu ba ūwam*	اُود *ūd*	وُ اُود *wu ūd*	اُودلي دي *ūdalai dai*
آوريدل *āwredal*	to hear	آورم *āwram*	واورم *wāwram*	وا به ورم *wā ba wram*	آوريد *āwred*	واوريد *wāwred*	آوريدلي دي *āwredalai dai*

INFINITIVE.		PRESENT.			PAST.		
		PRESENT.	AORIST.	FUTURE.	IMPERFECT.	PAST.	PERFECT.
پيرودل *pīrodal*	to buy	پيرم *pīram*	وُ پيرم *wu pīram*	وُ به پيرم *wu ba pīram*	پيرود *pīrod*	وُ پيرود *wu pīrod*	پيرودلي دي *pīrodalai dai*
پيژندل *peǰandal*	to know	پيژنم *peǰanam*	وُ پيژنم *wu peǰanam*	وُ به پيژنم *wu ba peǰanam*	پيژند *peǰand*	وُ پيژند *wu peǰand*	پيژندلي دي *peǰandalai dai*
پښتيدل *pukkhtedal*	to ask	پښتم *pukkhtam*	وُ پښتم *wu pukkhtam*	وُ به پښتم *wu ba pukkhtam*	پښتيد *pukkhted*	وُ پښتيد *wu pukkhted*	پښتيدلي دي *pukkhtedalai dai*
رودل *rawdal*	to reap to suck	رَوَم *rawam*	وُ رَوَم *wu rawam*	وُ به رَوَم *wu ba rawam*	رود *rawd*	وُ رود *wu rawd*	رودلي دي *rawdalai dai*
سپړدل *spaṛdal*	to unravel	سپړم *spaṛam*	وُ سپړم *wu spaṛam*	وُ به سپړم *wu ba spaṛam*	سپړد *spaṛd*	وُ سپړد *wu spaṛd*	سپړدلي دي *spaṛdalai dai*
لودل *lawdal*	to utter	لَوَم *lawam*	وُ لَوَم *wu lawam*	وُ به لَوَم *wu ba lawam*	لود *lawd*	وُ لود *wu lawd*	لودلي دي *lawdalai dai*
نغړدل *nghaṛdal*	to swallow	نغاړم *nghāṛam*	وُ نغاړم *wu nghāṛam*	وُ به نغاړم *wu ba nghāṛam*	نغړد *nghaṛd*	وُ نغړد *wu nghaṛd*	نغړدلي دي *nghaṛdalai dai*

d. Order IV. comprises verbs of two syllables, each of which is formed by the short vowel *zabar* ـَ *a*, in the infinitive mood. They form the present tenses by substituting the long vowel ا *ā* for the penultimate short one. Some of the verbs of this order are both transitive and intransitive. Examples :

INFINITIVE.		PRESENT.			PAST.		
		PRESENT.	AORIST.	FUTURE.	IMPERFECT.	PAST.	PERFECT.
دنگل *dangal*	to leap	دانگم *dāngam*	وُ دانگم *wudāngam*	وُ به دانگم *wu ba dāngam*	دنگل *dangal*	وُ دنگل *wu dangal*	دنگلي دي *dangalai dai*
غپل *ghapal*	to bark	غاپم *ghāpam*	وُ غاپم *wu ghāpam*	وُ به غاپم *wu ba ghāpam*	غپل *ghapal*	وُ غپل *wu ghapal*	غپلي دي *ghapalai dai*

INFINITIVE.	PRESENT.			PAST.		
	PRESENT.	AORIST.	FUTURE.	IMPERFECT.	PAST.	PERFECT.
لنبل *lanbal* } to bathe	لانبم *lānbam*	وُ لانبم *wu lānbam*	وُ به لانبم *wu ba lānbam*	لنبل *lanbal*	وُ لنبل *wu lanbal*	لنبلي دي *lanbalai dai*
نړل *naṛal* } to shout	نارم *nāṛam*	وُ نارم *wu nāṛam*	وُ به نارم *wu ba nāṛam*	نړل *naṛal*	وُ نړل *wu naṛal*	نړلي دي *naṛalai dai*
ويل *wayal* } to speak	وايم *wāyam*	وُ وايم *wu wāyam*	وُ به وايم *wu ba wāyam*	ويل *wayal*	وُ ويل *wu wayal*	ويلي دي *wayalai dai*

e. Order V. includes those verbs, whose root ending in ت *t*, change it to ز *z* or ځ *dz* in the present tenses. They are distinguished as having both a transitive and intransitive signification sometimes. The verb بوتلل *botlal* (to lead) drops both its final letters for the root. The verb نجتل *njatal* (to imbed) takes ن *n* instead of ز *z* or ځ *dz* in the present tenses. Examples :

INFINITIVE.	PRESENT.			PAST.		
	PRESENT.	AORIST.	FUTURE.	IMPERFECT.	PAST.	PERFECT.
ارتل *aratal* } to widen	ارزم *arzam*	وُ ارزم *wu arzam*	وُ به ارزم *wu ba arzam*	ارت *arat*	وُ ارت *wu arat*	ارتلي دي *aratalai dai*
بوتلل *botlal* } to lead	بوزم *bozam*	بوزم *bozam*	بو به زم *bo ba zam*	بوت *bot*	بوت *bot*	بوتللي دي *botlalai dai*
پرانتل *prānatal* } to open	پرانځم *prānadzam*	پرانځم *prānadzam*	پرا به نځم *prā ba nadzam*	پرانت *prānat*	پرانت *prānat*	پرانتلي دي *prānatalai dai*
ميتل *mītal* } to piss	ميځم *mīdzam*	وُ ميځم *wu mīdzam*	وُ به ميځم *wu ba mīdzam*	ميتل *mītal*	وُ ميتل *wu mītal*	ميتلي دي *mītalai dai*
نجتل *njatal* } to imbed	نجنم *njanam*	وُ نجنم *wu njanam*	وُ به نجنم *wu ba njanam*	نجت *njat*	وُ نجت *wu njat*	نجتلي دي *njatalai dai*

f. Order VI. comprises a few verbs which can be reduced to no general rule, as those of the preceding orders, or which are solitary examples of a particular formation. Examples:

INFINITIVE.		PRESENT.			PAST.		
		PRESENT.	AORIST.	FUTURE.	IMPERFECT.	PAST.	PERFECT.
بلل *balal*	to call	بولم *bolam*	وُ بولم *wu bolam*	وُ به بولم *wu ba bolam*	بلل *balal*	وُ بلل *wu balal*	بللي دي *balalai dai*
موندل *mūndal*	to find	مومم *mūmam*	مومم *mūmam*	وُ به مومم *wuba mūmam*	موندل *mūndal*	موندل *mūndal*	موندلي دي *mūndalai dai*
نيول *nīwul*	to catch	نسم *nisam*	وُ نسم *wu nisam*	وُ به نسم *wu ba nisam*	نيول *nīwul*	وُ نيول *wu nīwul*	نيولي دي *nīwulai dai*
وژلل *wajlal*	to kill	وژنم *wajnam*	وُ وژنم *wu wajnam*	وُ به وژنم *wu ba wajnam*	وژلل *wajlal*	وُ وژلل *wu wajlal*	وژلي دي *wajalai dai*

g. The Imperfect and Past Tenses of the verbs of Class I., as also of those in Orders IV. and VI. of Class II. are subject to change in the third person singular, as has been explained in Art. 75, *a*.

90. Class III. comprises those transitive verbs which (like their Persian originals) form their present and past tenses from separate infinitives, which by themselves alone are defective in one or other form of tense. The verbs of this class are not very numerous. The following list includes all those in common use, and shows how they are combined to complete the paradigm.

INFINITIVE.		PRESENT.			PAST.		
		PRESENT.	AORIST.	FUTURE.	IMPERFECT.	PAST.	PERFECT.
باسل	to	باسم	وُ باسم	وُ به باسم	*yūst*	*wu yūst*	*yastalai dai*
يستل	extract	*basām*	*wu bāsam*	*wu ba bāsam*	يوُست	وُ يوُست	يستلي دي
آغړل	to	آغړم	وُ آغړم	وُ به آغړم	*ākkhal*	*wu ākkhal*	*ākkhalai dai*
آښل	knead	*āghagam*	*wu āghagam*	*wu ba āghagam*	آښل	وُ آښل	آښلي دي

INFINITIVE.		PRESENT.			PAST.		
		PRESENT.	AORIST.	FUTURE.	IMPERFECT.	PAST.	PERFECT.
بيول بوتلل	to lead	بيايم *biyāyam*	بيايم *biyāyam*	به بيايم *ba biyāyam*	*bot* بوت	*bot* بوت	بيولي دي *biwulai dai*
پريږدل پريښودل	to let go	پريږدم *pregdam*	پريږدم *pregdam*	پري به ږدم *pre ba gdam*	*prekkhod* پريښود	*prekkhod* پريښود	*prekkhodalai dai* پريښودلي دي
ږدل يښودل	to place	ږدم *gdam*	ږدم *gdam*	به ږدم *ba gdam*	*yakkhod* يښود	*yckkhoa* يښود	*yakkhai dai* يښي دي
ښيل ښوول	to show	ښيم *kkhayam*	وُ ښيم *wu kkhayam*	وُ به ښيم *wu ba kkhayam*	*kkhowah* ښووه	*wu kkhowah* وُ ښووه	*kkhowulai dai* ښوولي دي
کاږل ښکل	to pull to write	کاږم *kāgam*	وُ کاږم *wu kāgam*	وُ به کاږم *wu ba kāgam*	*kkhkal* ښکل	*wu kkhkal* وُ ښکل	*kkhkalai dai* ښکلي دي
ګورل کتل	to look	ګورم *goram*	وُ ګورم *wu goram*	وُ به ګورم *wu ba goram*	*kot* کوت	*wu kot* وُ کوت	*katalai dai* کتلي دي
obsolete ليدل	to see	وينم *wīnam*	وُ وينم *wu wīnam*	وُ به وينم *wu ba wīnam*	*līdah* ليده	*wu līdah* وُ ليده	*līdalai dai* ليدلي دي
ليږدل ليښل	to load	ليږدم *legdam*	وُ ليږدم *wu legdam*	وُ به ليږدم *wu ba legdam*	*lekkhah* ليښه	*wu lekkhah* وُ ليښه	*lekkhalai dai* ليښلي دي
وړل يوسل	to carry	وړم *wṛam*	وُ وړم *wu wṛam*	وُ به وړم *wu ba wṛam*	*yowuṛ* يووړ	*yowuṛ* يووړ	وړي دي *wṛai dai*

91. The Intransitive Verb (*f'iali-lāzimī*). The neuter or intransitive verb denotes action completed in the object itself without passing to another. It has only the Active Voice, and is distinguished by the termination of the infinitive mood in يدل *edal*, and sometimes in ل *al*. The former is added to nouns and adjectives to form them into verbs intransitive. Intransitives generally govern the dative or ablative case.

92. In regular intransitive verbs the tenses of present and past time are formed from the root and infinitive respectively, according to the general rules explained in Art. 74 and 75, and they are conjugated on

the model of the regular intransitive verb خوځيدل *khwadzedal* (to move), the paradigm of which is herewith subjoined.

INFINITIVE MOOD. خوځيدل *khwadzedal* (to move).

INDICATIVE MOOD.

Present Tense. I am moving, etc. — We are moving, etc.

	SINGULAR.	PLURAL.
	خوځيږم *khwadzegam*	خوځيږو *khwadzegū*
	خوځيږي *khwadzege*	خوځيږئ *khwadzega-ī*
	خوځيږي *khwadzegī*	خوځيږي *khwadzegī*

Aorist Tense. I move or may move, etc. — We move or may move, etc.

	SINGULAR.	PLURAL.
	وُ خوځيږم *wu khwadzegam*	وُ خوځيږو *wu khwadzegū*
	وُ خوځيږي *wu khwadzege*	وُ خوځيږئ *wu khwadzega-ī*
	وُ خوځيږي *wu khwadzegī*	وُ خوځيږي *wu khwadzegī*

Future Tense. I will or shall move, etc. — We will or shall move, etc.

	SINGULAR.	PLURAL.
	وُ به خوځيږم *wu ba khwadzegam*	وُ به خوځيږو *wu ba khwadzegū*
	وُ به خوځيږي *wu ba khwadzege*	وُ به خوځيږئ *wu ba khwadzega-ī*
	وُ به خوځيږي *wu ba khwadzegī*	وُ به خوځيږي *wu ba khwadzegī*

Imperfect Tense. I was moving, etc. — We were moving, etc.

	SINGULAR.	PLURAL.
	خوځيدلم *khwadzedalam*	خوځيدلو *khwadzedalū*
	خوځيدلي *khwadzedale*	خوځيدلئ *khwadzedala-ī*
m.	خوځيده *khwadzedah*	خوځيدل *khwadzedal*
f.	خوځيدله *khwadzedala*	خوځيدلي *khwadzedale*

Past Tense. I moved or did move, etc. — We moved or did move, etc.

	SINGULAR.	PLURAL.
	وُ خوځيدم *wu khwadzedam*	وُ خوځيدو *wu khwadzedū*
	وُ خوځيدي *wu khwadzede*	وُ خوځيدئ *wu khwadzeda-ī*
m.	وُ خوځيده *wu khwadzedah*	وُ خوځيدل *wu khwadzedal*
f.	وُ خوځيدله *wu khwadzedala*	وُ خوځيدلي *wu khwadzedale*

Continuative Past. I used to move, etc. — We used to move, etc.

	SINGULAR.	PLURAL.
	خوځيدم به khwadzedam ba	خوځيدوُ به khwadzedū ba
	خوځيدي به khwadzede ba	خوځيدئ به khwadzeda-ī ba
m.	خوځيده به khwadzedah ba	خوځيدل به khwadzedal ba
f.	خوځيدله به khwadzedala ba	خوځيدلي به khwadzedale ba

Perfect Tense. I have moved, etc. — We have moved, etc.

	SINGULAR.	PLURAL.
m.	خوځيدلي khwadzedalai { يم yam, يي ye, دي dai }	خوځيدلي khwadzedalī { يوُ yū, يئ ya-ī, دي dī }
f.	خوځيدلِ ده khwadzedali da	خوځيدلِ دي khwadzedali dī.

Pluperfect Tense. I had moved, etc. — We had moved, etc.

	SINGULAR.	PLURAL.
m.	خوځيدلي khwadzedalai { وُم wum, وې we, وُه wuh }	خوځيدلي khwadzedalī { وُو wū, وئ wa-ī, وُو wū }
f.	خوځيدلِ وَه ـ وَ khwadzedali wa	خوځيدلِ وي ـ وِ khwadzedali we, wi

Doubtful Past. I would have moved, etc. — We would have moved, etc.

	SINGULAR.	PLURAL.
m.	خوځيدلي به khwadzedalai ba { وُم wum, وې we, وُه wuh }	خوځيدلي به khwadzedalī ba { وُو wū, وئ wa-ī, وُو wū }
f.	خوځيدلِ به وَه ـ وَ khwadzedali ba wa	خوځيدلِ به وي ـ وِ khwadzedali ba we, wi

IMPERATIVE MOOD.

Move thou, let him move. — Move ye, let them move.

SINGULAR.	PLURAL.
وُ خوځيږه wu khwadzega	وُ خوځيږئ wu khwadzega-ī
or هغه دِ خوځي haghah di khwadzī or	or هغه دِ خوځي haghah di khwadzī or
or خوځيږي دِ khwadzegī di or	or خوځيږي دِ khwadzegī di or
وُ دِ خوځي wu di khwadzī	وُ دِ خوځي wu di khwadzī

SUBJUNCTIVE MOOD.

Present Tense. If I move, etc. — If we move, etc.

SINGULAR.	PLURAL.
که خوځیږم *ki khwadzegam*	که خوځیږو *ki khwadzegū*
که خوځیږې *ki khwadzege*	که خوځیږئ *ki khwadzega-ī*
که خوځیږي *ki khwadzegī*	که خوځیږي *ki khwadzegī*

Past Tense. If I had moved, etc. — If we had moved, etc.

	SINGULAR.			PLURAL.	
m.	که زه خوځیدلی *ki zah khwadzedalai*			که مونګ خوځیدلي *ki mūng khwadzedalī*	
وي	etc. که ته *ki tah*, etc.	wai	وي	etc. که تاسو *ki tāsū*, etc.	wai
f.	که هغه خوځیدلِ *ki hagha khwadzedali*			که هغه خوځیدلِ *ki hagha khwadzedali*	

Future Tense. If I would have moved, etc. — If we would have moved, etc.

	SINGULAR.		PLURAL.	
وُم		*wum*	وُو	*wū*
m. وي	که خوځیدلی به *ki khwadzedalai ba*	*we*	وئ — که خوځیدلي به *ki khwadzedalī ba*	*wa-ī*
وُه		*wuh*	وُو	*wū*

f. که خوځیدلِ به وَه-وَ *ki khwadzedali ba wa* — که خوځیدلِ به وې-وِ *ki khwadzedali ba we, wi*

POTENTIAL MOOD.

Present Tense. I can move, etc. — We can move, etc.

	SINGULAR.			PLURAL.	
m. شم	خوځیدلی *khwadzedalai*	*sham*	شُو	خوځیدلي *khwadzedalī*	*shū*
شې		*she*	شئ		*sha-ī*
f. شي	خوځیدلِ *khwadzedali*	*shī*	شي	خوځیدلِ *khwadzedali*	*shī*

Past Tense. I could move, etc. — We could move, etc.

	SINGULAR.			PLURAL.	
شوم		*shwam*	شوُو		*shwū*
m. شوې	خوځیدلی *khwadzedalai*	*shwe*	شوئ	خوځیدلي *khwadzedalī*	*shwa-ī*
شه		*shah*	شوُو		*shwū*

f. خوځیدلِ شوه-شَ *khwadzedali shwa, sha* — خوځیدلِ شوې-شِو *khwadzedali shwe, shwi*

Future Tense. I shall or will be moved, etc. — We shall or will be moved, etc.

	SINGULAR.			PLURAL.	
m. شم	خوځیدلی به *khwadzedalai ba*	*sham*	شُو	خوځیدلي به *khwadzedalī ba*	*shū*
شې		*she*	شئ		*sha-ī*
f. شي	خوځیدلِ به *khwadzedali ba*	*shī*	شي	خوځیدلِ به *khwadzedalī ba*	*shī*

GERUND.—*m.* خوځیدون *khwadzedūn*, *f.* خوځیدنه *khwadzedana*, a moving.

PRESENT PARTICIPLE.—*m.* خوځیده *khwadzedah*, *f.* خوځیدله *khwadzedala*, moved.

ACTIVE PARTICIPLE.—خوځیدونکي *khwadzedūnkai* or خوځیدوني *khwadzedūnai*, mover.

PASSIVE PARTICIPLE.—خوځیدلي *khwadzedalai* or خوځیدي *khwadzedai*, having moved.

a. The present tenses are sometimes contracted by adding the pronominal affixes direct to the root, as خوځم *khwadzam*, خوځي *khwadze*, etc.

b. In the imperfect and past tenses the final ل *al* of the infinitive is sometimes dropped as is shown in the past and continuative past tenses, and the passive participle.

93. All primitive intransitive verbs end in the infinitive mood in یدل *edal* or ل *al*. Those ending in یدل *edal* are, like the transitive verbs ending in ول *wul*, all regular. Those ending in ل *al*, also like transitive verbs of the same infinitive termination, are all irregular and defective. Intransitive verbs may therefore be divided into two classes.

94. CLASS I. comprises all primitive intransitives whose infinitive mood ends in یدل *edal*. They are all regularly conjugated in the same manner as خوځیدل *khwadzedal* (to move). Examples :—

INFINITIVE.		PRESENT.			PAST.		
		PRESENT.	AORIST.	FUTURE.	IMPERFECT.	PAST.	PERFECT.
بگنیدل *bugnedal*	to shy to wince	بگنیږم *bugnegam*	وُ بگنیږم *wu bugnegam*	وُ به بگنیږم *wu ba bugnegam*	بگنیدلم *bugned-alam*	وُ بگنیدلم *wu bug-nedalam*	بگنیدلي یم *bugnedalai yam*
بهیدل *bahedal*	to flow	بهیږم *bahegam*	وُ بهیږم *wu bahegam*	وُ به بهیږم *wu ba bahegam*	بهیدلم *bahed-alam*	وُ بهیدلم *wu bahedalam*	بهیدلي یم *bahedalai yam*
رپیدل *rapedal*	to shake	رپیږم *rapegam*	وُ رپیږم *wu rapegam*	وُ به رپیږم *wu ba rapegam*	رپیدلم *raped-alam*	وُ رپیدلم *wu rapedalam*	رپیدلي یم *rapedalai yam*
رژیدل *raĵedal*	to shed	رژیږم *raĵegam*	وُ رژیږم *wu raĵegam*	وُ به رژیږم *wu ba raĵegam*	رژیدلم *raĵed-alam*	وُ رژیدلم *wu raĵedalam*	رژیدلي یم *raĵedalai yam*
کړیدل *kaṛedal*	to pine	کړیږم *kaṛegam*	وُ کړیږم *wu kaṛegam*	وُ به کړیږم *wu ba kaṛegam*	کړیدلم *kaṛed-alam*	وُ کړیدلم *wu kaṛedalam*	کړیدلي یم *kaṛedalai yam*
لویدل *lwedal*	to fall	لویږم *lwegam*	وُ لویږم *wu lwegam*	وُ به لویږم *wu ba lwegam*	لویدلم *lwed-alam*	وُ لویدلم *wu lwedalam*	لویدلي یم, *lwedalai yam*

a. Many verbs of this class form the present tenses by rejecting the يدل *edal* of the infinitive, and adding the pronominal affixes direct to the verbal root thus derived. This form is generally used with reference to action of remote signification, or not occurring actually in the presence of the speaker. The first form on the other hand is used when the action occurs actually in the presence of the speaker, or in other words it has a proximate application. Ex. ځناور څو چه ساه لري خوځي *dzanāwar tso chi sāh larī khwadzī* (an animal as long as it has life moves); مړ نه دي ګوره خوځيږي *mur na dai gora khwadzegī* (he is not dead, see, he is moving).

b. Many verbs of this class, however, only use the contracted form for the present tenses without reference to the distinction above noted. Examples:—

INFINITIVE.		PRESENT.			PAST.		
		PRESENT.	AORIST.	FUTURE.	IMPERFECT.	PAST.	PERFECT.
اوسيدل *osedal*	to abide	اوسم *osam*	اوسم *osam*	به اوسم *ba osam*	اوسيدلم *osedalam*	اوسيدلم *osedalam*	اوسيدلي يم *osedalai yam*
درومېدل *drūmedal*	to depart	درومم *drūmam*	درومم *drūman*	به درومم *ba drūmam*	درومېدلم *drūmed-alam*	درومېدلم *drūmed-alam*	درومېدلي يم *drūmedalai yam*
زغليدل *zghaledal*	to run	زغلم *zghalam*	وُ زغلم *wu zghalam*	وُ به زغلم *wu ba zghalam*	زغليدلم *zghaled-alam*	وُ زغليدلم *wu zghal-edalam*	زغليدلي يم *zghaledalai yam*
ګرزيدل *girzedal*	to wander	ګرزم *girzam*	وُ ګرزم *wu girzam*	وُ به ګرزم *wu ba girzam*	ګرزيدلم *girzedalam*	وُ ګرزيدلم *wu girzedalam*	ګرزيدلي يم *girzedalai yam*

95. Class II. comprises all those intransitive verbs whose infinitive mood ends in ل *al.* They are not very numerous and may be included in four orders.

a. Order I. contains a couple of verbs whose present tenses are formed by substituting the affixed personal pronouns for the last three letters of the verbal root. They are the following:—

INFINITIVE.		PRESENT.			PAST.		
		PRESENT.	AORIST.	FUTURE.	IMPERFECT.	PAST.	PERFECT.
خملاستل *tsamlāstal*	to recline	خملم *tsamlam*	خملم *tsamlam*	به خملم *ba tsamlam*	خملاستم *tsam-lāstam*	خملاستم *tsam-lāstcm*	خملاستي يم *tsamlāstai yam*
ښکيناستل *kkhkenāstal*	to sit	ښکينم *kkhkenam*	ښکينم *kkhkenam*	ښکي به نم *kkhke ba nam*	ښکيناستم *kkhke-nāstam*	ښکيناستم *kkhke-nāstam*	ښکيناستي يم *kkhkenāstai yam*

b. Order II, contains those verbs, the last radical letter of which being ت *t*, change it to ز *z* in the present tenses, and the preceding short vowel *zabar* ـَ *a*, to *pesh* ـُ *u*. The verb ختل *khatal* (to rise) is an exception to this rule, and following its Persian original forms the present tenses by changing the radical ت *t* to ږ *ej*. Examples :—

INFINITIVE.		PRESENT.			PAST.		
		PRESENT.	AORIST.	FUTURE.	IMPERFECT.	PAST.	PERFECT.
آلوتل *ālwatal*	to fly	آلوزم *ālwuzam*	والوزم *wālwuzam*	وا به لوزم *wā ba lwuzam*	آلوتم *ālwatam*	والوتم *wālwatam*	آلوتلي يم *ālwatalai yam*
پريوتل *prewatal*	to fall on	پريوزم *prewuzam*	پري وُ وُزم *pre wu wuzam*	پري به وُزم *pre ba wuzam*	پريوتم *prewa-tam*	پري وُ وتم *pre wu watam*	پريوتلي يم *prewatalai yam*
جاروتل *iārwatal*	to return	جاروُزم *jārwuzam*	جار وُ وُزم *jār wu wuzam*	جار به وُزم *jār ba wuzam*	جاروتم *jār-watam*	جار وُ وتم *jār wu watam*	جاروتلي يم *jārwatalai yam*
ښکيوتل *kkhkewatal*	to fall into	ښکيوُزم *kkhke-wuzam*	ښکي وُ وُزم *kkhke wuwuzam*	ښکي به وُزم *kkhke ba wuzam*	ښکيوتم *kkhke-watam*	ښکي وُ وتم *kkhke wu watam*	ښکيوتلي يم *kkhkewata-lai yam*
ننوتل *nanwatal*	to enter	ننوُزم *nanwuzam*	ننَ وُ وُزم *nana wuwuzam*	وُ به ننوُزم *wu ba nanwuzam*	ننوتم *nan-watam*	ننَ وُ وتم *nana wu watam*	ننوتلي يم *nanwatalai yam*

INFINITIVE.		PRESENT.			PAST.		
		PRESENT.	AORIST.	FUTURE.	IMPERFECT.	PAST.	PERFECT.
وتل *watal*	to issue	وزم *wuzam*	وُ وزم *wu wuzam*	وُ به وزم *wu ba wuzam*	وتم *watam*	وُ وتم *wu watam*	وتلي يم *watalai yam*
ختل *khatal*	to rise	خيژم *khejam*	وُ خيژم *wu khejam*	وُ به خيژم *wu ba khejam*	ختم *khatam*	وُ ختم *wu khatam*	ختلي يم *khatalai yam*

N.B.—In the imperfect and past tenses of the verbs of Order II. the contracted forms are given throughout the examples, as آلوتم *ālwatam* for آلوتلم *ālwatalam*, etc. (Art. 92, *b.*) The verb ختل *khatal*, in the third person singular becomes خوت *khot* for the masculine in the imperfect and past tenses.

c. Order III. contains those intransitives whose verbal root ends in ښت *kkht*, which, as in transitives of the same form (Class II. Order II. Art. 89, *b.*), is changed to ړ *r* in the present tenses. The verb نښتل *nkkhatal* (to stick) is an exception, as it substitutes ل *l* for the terminal letters of the root. Examples :—

INFINITIVE.		PRESENT.			PAST.		
		PRESENT.	AORIST.	FUTURE.	IMPERFECT.	PAST.	PERFECT.
رغښتل *rghakkhtal*	to wallow	رغړم *rgharam*	وُ رغړم *wu rgharam*	وُ به رغړم *wu ba rgharam*	رغښتم *rghakkhtam*	وُ رغښتم *wu rghakkhtam*	رغښتلي يم *rghakkhtalai yam*
غښتل *ghakkhtal*	to coil	غړم *gharam*	وُ غړم *wu gharam*	وُ به غړم *wu ba gharam*	غښتم *ghakkhtam*	وُ غښتم *wu ghakkhtam*	غښتلي يم *ghakkhtalai yam*
لوښتل *lwukkhtal*	to part	لوړم *lwuram*	وُ لوړم *wu lwuram*	وُ به لوړم *wu ba lwuram*	لوښتم *lwukkhtam*	وُ لوښتم *wu lwukkhtam*	لوښتلي يم *lwukkhtalai yam*
نښتل *nkkhatal*	to hitch	نښلم *nkkhlam*	وُ نښلم *wu nkkhlam*	وُ به نښلم *wu ba nkkhlam*	نښتم *nkkhatam*	وُ نښتم *wu nkkhatam*	نښتلي يم *nkkhatalai yam*

d. Order IV. contains a few irregular and defective verbs. Most of them are included in the annexed list.

INFINITIVE.		PRESENT.			PAST.		
		PRESENT.	AORIST.	FUTURE.	IMPERFECT.	PAST.	PERFECT.
تلل لاړل	to go	خم *dzam*	خم *dzam*	به خم لاړ به شم *lāṛ ba sham*	تللم *tlalam*	*lāṛam* لاړم	تللي يم *tlalai yam*
درتلل درغلل	to go to thee	درخم *dardzam*	درخم *dardzam*	در به شم *dar ba sham*	درتللم *dartlalam*	*daraghlam* درغلم	*daraghlalai yam* درغللي يم
راتلل راغلل	to come	راخم *rādzam*	راخم *rādzam*	را به شم *rā ba sham*	راتلم *rātlam*	*rāghlam* راغلم	*rāghlai yam* راغلي يم
ورتلل ورغلل	to go to him	ورخم *wardzam*	ورخم *wardzam*	ور به شم *war ba sham*	ورتلم *wartlam*	*waraghlam* ورغلم	*waraghlai yam* ورغلي يم
زغليدل زغاښتل	to run	زغلم *zghalam*	وُ زغلم *wu zghalam*	وُ به زغلم *wu ba zghalam*	*zghākkhtam* زغاښتم	*wu zghākkhtam* وُ زغاښتم	*zghākkhtalai yam* زغاښتلي يم
زيږيدل زوول	to be born	زيږيږم *zegegam*	وُ زيږيږم *wu zegegam*	وُ به زيږيږم *wu ba zegegam*	زيږيدلم *zegedalam* زوولم *zowulam*	وُ زيږيدلم *wu zegedalam* وُ زوولم *wu zowulam*	زيږيدلي يم *zegedalai yam* زوولي يم *zowulai yam*
چاودل *chāwdal*	to split	چوَم *chawam*	وُ چوَم *wu chawam*	وُ به چوَم *wu ba chawam*	چاودم *chāwdam*	وُ چاودم *wu chāwdam*	چاودلي يم *chāwdalai yam*
سول *swal*	to burn	سوَخم *swadzam*	وُ سوَخم *wu swadzam*	وُ به سوَخم *wu ba swadzam*	سوَلم *swalam*	وُ سوَم *wu swam*	سوَي يم *sawai yam*

N.B. In the third person masculine singular in the imperfect and past tenses these verbs use a contracted form by substituting ز *zāhir* for the ل *al* of the infinitive. The verb تلل and its compounds still further contract this form to تهٔ *tah*, راتهٔ *rātah*, etc., in the imperfect tense. The verb راغلل, *rāghlal*, uses the form راغي *rāghai*, ورغي *wuraghāi*, etc., for the third person singular masculine of the past tense. Similarly the other verbs contract the same person singular masculine to زغاښت *zghākkht*, زووهٔ *zowah*, چاوډ *chāwd*, سهٔ *sah*, respectively in the imperfect and past tenses.

96. The Derivative Verb (*f'iali-mushtaq*). The compound or derivative verb may be either transitive or intransitive. It is formed by conjugating a noun or adjective with the auxiliaries کول *kawul* and کړل *kṛal* (to do) with the present and past tenses respectively, if transitive, and with the auxiliaries کيدل *kedal* and شول *shwal* (to be or become) with the present and past tenses respectively, if intransitive.

a. With the derivatives are included nominals or verbs which are combined with a noun to express compound action, intensity, or speciality, etc., as غوټه وهل *ghoṭa-wahal* (to dive), پور آخستل *por-ākhistal* (to borrow), سندري ويل *sandare-wayal* (to sing), etc.

97. The conjugations of the intransitive auxiliaries کيدل *kedal* and شول *shwal* have been given in the preceding pages (Art. 81 and 82). It is necessary now to shew the conjugations of the transitive auxiliaries کول *kawul* and کړل *kṛal* in order to illustrate the paradigms of derivative verbs.

98. The transitive verb کول *kawul* (to do), which is used as an auxiliary in forming the tenses of present time in derivative verbs, is defective in the compound past tenses, and has only the active voice. It is thus conjugated.

INFINITIVE MOOD. کول *kawul* (to do).

INDICATIVE MOOD.

PRESENT TENSE. I do or am doing, etc.	We do or are doing, etc.
SINGULAR.	PLURAL.
کوم - کم *kawam, kam*	کوو - کو *kawū, kū*
کوي - کي *kawe, ke*	کوئ - کئ *kawa-ī, ka-ī*
or کاندِ or کي - کوي *kawī, kī*, or *kāndi*	or کاندِ or کي - کوي *kawī, kī*, or *kāndi*
or کا or کَ *kā* or *ka*	or کا or کَ *kā* or *ka*

Aorist Tense. I may do, etc.	We may do, etc.
SINGULAR.	PLURAL.
وُ کوم - وُ کم *wu kawam, wu kam*	وُ کوؤ - وُ کؤ *wu kawū, wu kū*
وُ کوي - وُ کي *wu kawe, wu ke*	وُ کوئ - وُ کئ *wu kawa-ī, wu ka-ī*
or وُ کوي - وُ کي *wu kawī, wu kī* or	or وُ کوي - وُ کي *wu kawī, wu kī* or
etc. وُ کاندِ or وُ کا *wu kāndi* or *wu kā*, etc.	etc. وُ کاندِ or وُ کا *wu kānai* or *wu kā*, etc.

Future Tense. I shall or will do, etc.	We shall or will do, etc.
SINGULAR.	PLURAL.
کم or وُ به کوم *wu ba kawam* or *kam*	کؤ or وُ به کوؤ *wu ba kawū* or *kū*
کي or وُ به کوي *wu ba kawe* or *ke*	کئ or وُ به کوئ *wu ba kawa-ī* or *ka-ī*
or کي or وُ به کوي *wu ba kawī* or *kī* or	or کي or وُ به کوي *wu ba kawī* or *kī* or
etc. وُ به کاندِ *wu ba kāndi*, etc.	etc. وُ به کاندِ *wu ba kāndi*, etc.

Imperfect Tense. I was doing, etc. — We were doing, etc.

SINGULAR.

		Pronoun	
m.	کول	ما *mā*	*kawul*
	کاوه	تا *tā*	*kāwah*
		هغه *haghah*	
		مونګه *mūnga*	
		تاسو *tāsū*	
f.	کوله	هغو *hagho*	*kawula*

PLURAL.

	Pronoun	
کول	ما *mā*	*kawul*
	تا *tā*	
	هغه *haghah*	
	مونګه *mūnga*	
	تاسو *tāsū*	
کولي	هغو *hagho*	*kawule*

Past Tense. I did or did do, etc. — We did or did do, etc.

SINGULAR.

		Pronoun	
m.	وُ کول	ما *mā*	*wu kawul*
	وُ کاوه	تا *tā*	*wu kāwah*
		هغه *haghah*	
		مونګه *mūnga*	
		تاسو *tāsū*	
f.	وُ کوله	هغو *hagho*	*wu kawula*

PLURAL.

	Pronoun	
وُ کول	ما *mā*	*wu kawul*
	تا *tā*	
	هغه *haghah*	
	مونګه *mūnga*	
	تاسو *tāsū*	
وُ کولي	هغو *hagho*	*wu kawule*

Continuative Past Tense. I used to do, etc. We used to do, etc.

	SINGULAR.			PLURAL.	
m.	به کول / به کاوه	ما *mā*	*ba kawul* / *ba kāwah*	به کول	ما *mā*	*ba kawul*
		تا *tā*			تا *tā*	
		هغه *haghah*			هغه *haghah*	
		مونکه *mūnga*			مونکه *mūnga*	
		تاسو *tāsū*			تاسو *tāsū*	
f.	به کوله	هغو *hagho*	*ba kawula*	به کولي	هغو *hagho*	*ba kawule*

IMPERATIVE MOOD.

Do thou; let him do. — Do ye; let them do.

SINGULAR.

وُ کوه - وُ که *wu kawa, wu ka*
or کي or هغه دِ وُ کوي *haghah di wu kawī*
or *kī* or
کَ or کا or کاندِ *kāndi* or *kā* or *ka*
etc. وُ دِ کوي - کي - کاندِ *wu di kawī* or *kī*
or *kāndi*, etc.

PLURAL.

وُ کوئ - وُ کئ *wu kawa-ī, wu ka-ī*
or کي or هغه دِ وُ کوي *haghah di wu kawī*
or *kī* or
کَ or کا or کاندِ *kāndi* or *kā* or *ka*
etc. وُ دِ کوي or کي or کاندِ *wu di kawī* or *kī* or
kāndi, etc.

SUBJUNCTIVE MOOD.

Present Tense. If I do, etc. — If we do, etc.

SINGULAR.

که *ki* { کوم *kawam* / کوې *kawe* / کوي - کاندِ etc. *kawī, kāndi*, etc. }

PLURAL.

که *ki* { کوُ *kawū* / کوئ *kawa-ī* / کوي - کاندِ etc. *kawī, kāndi*, etc. }

Past Tense. If I had done, etc. — If we had done, etc.

SINGULAR.

m. که کولی *ki kawulai* } وې *wai*
f. که کولِ *ki kawuli* }

PLURAL.

m. که کولي *ki kawulī* } وې *wai*
f. که کولِ *ki kawuli* }

Future Tense. If I would have done, etc. — If we would have done, etc.

SINGULAR.

m. کولی وَه } که به *ki ba* { *kawulai wuh*
f. کولِ وَه } { *kawuli wa*

PLURAL.

m. کولي وُو } که به *ki ba* { *kawulī wū*
f. کولِ وې - وِ } { *kawuli we, wi*

POTENTIAL MOOD.

PRESENT TENSE. I can do, etc. We can do, etc.

	SINGULAR.			PLURAL.	
m. شم	کولي *kawulai*	*sham*	شُو	کولي *kawulī*	*shū*
شي		*she*	شئ		*sha-ī*
f. شي	کولِ *kawuli*	*shī*	شي	کولِ *kawuli*	*shī*

PAST TENSE. I could have done, etc. We could have done, etc.

	SINGULAR.			PLURAL.	
m. کولي شه	ما *mā*	*kawulai shah*	کولي شُوُو	ما *mā*	*kawulī shwū*
	تا *tā*			تا *tā*	
	هغه *haghah*			هغه *haghah*	
	مونګه *mūnga*			مونګه *mūnga*	
	تاسو *tāsū*			تاسو *tāsū*	
f. کولِ شوه	هغو *hagho*	*kawuli shwa*	کولِ شوي	هغو *hagho*	*kawuli shwe*

FUTURE TENSE. I would have done, etc. We would have done, etc.

	SINGULAR.			PLURAL.	
m. به کولي	ما *mā*	*ba kawulai*	به کولي	ما *mā*	*ba kawulī*
وُه	تا *tā*	*wuh*	وُو	تا *tā*	*wū*
	هغه *haghah*			هغه *haghah*	
	مونګه *mūnga*			مونګه *mūnga*	
f. به کولِ	تاسو *tāsū*	*ba kawuli*	به کولِ	تاسو *tāsū*	*ba kawuli*
وَه	هغو *hagho*	*wa*	وي	هغو *hagho*	*we*

GERUND.—*m.* کوُون *kawūn*, *f.* کوُونه *kawūna*, a doing.

PRESENT PARTICIPLE.—*m.* کاوه *kāwah*, *f.* کوله *kawala*, done.

ACTIVE PARTICIPLE.—کوُونکي *kawūnkai* or کوُوني *kawūnai*, doer.

PASSIVE PARTICIPLE.—کولي *kawulai*, having done.

a. In the Imperative Mood plural the form وُ کانړئ *wu kāṉra-ī* is sometimes used for وُ کوئ *wu kawa-ī* (do ye).

99. The transitive verb کړل *kṛal* (to do or perform) has both an active and a passive voice and is regular in all its moods and tenses. It is used as an auxiliary in forming the past tenses of derivative verbs. It

is conjugated in the same manner as وهل, *wahal* (to strike). See Art. 84 and 85. Its tenses of present and past time are formed according to the rules explained in Art. 74 and 75, as is shown in the subjoined skeleton of the paradigm.

ACTIVE VOICE.

INFINITIVE MOOD. کړل *kṛal* (to do).

INDICATIVE MOOD.

Present Tense. I do or am doing, etc.

SINGULAR.	PLURAL.
کړم *kṛam*	کړو *kṛū*
کړې *kṛe*	کړئ *kṛa-ī*
کړي *kṛī*	کړي *kṛī*

Imperfect Tense. Was doing me, etc. — Was doing us, etc.

	SINGULAR.	PLURAL.
	کړلم - کړم *kṛalam, kṛam*	کړلو - کړو *kṛalū, kṛū*
	کړلې - کړې *kṛale, kṛe*	کړلئ - کړئ *kṛala-ī, kṛa-ī*
m.	کړ - کړه - کړل *kṛal, kṛah, kaṛ*	کړل - کړه *kṛal, kṛah*
f.	کړله - کړه *kṛala, kṛa*	کړلې - کړې *kṛale, kṛe*

Perfect Tense. Has done me, etc. — Has done us, etc.

	SINGULAR.	PLURAL.
m.	یم / یې / دی } کړی *kaṛai* { *yam* / *ye* / *dai*	یو / یئ / دي } کړي *kaṛī* { *yū* / *ya-ī* / *dī*
f.	کړې ده *kiṛi da*	کړې دي *kiṛi dī*

IMPERATIVE MOOD.

Do thou; let him do. — Do ye; let them do.

SINGULAR.	PLURAL.
وُ کړه - کړه *wu kṛa, kṛa*	وُ کړئ - کړئ *wū kṛa-ī, kṛa-ī*
or هغه دِ وُ کړي *haghah di wu kṛī*, or	or هغه دِ وُ کړي *haghah di wu kṛī*
وُ دِ کړي *wu di kṛī*	وُ دِ کړي *wu di kṛī*

SUBJUNCTIVE MOOD.

Present Tense. If I do, etc. — If we do, etc.

SINGULAR.			PLURAL.		
کړم	که ki	*kṛam*	کړُو	که ki	*kṛū*
کړې		*kṛe*	کړئ		*kṛa-ī*
کړي		*kṛī*	کړي		*kṛī*

Past Tense. If I had done, etc. — If we had done, etc.

	SINGULAR.		PLURAL.	
m.	که کړی *ki kaṛai*	وي *wai*	که کړي *ki kaṛī*	وي *wai*
f.	که کړې *ki kiṛi*		*که کړې *ki kiṛi*	

Future Tense. If I would have done, etc. — If we would have done, etc.

	SINGULAR.	PLURAL.
m.	که به کړی وُه *ki ba kaṛai wuh*	که به کړي وُو *ki ba kaṛī wū*
f.	که به کړې وه *ki ba kiṛi wa*	که به کړې وي *ki ba kiṛi we*

POTENTIAL MOOD.

Present Tense. I can do, etc. — We can do, etc.

SINGULAR.			PLURAL.		
شم	کړی *kaṛai*	*sham*	شُو	کړي *kaṛī*	*shū*
شې		*she*	شئ		*sha-ī*
شي	کړې *kiṛi*	*shī*	شي	کړې *kiṛi*	*shī*

Past Tense. I could have done, etc. — We could have done, etc.

	SINGULAR.	PLURAL.
m.	کړی شه *kaṛai shah*	کړي شوُ *kaṛī shwū*
	کړې شوه *kiṛi shwa*	کړې شوې *kiṛi shwe*

Future Tense. I would have done, etc. — We would have done, etc.

	SINGULAR.	PLURAL.
m.	به کړی شه *ba kaṛai shah*	به کړي شوُ *ba kaṛī shwū*
f.	به کړې شوه *ba kiṛi shwa*	به کړې شوې *ba kiṛi shwe*

Gerund.—*m.* کړُون *kṛūn* (obsol.), *f.* کړنه *kaṛana*, a doing.

Present Participle.—*m.* کړه *kṛah*, *f* کړله *kṛala*, done.

* Though generally met with as given in the text the plural feminine should properly be کړي *kiṛī*.

ACTIVE PARTICIPLE.—كړونكي *krūnkai* or كړوني *krūnai*, a doer.
PASSIVE PARTICIPLE.—كړلي *kralai* or كړي *karai*, having done.

100. The Passive Voice of the verb كړل *kral* is formed by conjugating the past participle with the auxiliaries يم *yam* and شول *shwal*.

PASSIVE VOICE.

INFINITIVE MOOD. كړي كيدل *karai kedal* (to be done).

INDICATIVE MOOD.

PRESENT TENSE. I am done, etc. — We are done, etc.

	SINGULAR.			PLURAL.	
m.	يم / يي / دئ	كړئ *karai*	*yam* / *ye* / *dai*	يو / يئ / دي	كړي *karī*	*yū* / *ya-ī* / *dī*
f.	كړِ ده *kiri da*			كړِ دي *kiri dī*	

IMPERFECT TENSE. I was being done, etc. — We were being done, etc.

	SINGULAR.			PLURAL.	
m.	كيدلم / كيدلي / كيدل - كيده	كړئ *karai*	*kedalam* / *kedale* / *kedal, kedah*	كيدلو / كيدلئ / كيدل	كړي *karī*	*kedalū* / *kedala-ī* / *kedal*
f.	كړِ كيدله *kiri kedala*			كړِ كيدلِ *kiri kedali*	

PERFECT TENSE. I have been done, etc. — We have been done, etc.

	SINGULAR.			PLURAL.	
m.	يم / يي / دئ	كړئ شوئ *karai shawai*	*yam* / *ye* / *dai*	يو / يئ / دي	كړي شوي *karī shawī*	*yū* / *ya-ī* / *dī*
f.	كړِ شوِ ده *kiri shiwi da*			كړِ شوِ دي *kiri shiwi dī*	

IMPERATIVE MOOD.

Be thou done; let him be done.	Be ye done; let them be done.
SINGULAR.	PLURAL.
وُ كړَيْ شه *wu karai sha*	وُ كړي شئ *wu karī sha-ī*
or هغه دِ كړَيْ شي *haghah di karai shī*, or	or هغه د كړي شي *haghah di karī shī*, or
وُ دِ كړَيْ شي *wu di karai shī*	وُ دِ كړي شي *wu di karī shī*

SUBJUNCTIVE MOOD.

PRESENT TENSE. If I were done, etc. — If we were done, etc.

	SINGULAR.		PLURAL.	
m.	شم / شې / شي	كه كړَيْ *ki karai* / كه كړِ *ki kiri* (f.) — *sham* / *she* / *shī*	شُو / شئ / شي	كه كړي *ki karī* / كه كړِ *ki kiri* — *shū* / *sha-ī* / *shī*

PAST TENSE. If I had been done, etc. — If we had been done, etc.

	SINGULAR.	PLURAL.
m.	كه كړَيْ شوَيْ *ki karai shawai*	كه كړي شوي *ki karī shawī*
	وَيْ *wai*	وَيْ *wai*
f.	كه كړِ شوِ *ki kiri shiwi*	كه كړِ شوِ *ki kiri shiwi*

FUTURE TENSE. If I should have been done, etc. — If we should have been done, etc.

	SINGULAR.	PLURAL.
m.	وُم / وې / وُه كه كړَيْ شوَيْ به *ki karai shawai ba* — *wum* / *we* / *wuh*	وُو / وئ / وُو كه كړي شوي به *ki karī shawī ba* — *wū* / *wa-ī* / *wū*
f.	كه كړِ شوِ به وَه *ki kiri shiwi ba wa*	كه كړِ شوِ به وې *ki kiri shiwi ba we*

PASSIVE PARTICIPLE.—كړَيْ شوَيْ *karai shawai*, been done.

101. Derivative verbs may be either transitive or intransitive according as the adjectives or nouns from which they are formed happen to be conjugated with the transitive auxiliary كول *kawul* or the intransitive auxiliary كيدل *kedal*.

a. In forming the infinitive mood of such verbs, the auxiliaries are combined with the feminine form of those adjectives and nouns whose masculine ends in a consonant, by rejecting both the final ه *khafī* of the feminine, and the initial ک *k* of the auxiliary, as shown in the following examples :—

m. پوخ *f.* پښه ripe, پښول to cook, پښيدل to ripen.
m. ړوند *f.* ړنده blind, ړندول to blind, ړنديدل to be blind.
m. کوږ *f.* کږه crooked, کږول to distort, کږيدل to be bent.
m. پلن *f.* پلنه broad, پلنول to widen, پلنيدل to become wide.
m. لنډ *f.* لنډه short, لنډول to shorten, لنډيدل to become short.

b. In those derivative verbs formed from nouns or adjectives that end in a long vowel or ه *z̤āhir* (and which are both masculine and feminine) no such combination takes place. The auxiliaries are in such cases merely coupled with the nouns, etc., and thus conjugated with them. Examples :

اوده *ūdah*, sleep, اوده کول to put to sleep, اوده کيدل to go to sleep.
تږي *tigai*, thirsty, تږي کول to make thirsty, تږي کيدل to become thirsty.
خپه *khapah*, angry, خپه کول to make angry, خپه کيدل to be angry.
رڼا *ranṛā*, light, رڼا کول to make light, رڼا کيدل to be light.

c. All causal verbs derived from primitive intransitives that end in ل *al*, excepting those of Class II. Order III. (which are both transitive and intransitive), form their infinitives by adding the termination ول *wul* to the present tense of the intransitive deprived of its pronominal affix. The exceptional verbs above noted form their causals simply by changing the terminal ل *al* of the infinitive to ول *wul*. These changes are shown in the subjoined examples, which are conjugated like regular transitive verbs.

INTRANSITIVES.	CAUSALS.	PRESENT.	IMPERFECT.	PERFECT.
څملاستل to recline,	څملول to lay down.	څملوم	څملاوه	څملولي دي
کښيناستل to sit,	کښينول to seat.	کښينوم	کښيناوه	کښينولي دي
ختل to rise,	خيژول to raise.	خيژوم	خيژاوه	خيژولي دي
آلوتل to fly,	آلوزول to make fly.	آلوزوم	آلوزاوه	آلوزولي دي
زغاښتل to run,	زغلول to make run.	زغلوم	زغلاوه	زغلولي دي
نښتل to hitch,	نښلول to entangle.	نښلوم	نښلاوه	نښلولي دي
دنگل to jump,	دنگول to make jump.	دنگوم	دنگاوه	دنگولي دي
خندل to laugh,	خندول to make laugh.	خندوم	خنداوه	خندولي دي
ژړل to cry,	ژړول to cause to cry.	ژړوم	ژړاوه	ژړولي دي
زنگل to swing,	زنگول to make swing.	زنگوم	زنگاوه	زنگولي دي

102. In derivative verbs the tenses of present time are formed from the infinitive according to general rules. But those of past time are formed from the auxiliaries کړل *kṛal* and شول *shwal* for transitives and intransitives respectively, both noun and verb being inflected for gender and number.

103. The subjoined skeleton conjugations of a transitive and intransitive derivative verb, show how the tenses are formed, and also the changes for gender and number.

TRANSITIVE DERIVATIVE.

INFINITIVE MOOD. پښول *paḵẖawul* (to cook).

INDICATIVE MOOD.

PRESENT TENSE.

SINGULAR.	PLURAL.
پښوم *paḵẖawam*	پښوو *paḵẖawū*
پښوې *paḵẖawe*	پښوئ *paḵẖawa-ī*
پښوي *paḵẖawī*	پښوي *paḵẖawī*

IMPERFECT TENSE.

	SINGULAR.	PLURAL.
m.	پښول - پښوه or *paḵẖawul, paḵẖawah* or پوخ کړه or کړ *poḵẖ kṛah* or *kaṛ*	پښول or *paḵẖawul* or پاخه کړل or کړه *pāḵẖah kṛal* or *kṛah*
f.	پښوله or *paḵẖawula* or پښه کړله or کړ *paḵẖa kṛala* or *kṛa*	پښولې - پښولِ or *paḵẖawule, paḵẖawuli* پښې کړلې or کړې *paḵẖe kṛale* or *kṛe*

PERFECT TENSE.

	SINGULAR.	PLURAL.
m.	پښولی or پښلی دی *paḵẖawulai* or *paḵẖalai dai* or پوخ کړی دی or *poḵẖ kaṛai dai*	پښولي or پښلي دي *paḵẖawulī* or *paḵẖalī dī* or پاخه کړي دي *pāḵẖah kaṛī dī*
f.	پښولِ or پښلِ ده *paḵẖawuli* or *paḵẖali da* or پښه کړِ ده *paḵẖa kiṛi da*	پښولِ or پښلِ دي *paḵẖawuli* or *paḵẖali dī* or پښې کړِ دي *paḵẖe kiṛi dī*

IMPERATIVE MOOD.

SINGULAR.	PLURAL.
or ښخوه *pakhawa* or	or ښخوئ *pakhawa-ī* or
ښخه کړه or پوخ *pokh* or *pakha kṛa*	ښخي کړئ or پاخه *pākhah* or *pakhe kṛa-ī*
or هغه دِ ښخوي *haghah ḍi pakhawī* or	or هغه دِ ښخوي *haghah di pakhawī* or
or دِ ښخوي *pakhawī di* or	or دِ ښخوي *pakhawī di* or
ښخه کړي or هغه دِ پوخ *haghah di pokh* or *pakha kṛī*	ښخي کړي or هغه دِ پاخه *hagah di pākhah* or *pakhe kṛī*
ښخه دِ کړي or پوخ *pokh* or *pakha di kṛī*	ښخي دِ کړي or پاخه *pākhah* or *pakhe di kṛī*

SUBJUNCTIVE MOOD.

PRESENT TENSE.

	SINGULAR.		PLURAL.	
m.	کړم	که پوخ *ki pokh*	*kṛam*	کړو	که پاخه *ki pākhah*	*kṛū*
	کړې		*kṛe*	کړئ		*kṛa-ī*
f.	کړي	که ښخه *ki pakha*	*kṛī*	کړي	که ښخي *ki pakhe*	*kṛī*

PAST TENSE.

	SINGULAR.			PLURAL.	
m.	وئ	که ښخولی *ki pakhawulai*	*wai*	وئ	که ښخولي *ki pakhawulī*	*wai*
		که پوخ کړی *ki pokh karai*			که پاخه کړي *ki pākhah kaṛī*	
f.		که ښخوله *ki pakhawuli*			که ښخولې *ki pakhawuli*	
		که ښخه کړه *ki pakha kiṛi*			که ښخي کړې *ki pakhe kiṛi*	

POTENTIAL MOOD.

PRESENT TENSE.

	SINGULAR.			PLURAL.	
m. شم	ښخولی *pakhawulai*	*sham*	شو	ښخولي *pakhawulī*	*shū*
شې	پوخ کړی *pokh karai*	*she*	شئ	پاخه کړي *pākhah kaṛī*	*sha-ī*
f. شي	ښخوله *pakhawuli*	*shī*	شي	ښخولې *pakhawuli*	*shī*
	ښخه کړه *pakha kiṛi*			ښخي کړې *pakhe kiṛi*	

PAST TENSE.

	SINGULAR.			PLURAL.	
m. شه	پخولی pakhawulai / پوخ کړی pokh karai	shah	شوو	پخولي pakhawulī / پاخه کړي pākhah karī	shwū
f. شوه	پخولِ pakhawuli / پخه کړِ pakha kiri	shwa	شوي	پخولِ pakhawuli / پخې کړِ pakhe kiri	shwe

Gerund.—*m.* پخوون *pakhawūn*, *f.* پخوونه *pakhawūna*, a cooking.

Present Participle.—*m.* پخاوه *pakhāwah*, *f.* پخوله *pakhawala*, cooked.

Active Participle.—پخوونکی *pakhawūnkai* or پخووني *pakhawūnai*, cooker.

Passive Participle.—پخولی *pakhawulai* or پخلی *pakhalai*, having cooked.

INTRANSITIVE DERIVATIVE.

INFINITIVE MOOD. پخیدل *pakhedal* (to ripen).

INDICATIVE MOOD.

PRESENT TENSE.

SINGULAR.	PLURAL.
پخیږم *pakhegam*	پخیږو *pakhegū*
پخیږې *pakhege*	پخیږئ *pakhega-ī*
پخیږي *pakhegī*	پخیږي *pakhegī*

IMPERFECT TENSE.

	SINGULAR.	PLURAL.
m.	پخیدل - پخیده *pakhedal, pakhedah*	پخیدل *pakhedal*
	پوخ شه *pokh shah*	پاخه شوو *pākhah shwū*
f.	پخیدله *pakhedala*	پخیدلِ *pakhedali*
	پخه شوه *pakha shwa*	پخې شوې *pakhe shwe*

PAST TENSE.

	SINGULAR.			PLURAL.	
m. دی	پخیدلی *pakhedalai* / پوخ شوی *pokh shawai*	dai	دي	پخیدلي *pakhedalī* / پاخه شوي *pākhah shawī*	dī
f. ده	پخیدلِ *pakhedali* / پخه شوِ *pakha shiwi*	da	دي	پخیدلِ *pakhedali* / پخې شوِ *pakhe shiwi*	dī

IMPERATIVE MOOD.

SINGULAR.	PLURAL.
پخيږه - وُ پخيږه *pakhega, wu pakhega* or	پخيږئ - وُ پخيږئ *pakhega-ī, wu pakhega-ī*
پوخ or پخه شه *pokh* or *pakha sha*	پاخه or پخي شئ *pākhah* or *pakhe sha-ī*
or هغه دِ پخيږي *haghah di pakhegī* or	هغه دِ پخيږي *haghah di pakhegī*
or پخيږي دِ *pakhegī di*	وُ دِ پخيږي *wu di pakhegī*
هغه دِ پوخ or پخه شي *haghah di pokh* or *pakha shī*	هغه دِ پاخه or پخي شي *haghah di pākhah* or *pakhe shī*
پوخ or پخه دِ شي *pokh* or *pakha di shī*	پاخه or پخي دِ شي *pākhah* or *pakhe di shī*

SUBJUNCTIVE MOOD.

PRESENT TENSE.

SINGULAR.			PLURAL.		
پخيږم	که *ki*	*pakhegam*	پخيږو	که *ki*	*pakhegū*
پخيږې		*pakhege*	پخيږئ		*pakhega-ī*
پخيږي		*pakhegī*	پخيږي		*pakhegī*

PAST TENSE.

	SINGULAR.			PLURAL.	
m. وي	که پخيدلي *ki pakhedalai*	*wai*	وي	که پخيدلي *ki pakhedalī*	*wai*
	که پوخ شوي *ki pokh shawai*			که پاخه شوي *ki pākhah shawī*	
f.	که پخيدلِ *ki pakhedali*			که پخيدلِ *ki pakhedali*	
	که پخه شِوِ *ki pakha shiwi*			که پخي شِوِ *ki pakhe shiwi*	

POTENTIAL MOOD.

PRESENT TENSE.

	SINGULAR.			PLURAL.	
m. شم	پخيدلي *pakhedalai*	*sham*	شو	پخيدلي *pakhedalī*	*shū*
شې	پوخ شوي *pokh shawai*	*she*	شئ	پاخه شوي *pākhah shawī*	*sha-ī*
f. شي	پخيدلِ *pakhedali*	*shī*	شي	پخيدلِ *pakhedali*	*shī*
	پخه شِوِ *pakha shiwi*			پخي شِوِ *pakhe shiwi*	

PAST TENSE.

	SINGULAR.			PLURAL.	
m. شه	پخيدلي *pakhedalai*	*shah*	شوو	پخيدلي *pakhedalī*	*shwū*
	پوخ شوي *pokh shawai*			پاخه شوي *pākhah shawī*	
f. شوه	پخيدلِ *pakhedali*	*shwa*	شوي	پخيدلِ *pakhedali*	*shwe*
	پخه شِوِ *pakha shiwi*			پخي شِو *pakhe shiwi*	

GERUND.—*m.* پخيدون *pa<u>kh</u>edūn*, *f.* پخيدنه *pa<u>kh</u>edana*, a ripening.
PRESENT PARTICIPLE.—*m.* پخيده *pa<u>kh</u>edah*, *f.* پخيدله *pa<u>kh</u>edala*, ripened.
ACTIVE PARTICIPLE.—پخيدونکي *pa<u>kh</u>edūnkai* or پخيدوني *pa<u>kh</u>edūnai*, ripener.
PASSIVE PARTICIPLE.—پخيدلي *pa<u>kh</u>edalai* or پوخ شوي *po<u>kh</u> <u>sh</u>awai*, having ripened.

104. Negation and Prohibition (*nafī wa nahī*) are expressed by the use of the adverbs نه *na* and مه *ma*, with the several forms of the verbs.

a. The adverb or particle of prohibition مه *ma*, is only used with the second person of the imperative mood alone, and it always precedes the verb with which it often coalesces by rejecting its final ه *h*. Ex. مه ژاړه or مژاړه *ma ĵāṛa* (don't cry), مه کوئ or مکوئ *ma kawa-ī* (don't ye), etc.

b. The adverb of negation نه *na*, is used with all other formations of the verb, and, like the preceding, is often joined to it by the rejection of the terminal ه *h*. It denotes simple negation. In the simple tenses of present time it precedes the verb, as, نه وينم *na wīnam* (I do not see), نه پوهيږي *na pohegī* (he does not understand), etc. In those tenses which take the prefix و *wu*, the particle نه *na* intervenes between it or its combinations and the verb itself, as و نه کوت *wu na kot* (he did not look), وا به نه خلم *wā ba na <u>kh</u>lam* (I will not take), و به نه وهي *wu ba na wahī* (he will not strike), etc. But in those verbs that reject the prefix و *wu* as redundant, the particle of negation intervenes between the first and second syllables of the verb itself, including the combination of the former with the future sign به *ba*, as, پري نه وت *pre na wat* (he did not fall), ښکي به نه نم *<u>kkh</u>ke ba na nam* (I will not sit down), etc. In compound tenses whether present or past, of the active or passive voice, the particle of negation intervenes between the participle and the auxiliary forming the tense, as, وهلِ شوِ نه ده *wahali <u>sh</u>iwi na da* (she has not been struck), سري آس نيولي نه شه *sarī ās nīwulai na <u>sh</u>ah* (the man could not catch the horse), لاس دِ خوږ شوي به نه وي *lās di <u>kh</u>ūg <u>sh</u>awai ba na wī* (your hand will not have been hurt), etc.

SECTION IV.

THE PARTICLE (*harf*).

105. The particle is a word which, by itself being indeclinable and without independent meaning, is added to another word to denote some quality, condition, or other circumstance connected with it. Under the term particle are included the adverb, interjection, conjunction, and preposition.

106. The Adverb (*zaraf*). As a rule the adverbs are indeclinable, but those that end in a consonant are subject to inflection when coupled with another word commencing with one, as اوس *os* (now), تر اوسَ پوري *tar osa pore* (until now), تل *tal* (always), ترتله *tartala* (for ever). Some few nouns and adjectives are used as adverbs, and subject to all the changes for gender and number as those parts of speech, as, هر *har* (every), هره ورځ *hara wradz* (every day), etc.

107. The adverbs both simple and compound form a numerous class, and they include besides some purely Pukkhto words a number which have been derived from the Arabic and Persian. These last, however, are, generally speaking, only met with in books or are used in composition. The adverbs may be classed as those of time, place, quantity, similitude and affirmation. The following lists of these several classes include those in general use in Pukkhto.

a. The Adverbs of Time (*zurūfu-z-zamān*) are the following:

آخر *ākhir*, at last.	برايه ـ برني *barāya, barane*, last night.
اوس *os*, now.	بربر *barbar*, repeatedly.
تر اوسَ پوري *tar osa pore*, until now.	بيا *biyā*, again, then.
لا تر اوسَ *lā tar osa*; even till now.	پارون *pārūn*, yesterday.
باري *bāre*, then.	پس *pas*, therefore, next.

پله پسي *pala pase*, successively.
پخوا *pakhwā*, formerly.
پلغت *palaghat*, at once.
تل *tal*, always.
ترتله *tartala*, for ever.
چري *chare*, ever.
هيڅري *hechare*, never.
رو رو *ro ro*, slowly.
زر زر *zar zar*, quickly.
سم دَ لاسَ *sam da lāsa*, forthwith.
څو ځله *tso dzala*, how often?
يو ځل *yo dzal*, once.
صبا *ṣabā*, to-morrow.
بل صبا *bul ṣabā*, next day.
نن صبا *nan ṣabā*, nowadays.
كله *kala*, ever? when?
كله كله *kala kala*, sometimes.
كله نه كله *kala na kala*, occasionally
تر كله پوري *tar kala pore*, till when?
هر كله *har kala*, always.
هر كله چه *har kala chi*, whenever.
هيڅ كله *hets kala*, at no time.
نن *nan*, to-day.
نن ورځ *nan wradz*, this day.
ورمه ورځ *warama wradz*, day before last.
لا ورمه ورځ *lā waṛama wradz*, three days ago.
لالا ورمه ورځ *lālā waṛama wradz*, four days ago.
لري *lire*, far.
لري لارغه *lire lārghah*, long ago.
لرغوني *larghūne*, long since.
نا څاپه *nā tsāpa*, suddenly.
ناگاه *nāgāh*, unawares.
ناگهان *nāgahān*, unexpectedly.
هاله *hāla*, then.
هډو *haḍo*, never.
هره پلا *hara plā*, each time.
هر ځل *har dzal*, every time.
وار په وار *wār pa wār*, in turn.
وختي *wakhtī*, early.
وړنبي *wṛunbe*, firstly.

b. The Adverbs of Place (*ẕurūfu-l-makān*) are the following:

باندي *bānde*, on, upon.
بهر *bahar*, outside.
بيرته *biyarta*, aback.
پوري *pore*, up to.
په *pa*, on, upon.
پورته *porta*, above, on.
په ښكي *pa kkhke*, within, in.
تر *tar*, to, as far as.
تر دي پوري *tar de pore*, to this degree.
تر هغه پوري *tar haghah pore*, to that degree.
تر حدّ پوري *tar ḥadda pore*, to the utmost.
پوري اوري *pore ore*, out and out.
چاپيره *chāpera*, all round.
چرته *charta*, where.
بل چرته *bul charta*, elsewhere.
هر چرته *har charta*, everywhere.

هيچرته *hecharta*, nowhere.
دلته ـ دلي *dalta, dale*, here.
دننه *danana*, inside.
يواځي *yawādzai*, alone.
دلته هلته *dalta halta*, here and there.
دي پلو *de palaw*, this side.
دي خوا *de khwā*, this way.
هغه پلو *haghah palaw*, that side.
هغه خوا *hagha khwā*, that way.
سره *sara*, together.
ښکته *kkhkata*, below.
ښکيه *kkhkea*, under.

ښکي *kkhke*, in, within.
لاندي *lānde*, under.
لاندي باندي *lānde bānde*, over and under
لري *lire*, afar.
له ورايه *la warāya*, from afar.
نژدي *nijde*, near.
وراندي *wrānde*, in front.
ورستو *wrusto*, in rear.
هلته *halta*, here.
هوري *hūre*, there.
هيسته *hīsta*, here.
ورهيسته *warhīsta*, towards him.

c. The Adverbs of Quantity (*zurūfu-l-miqdār*) are the following :

ډير *der*, very.
ډير ځله *der dzala*, very often.
دومره *domra*, this much.
څومره *tsomra*, how much ?
هومره *homra*, that much.
هر څومره *har tsomra*, however much.
لا *lā*, even, yet.
هر *har*, every.
هر څو *har tso*, however many.

لا زيات *lā ziyāt*, even more.
هر څه *har tsa*, whatever.
هر يو *har yo*, every one.
يو يو *yo yo*, singly.
لږکوتي *lagkūtī*, a little.
زيات *ziyāt*, more.
تر حدّ زيات *tar hadda ziyāt*, beyond degree.

d. The Adverbs of Similitude (*zurūfu-l-tashbīh*) are the following :

به وي *ba wī*, may be.
بويه *boya*, it behoves.
بيدوُ *bedū*, exactly.
بي شک *be-shakh*, doubtless.
څه دَپاره *tsa dapāra*, for what.
څه له *tsa la*, why ?
جوړ *joṛ*, then, well.
خو *kho*, at least.

رښتيا *rikkhtiyā*, indeed.
ښائي *kkhā-ī*, perhaps.
ولي *wale*, but, why ?
خداي خبر *khudāe khabar*, } God knows
خداي زده *khudāe zdah*, } God knows
خداي رو *khudāe go*, by God.
له سره *la sara*, not at all.
ګوندي *gūnde*, likely.

مه *ma*, don't.
نه دِ وي *na di·wī*, perhaps not.
هرگوره *har gora*, at all events.
هو ـ آري *ho, āre*, yes, aye.
يه ـ نه ـ آيا *ya, na, āyā*, no, nay.
يره *yara*, verily.

108. The Interjection (*ḥarfi-ṣaut*). The exclamations commonly used in Pukkhto are the following, among many others :—

آخ ـ اخښ *ākh, akhkkh*, excellent!
آپرين *āparīn*, well done!
شاباش *shābāsh*, bravo!
آمين *āmīn*, amen!
آيا *āyā*, no! is it?
بس که *bas ka*, have done!
بيدار شه *baidār sha*, look out!
بيرته شه *biyarta sha*, avaunt!
پهم که *pahm ka*, have a care!
پيتي مو شه *peṭī·mo sha*, for shame!
پوه شه *poh sha*, mark!
کاشکي *kāshke*, would to God!
الله *allah*, oh God!
توبه *tobah*, fie!
لري شه *lire sha*, begone!
افسوس *afsos*, pity!
چخه *chikha*, away!
هائي هائي *hā-ī hā-ī*, alas! alas!
وائي وائي *wā-ī wā-ī*, oh my!
ميرات شه *mīrāt sha*, death to thee!

a. The interjections او *o* and اي *ai* have already been described as signs of the vocative case (Art. 36). They also have the meaning of Oh you! Holloa! when used to attract attention or as a call.

109. The Conjunction (*ḥarfi-'aṭf*) is a word used to connect sentences and phrases. Those commonly used are as follows :—

او *o* or *aw*, and, also.
بلکه *balki*, but, rather.
پس *pas*, therefore.
پرته *prata*, besides.
بي له *be la*, without.
ترو *tro*, then, thence.
ځکه *dzaka*, because.
چه *chi*, that, for.
سوا *siwā*, except.
منگر *mangar*, unless.
که *ki*, if.
که نه ـ کنړه *ki na, kanṟa*, otherwise.
ليکن *lekin*, but, but if.
هم *hum*, also, even.
ولي *wale*, but, then.
يا *yā*, or, either.

110. The Preposition (*ḥarfi-m'anawī*) includes both prefixes and affixes or post-positions. Some adverbs are also used as prepositions. Those

prepositions that are formed by the union of a word with the particle په *pa* or تر *tar*, require that the noun they qualify should intervene between the two component parts of such prepositions. Ex. په سر باندي *pa sar bānde* (on the head), تر کټَ لاندي *tar kaṭa lānde* (under the bed), etc. The prepositions commonly used in Pukkhto are the following:

په *pa*, on, in, upon.	څخه-خڅه *tsakha*, *khatsa*, with, at, near
په ښکي *pa kkhke*, in, within.	سره *sara*, along with.
پري *pre*, on, upon.	دَ پاره *da pāra*, on account of.
تري *tre*, } from.	دَ پاسَ *da pāsa*, above.
تري نه *tre na*, } from.	دَ لاندي *da lānde*, below.
تِنه *tina*, } from.	ښکي *kkhke*, in, within.
تر *tar*, to, up to.	تر لاندي *tar lānde*, under.

111. Besides the prepositions and post-positions above mentioned, there are several particles only used as affixes to nouns, etc. for the formation of diminutives and derivatives from them.

112. The Diminutive Particle (*ḥarfi-tasghīr*) in Pukkhto always ends in ۍ *ai* or ئ *a-ī*, for the masculine and feminine respectively. The diminutive particles commonly used are as follows.

a. ړئ *ṛa-ī*. This is not a common form. It is added to nouns denoting inanimate objects, and is always of the feminine gender. Ex.—

کوزه *kūza*, a gugglet,	کوزه ړئ a small gugglet.
کندو *kandū*, a corn bin,	کندوړئ a small corn bin.
خس *khas*, a straw,	خسړئ a mote in the eye.
چک *chak*, a lump,	چکړئ a clot.

b. ي *ai*. This affix is of the masculine gender and is added to some nouns that end in a consonant and denote inanimate objects. Ex.—

توپک *ṭopak*, musket,	توپکي a small musket.
ښانک *kkhānak*, platter,	ښانکي a small platter.
کندول *kanḍol*, bowl,	کندولي a cup.

c. كي *kai* is a common diminutive affix, subject to change for gender and number, and used with nouns denoting both animate and inanimate objects. If the noun end in ي or ه they are rejected before this affix. Ex.—

پندوس *pandos*, a ball,	پندوسكي a little ball.
مندوس *mandos*, a turband,	مندوسكي a small turband.
كټ *kaṭ*, a cot,	كټكي a child's cot.
كور *kor*, a house,	كوركي a small cabin.
پوزه *poza*, a nose,	پوزكئ a little nose.
جنئ *jina-ī*, a girl,	جنكئ a little girl.

d. گي *gai* is only added to nouns denoting animate objects, and is subject to change for gender and number, etc. Ex.—

ټټو *ṭaṭū*, a pony,	ټټوگي a little pony.
جولا *jolā*, a weaver,	جولاگي a little weaver.
ملا *mullā*, a priest,	ملاگي a young priest.
كافر *kāfir*, an infidel,	كافرگي a little infidel.
هندو *hindū*, a pagan,	هندوگي a young pagan.

e. وټي *oṭai* is added to nouns ending in ي, whether denoting animate or inanimate objects, that letter itself being rejected. Ex.—

سړي *saṛai*, a man,	سړوټي a very small man.
لرگي *largai*, a stick,	لرگوټي a little stick.
جنئ *jina-ī*, a girl,	جنوټئ a very little girl.
منگي *mangai*, a pitcher,	منگوټي a little pitcher.

f. وري *ūrai*, وړي *ūṛai*, and گوري *gūrai*, are applied to nouns that end in a consonant and denote animate objects. They are subject to change for gender and number. Ex.—

چرگ *chirg*, a cock,	چرگوري a chicken.
هلك *halak*, a boy,	هلكوري a little boy.
گډ *ga-aḍ*, a sheep,	گډوري a lamb.
مږك *magak*, a rat,	مږكوري a young rat.
بز *buz*, a goat,	بزگوري a kid.

g. وکي *ūkai* is applied mostly to nouns denoting inanimate objects. Nouns ending in ي drop that letter before this diminutive affix, and those ending in ه, whose penultimate syllable is formed by the long vowel ا *ā*, drop the ه *h* and change the long vowel to its corresponding short one. Ex.—

ډنډ *ḍanḍ*, a pool,	ډنډوکي a puddle.
چاړه *chāṛa*, a long knife,	چړوکي a penknife.
وړ *waṛ*, small,	وړوکي very small.
هډ *haḍ*, a bone,	هډوکي a small bone.

113. The Derivative Particle (*ḥarfi-muẓāf*). Pukkhto is very rich in derivative and compound words. For the most part they have been adopted into the language from the Arabic and Persian, and are usually modified by the addition to the original of certain terminal particles also derived from the Arabic or Persian. These particles may be considered as of two classes, viz., those used in the construction of abstract nouns from adjectives or primitive nouns, and those used in the construction of adjectives from primitive nouns or adverbs.

114. The Abstract Noun (*ismi-muẓāf*). Abstract nouns are formed from primitive nouns and adjectives by one or other of the following affixes:

a. توب *tob* (A. طبع) added to a noun or adjective denotes disposition, nature, calling, or occupation. Ex.—

آشنا *āshnā*, a friend,	آشناتوب friendliness.
سړي *saṛai*, a man,	سړيتوب human nature.
سپاهي *spāhī*, a soldier,	سپاهيتوب military life.
ليوني *lewanai*, mad,	ليونتوب madness.
مين *mayan*, loving,	مينتوب love, courtship.

b. تيا *tiyā*. This particle is mostly added to adjectives alone, in forming abstract nouns, denoting possession of the quality or property signified by the adjective to which it is affixed. It is occasionally changed to سيا *siyā* and ستيا *stiyā*. Ex.—

آسان *āsān*, easy, آسانتيا easiness.
زوړ *zoṛ*, old, زوړتيا oldness.
ناجوړ *nājoṛ*, sick, ناجوړتيا sickness.
موړ *moṛ*, satiated, موړتيا satiety.
تنګ *tang*, narrow, تنګسيا narrowness.
ميلمه *melmah*, a guest, ميلمستيا hospitality.

c. والي *wālai* (H. والا). This particle is only added to adjectives in forming the abstract nouns denoting possession of the quality signified by them. Ex.—

اوږد *ūgd*, long, اوږد والي length.
پلن *plan*, broad, پلن والي breadth.
سور *sūr*, red, سور والي redness.
کلک *klak*, firm, کلک والي firmness.

NOTE.—This particle is sometimes changed to يالي *yālai* as in the following examples :—

ننګ *nang*, honour, ننګيالي honourable.
جنګ *jang*, quarrel, جنګيالي quarrelsome.
برګ *brag*, spotted, برګيالي spotted, mottled.
زغره *zghara*, armour, زغريالي armour-clad.
توره *tūra*, sword, توريالي sword-armed.

d. ولي *walī* or ګلوي *galwī* is added to nouns denoting animate beings to signify relationship, nationality, society, or confederation. Ex.—

عزيز *'azīz*, a relative, عزيزولي relationship.
خپل *khpul*, own, خپلولي family tie.
قام *qām*, clan, قامولي clanship.
ورور *wror*, brother, وروروړي brotherhood.

e. تون *tūn* is added to a few nouns to denote state or place. Ex.—

بيل *bīyal*, separate, بيلتون separation.
ځاي *dzāe*, place, ځاي تون abode, resort.
ميږي *megai*, ant, ميږتون ant's nest.
کنډه *kunḍa*, widow, کنډتون widowhood.

115. Adjectives are formed from primitive nouns and adverbs by the affix of one or other of the following particles or letters:

a. جن *jan* or ژن *jan* is added to nouns to form adjectives denoting possession of the property signified by the noun. Ex.—

اوبه *oba*, water,	اوبجن watery.
غم *gham*, grief,	غمجن grief struck.
نول *nūl*, sorrow,	نولجن sorrowful.
كبر *kibr*, pride,	كبرجن arrogant.
تبه *taba*, fever,	تبجن feverish.
مكر *makr*, hypocrisy,	مكرجن hypocritical.

b. من *man* or مند *mand* is added to nouns to form adjectives signifying endowment or possession of the property denoted by them. Ex.—

دولت *daulat*, wealth,	دولتمن wealthy.
سود *sūd*, profit,	سودامن profitable.
خوږ *khūg*, pain,	خوږمن painful.
يره *yara*, fear,	يرمن timid.

c. ناك *nāk* is added to nouns to form adjectives denoting fullness or possession of the property signified by the noun, and is sometimes interchanged with the particle جن (Art. 115, *a.*). Ex.—

قهر *qahr*, wrath,	قهرناك wrathful.
خوف *khof*, fear,	خوفناك fearful.
زيم *zyam*, moisture,	زيمناك moist.
سليخ *salekh*, glue,	سليخناك sticky.
بوئي *bū-ī*, smell,	بوئي ناك full of smell.

d. دار *dār* is added to nouns to denote possession of the property denoted by the noun, and also signifies keeper, possessor, etc. Ex.—

دنيا *duniyā*, wealth,	دنيادار wealthy.
مال *māl*, property,	مالدار rich in cattle, etc.
پهره *pahra*, guard,	پهره‌دار sentinel.
طرف *taraf*, side,	طرفدار partizan.

e. In the same manner the letters ن *an*, ني *nai*, and ي *ai* are added to nouns in transforming them to adjectives. Ex.--

پم	*pam*, mange,	پمن	mangy.
پورته	*porta*, up, above.	پورتني	superior.
خيره	*khīra*, dirt,	خيرن	dirty.
پخوا	*pakhwā*, formerly,	پخواني	ancient.
صبا	*ṣabā*, morning,	صباني	matutinal, of to-morrow.
نن	*nan*, to-day,	نني	hodiernal.
پوهړ	*pūhaṛ*, a sloven,	پوهړي	slovenly.

116. Patronymics are not common in Pukkhto. A man's nationality or country is expressed by placing the noun in the genitive case, as دَ کابل سړي *da kābul saṛai*, etc. But they are sometimes formed by adding the particles وال *wāl* and ي *ai*, subject to inflection for gender, to the terminal letter of the noun. The former is used in the Eastern parts of the country and the latter in the Western. Examples:

سواتي *swātai*, a man of Swat. عشنغري *'ashnagharai*, a man of 'Ashnaghar.
بنيروال *bunerwāl*, a man of Buner. چمله وال *chamla-wāl*, a man of Chamla.

PUKKHTO CALENDAR.

117. The Afghans use the Muhammadan calendar for all purposes, religious and secular. But they have different names for the months from the Arabic ones. The following list shows the names of the Afghan months with their corresponding Arabic ones.

PUKKHTO.			ARABIC.		
حسن حسين	*ḥasan-ḥusain* . .	30	محرّم	*muḥarram* . . .	30
صفره	*ṣafara*	29	صفر	*ṣafar*	29
ورنبي خور	*wṛunba-ī khor* .	30	ربيع الاوّل	*rabī'-ul-awwal* .	30
دويمه خور	*dwayama khor* .	30	ربيع الثاني	*rabī'-uṣ-ṣānī* . .	30
دريمه خور	*driyama khor* .	30	جماد الاوّل	*jumād-ul-awwal* .	30
څلورمه خور	*tsalorama khor* .	29	جماد الثاني	*jumād-uṣ-ṣānī*. .	29
دَ خداي مياشت	*da khudāe myāsht*	30	رجب	*rajab*	30
شو قدر or برات	*sho-qadr* or *barāt*	29	شعبان	*sha'bān*. . . .	29
روژه	*roĵa*	30	رمضان	*ramẓān*. . . .	30
وروکي اختر	*wṛūkai akhtar* .	29	شوال	*shawāl*	29
ميانه	*miyāna* . . .	30	ذي قعده	*zī-q'ada* . . .	30
لوي اختر	*loe akhtar* . .	29	ذي حجّه	*zī-ḥijja*	29

118. By the Eastern Afghans the months of the Hindu calendar are used, principally with reference to the seasons and agriculture. The following list gives their names, with the corresponding Hindī ones. These are fixed or solar months.

PUKKHTO.	ENGLISH.	HINDĪ.
بيساك ـ وساك *baisāk, wisāk*	April	بيساكه *baisākh*
جيټ *jeṭ*	May	جيټه *jeṭh*
هاړ ـ آړ *hāṛ, āṛ*	June	اساړه *asāṛh*
پشكال ـ ساوڼ *pas͟hakāl, sāwaṉr*	July	ساون *sāwan*
بادرو *bādro*	August	بهادون *bhādon*
اسو *asū*	September	آسن *āsan*
كتك *katak*	October	كاتك *kātik*
مگر *magar*	November	اگهن *ag͟han*
پوه *poh*	December	پوس *pos*
ماه *māh*	January	ماگه *māgh*
پگڼر *pagaṉr*	February	پهاگن *phāgun*
چيتر *c͟hetar*	March	چيت *c͟hait*

119. The Pukkhto days of the week are shewn in the subjoined Table with the corresponding Persian and English names.

PUKKHTO.	ENGLISH.	PERSIAN.
خالي *k͟hālī*	Saturday	شنبه *s͟hamba*
اتبار *itbār*	Sunday	يكشنبه *yak·s͟hamba*
گل ـ پير *gul, pīr*	Monday	دو شنبه *do·s͟hamba*
نهه *naha*	Tuesday	سه شنبه *sih·s͟hamba*
چار شنبه *c͟hār·s͟hamba*	Wednesday	چهار شنبه *c͟hahār·s͟hamba*
دَ زيارت ورځ *da ziyārat wradz*	Thursday	پنجشنبه *panj·s͟hamba*
جمعه *jum'a*	Friday	آدينه *ādīna*

120. The seasons in the Pukkhto are the following, viz.:

پسرلي *psarlai* or سپرلي *sparlai*, spring (February, March, April).

اوري *orai*, summer [including دوبي *dūbai*, hot weather (of May and June) and پشكال *pas͟hakāl*, rainy weather (of July and part of August)].

مني *manai*, autumn (August, September, October).
ژمي *ǰamai* or *ǰimai*, winter (November, December, January).

121. The Cardinal points are the following:

قطب خوا *quṭb kh̲wā*, or ښي طرف *kkhai ṯaraf*, the north.
سهيل دډه *suhel ḍaḍa*, or کين طرف *kīnr ṯaraf*, the south.
نمر خاته or نور *nwar* or *nmar kh̲ātah*, the east.
نور پريواته *nwar prewātah*, or قبله خوا *qibla kh̲wā*, the west.

EXERCISES.

122. LESSON I.—CONCORD OF NOUN, ADJECTIVE, AND VERB.

Life is sweet.	Ĵwandūn khog dai.
This water is sweet.	Dā oba khwaga da.
These curds are not sweet.	Daghah māsta-ah khwāgah na dī.
Those fruits are sweet.	Haghe mewe khwage dī.
The sky is clear (green).	Āsmān shīn dai.
One tree was green.	Yawa wana shna wa.
The sticks are all green.	Largī wāṛa-ah shnah dī.
All the leaves were green.	Ṭole pānre shne we.
The sword may be blunt.	Tūra pa-atsa (*or* p-utsa) wī.
The swords will become blunt.	Tūre ba pa-atse (*or* p-utse) shī.
The air was very hot.	Bād ḍer tod wuh.
The water is very hot.	Oba ḍera tauda da.
Your horse was lame.	Stā ās guḍ wuh.
Was your mare lame?	Āspa di guḍa wa?
My father is blind.	Plār mi ṛūnd dai.
And his mother also is blind.	Aw da dah mor hum ṛanda da.
So-and-so's parents are both blind.	Da palānkī plār mor dwāṛah ṛāndah dī.
The camels were mangy.	Ūkkhān pama-an wū.
All the cows were lean.	Ṭole ghwāwe ḍangare we.
Take the bread from these deaf women and give it to those weary men.	La dagho kanro kkhadzo na ḍoḍa-ī wākhla aw hagho staṛo saṛīo ta e warkā.
These are fine young men.	Dwī kkhāyasta-ah zalmī dī.
You are foolish women.	Tāsū kam-'aqle kkhadze ya-ī.
Amongst them are some good and some bad.	Da hagho pa mandz kkhke dzane kkhah wī dzane bad.
He will become a rich man.	Daulat-man saṛai ba shī.
She may be a rich woman.	Daulat-mana kkhadza ba wī.

123. LESSON II.—DEGREES OF COMPARISON.

The man is taller than the woman.	Saṛai la kkhadze na dang dai.
The woman is stouter than the man.	Kkhadza la saṛī na ghaṭa da.
The horse is more noble than the ass.	Ās la khra na ashrāf dai.
Thy asses are smaller than my colts.	Stā khrah khare dzamā bihānro na la-ag dī.
Women are weaker than men.	Kkhadze la saṛio na kam·zore dī.
Iron is heavier and harder than wood.	Ospana tar largī drana aw klaka da.
You are bolder than lions.	Tar zmaro ziyāta maṛanī ya-ī.
This person's beeves are fatter than any other cattle in the district.	La noro ḍangaro na chi pa tape kkhke wī da dah skhwanda-ar tsārbah dī.
The hawk is faster in flight than the wind.	Bāz pa ālwatu la bāda zir dai.
You are worse than dogs.	Tāsū la spīo na bad ya-ī.
The maidens are handsomer than the youths.	Peghle la zalmīo na kkhāyaste dī.
The elephant is the largest of all animals.	Da ṭolo wāṛo dzanāwarāno hātī loe dai.
That tree is higher than the others.	Hagha wana la noro na tchata da.
Health though it be with poverty is still better than sickness with wealth.	Joṛ·tiyā sara da gadā·tob ki wī hum ghwara da la nārogh·tiyā sara da daulat.
The jackal is not so fleet as the dog, but he is more cunning.	Gīdaṛl aka spai hombra gaṛandai na dai, lekin tre (*or* tar e) ziyāt dai pa hokkhyārtiyā.
Thou art cleverer than so-and-so.	La palānkī na tah pohānd ye.
Yours is the largest share of the meat.	Da ghwakkhe stā brakha ziyāta da.
He is a most slovenly man.	Be ḥadda pūhaṛ saṛai dai.
Thou art most wise.	Be shāna hokkhyār ye.
This is good, that is better (*f.*), these are better than all (or best).	Daghah kkhah dai, dā lā kkha da, dwī la ṭolo wāṛo na kkha-ah dī.
In my opinion this is the best sword.	Dzamā pa fikr kkhke dagha tūra ghwara da.

124. LESSON III.—THE PRONOUNS.

a. PERSONAL PRONOUNS.

He is my brother.	Dzamā wror dai.
She is his mother.	Da dah mor da.
They are your brethren.	Da stāsū wrūnra dī.
They are our cows.	Dzamūnga ghwāwe dī.
My father is an old grey-beard.	Plār mi zoṛ spīn·gīrai dai.

Thy mother is become white-headed (aged).	Mor di spīn-saṛa shwa.
His sister is a widow.	Khor e kūnḍa da.
Their horses are very lean.	Āsūna e ḍer khwār dī.

b. DEMONSTRATIVE PRONOUNS.

This is my bread, that is yours.	Dagha dzamā ḍoḍa-ī da, hagha da stā da.
This is wood, it is not stone.	Dā largai dai, kāṇrai na dai.
That is the man, I recognize him.	Haghah daghah saṛai dai, zah e pejanam.
This is it, it was lying on the road.	Hāyah dai, pa lāri prot wuh.

c. INTERROGATIVE PRONOUNS.

Who says so?	Tsok dā hase wāyī?
Who called you?	Chā balalī ya-ī?
Whom dost thou suspect?	Gumān di pa chā bāndi kegī?
How many men does he require?	Tso tana saṛī ghwāṛī?
Which mare is lame?	Kūma āspa guḍa da?
What is the name of this tree?	Da daghe wane nūm tsa dai?
What does he know of this business?	Da de kār haghah tsa pohegī?
Is there anything in it?	Tsa shai pa kkhke shta?
How many bits may there be?	Tso dāne ba wī?

d. RELATIVE PRONOUNS.

The man who does so is deserving of severe punishment.	Kūm saṛai chi dā hase kawī haghah lā-iq da sakhte sazā dai.
Show me the shortest road.	Kūma lār chi lanḍa da hagha rā ta wu-kkhāya.
Let him cut down the trees that are dry and leave the others.	Kūme wane chi wuche dī haghe di pre-kawī, nore di pregdī.
Those who have wealth have also power.	Chā tsakha chi zar wī hagho tsakha ham zor wī.

125. LESSON IV.—NOUN WITH INTRANSITIVE VERB.

I dwell in that house.	Zah pa haghah kor kkhke osam.
The river flows very fast.	Sīnd ḍer zir (*or* zir zir) bahegī.
The water is now boiling.	Oba os khuṭ-kegī.
We are going to the city in the evening.	Makkhām mūng kkhahr lara dzū.
The master of the house will arrive the day after to-morrow.	Da kor tsakkhtan ba bul sabā (*or* pas sabā) rāshī.

Come, let us run after the horses.
Rādza chi āsūno pase wu zghalū.

The trees were bowed by the storm.
Wane pa sīla-ī ṭīṭe shwale (*or* shwe).

A storm bent down the trees.
Sīla-ī wane ṭīṭe kṛale (*or* kṛe).

My brother voluntarily went up to the top of the hill all alone.
Wror mi pakhpula yawādzai da ghra sar ta wu khot.

The water rose so high in the well that it overflowed its mouth.
Oba tar hase ḥadda pa kūhī kkhke wu khatala chi la khule na e toya shwa.

We will start for the hill to-morrow, let the huntsman go up to-day.
Mūng ba sabā ghra ta rawān shū, kkhkāriyān di nan wu khejī.

When he sat down on the ground then I rose up and went away.
Haghah chi pa zmake bāndi kkhkenāstedah pas zah pātsedam aw lāṛam.

The dog ran away from me, and the pigeon flying up, perched upon that high branch of this tree.
Spai rā na wu takkhtedah, aw kauntar ālwatalai, da daghe wane pa haghe ūchate kkhākhe bāndi kkhkenāst.

The tree has fallen down by reason of the force of the wind.
Wana da bād da zor la kabala prewatali (*or* prewati) da.

Having stumbled against a stone he fell, but he was not much hurt.
Pa kāṇrī bāndi tīndak khwuṛalai prewat, magar ḍer khūg shawai na wuh.

I am standing exactly on that spot, and have not moved at all.
Jukht pa haghah dzāe bāndi wulāṛ yam, aw lasara na yam khwadzedalai.

The mare was galloping very fast, when all of a sudden shying at a dog, which was lying concealed in the grass, she threw me over her head, and then stood still on the road.
Āspa ḍer pa gaṛandī tlala, chi nā gumāna pa spī bāndi, chi dah pa wākkho ghalai prot wuh, bugnedali, zah e khpul sar dapāsa wughurzawulam, aw biyā e pa lāri wudredala.

If I were a rich man, I would not now be lying on the bare ground.
Ki zah daulat-man wai, os ba pa baṛbande zmake mlāst na wum.

If thou hadst understood me, thou wouldst not have done this wrong act.
Ki tah pa mā pohedalai wai, dā bad kār ba di kaṛai na wai.

126. LESSON V.—NOUN WITH TRANSITIVE VERB.

He is carrying grass to the cattle.
Haghah ḍangaro lara wākkhah wṛī.

Why art thou sharpening thy sword?
Tūra di tsala tera kawe (*or* ke *or* kṛe)?

The camel-men will take the camels to graze in the evening.
Ūkkhbānah ba mākkhām ūkkhān tsaralu la biyāyī.

The milk-maids will milk the cows in the morning.
Ghobane ba ṣaḥār ghwāwe wulwashī.

Let him summon the witnesses to-morrow.
Haghah di shāhidān sabā rāwubolī.

The boy was shaking the tree when I saw him.	Halak chi mā e wulīdah, wana e wu rapawula.
That man called us, and seated us in this place.	Mūng haghah saṛī rābalalū, aw pa de dzāe bāndi kkhkenawulū.
The man killed his own wife.	Saṛī khpula kkhadza mṛa kṛa (*or* kṛala).
My enemy cut me with a blow of his sword.	Dukkhman mi, da tūre pa guẓār ghwuts kṛalam.
Why didst thy father beat thee?	Plār di tsala wu wahale?
Who has called these men here?	Cha dwī saṛī dalta balalī dī?
I have given him three rupees, and will not give him a farthing more.	Dre rūpa-ī me war kirī dī, aw yawa kun-jaka nora ba war na kawam (*or* kam).
He stirred the curds with such force that they are completely broken up.	Māstah e dombra pa zor sara laṛalī wū chi amānī māt shawī dī.
If I had struck him, the marks of the blows would be visible on his person.	Ki mā e wu wahalai wai, da guẓāruno nakkhe ba pa ṣūrat e tsargande we.
The marks are not apparent, but he has struck me.	Nakkhe kkhkāre na dī, magar zah e wa-halai yam.
We are weak, and therefore the Pathans have ejected us from the village, were it otherwise, they could not have turned us out, for even Pathans are but men.	Mūng kam-zor yū, aw dzaka pukkhtane la kilī na shaṛalī yū, ki pa bul shān wai, hagho mūng shaṛalī na shwū, wale chi pukkhtānah hum basha-ar dī.
Those women first abused me, and then they threw earth upon me.	Hagho kkhadzo zah wṛūnbe kkhkandzalam, aw biyā e rābāndi khāwre wulawastali.
How often have I told thee not to do so?	Mā darta tso dzala wayalai dai, chi dā hase makawa?
Do you know Pukkhto? It is a difficult language.	Pukkhto de zda da? grāna jiba da.

127. LESSON VI.—ADVERBS, PREPOSITIONS, ETC.

How far may it be from this place to the city?	La de dzāya tar kkhahra pore ba tsomra liri wī?
Sometimes they speak in one way, and sometimes in another.	Kala kala pa yo shān wāyī, aw kala kala pa bul.
The case may be so now, but it was otherwise formerly (in other times).	Os ba ḥāl daghah hase wī, wale nor kala pa bul shān wuh.
Let him eat as much as he likes.	Tsombra chi zṛah e ghwāṛī, hombra di wu khwurī.
They have all crossed to the other side of the river, and now no one else is left on this side but ourselves.	Hagha-ah ṭol da sīnd pore ghāre ta tlalī dī, aw os siwā la mūnga bul hets tsok rā-pore pātai na dai.

What has become of my sword? I don't see it. I put it under the bed before I went to sleep.

Tūra mi tsa shwa? Na e wīnam. Chi lā ūdah na wum, mā e tar kaṭa lāndi īkkhi da.

Don't shoot at the people, fire your matchlocks over their heads.

Pa khalqo bāndi ma wula-ī, da deo da sar dapāsa ṭopakūna muh khalāṣawa-ī.

What can I do? whichever way I turn they follow after me.

Zah tsa kawam? hara khwā chi girzam, dwī rā pase dī.

It is not so light a matter as you suppose, that I can tell you.

Hombra spuka khabara na da, laka chi tah e ganre, dā darta zah wāyam.

The upper people gained the victory because they were the most numerous, and, in a difficult country, as bold as lions; as for the lower people they met with defeat because they were at feud with each other, and moreover were afraid of treachery on the part of their own clansmen.

Bar 'alam barai gaṭalai dai, dzaka chi dwī ḍer ganr wū, aw pa sakht mulk kkhke, maṛanī laka zmarīo, har chi lar 'alam dī, hagho larai mūndalai dai, dzaka chi yo tar bula pa mandz kkhke patne we, aw nor, dwī da khpulo 'azīzāno la ṭaga-ī na wu weredal.

Yesterday the water was hidden under the ground, to-day it is congealed on its surface and has become ice, to-morrow it will spurt up into the sky in jets.

Pārūn oba tar zmake lāndi puṭa wa, nan dapāsa pre bāndi ṭīnga sha, kangal dai, sabā ba pa porta āsmān ta dāre wahī.

He has influence with the people of this district because he takes part more or less in their deliberative assemblies.

Haghah da de tape khalqo sara khula-larī, wale chi tsa la-ag ziyāt da dwīo pa jirgo kkhke kkhkata porta kegī.

No, I don't know where the needles are, and I have not got any now, but I saw some in the casket the day before yesterday.

Na na-yam khabar chi stani charta dī, aw dā sā'at rā tsakha tsa nishta dī, lekin waṛama wradz mā pa haṛpa-ī kkhke dzane wulīdali.

Well, go buy some sticks from him, and bring them to me, I will show them to my father and he will tell you what to do with them.

Joṛ, lāṛ sha pa baie tina tsa largī wākhla, aw biyā e rā khatsa rāwṛa, zah ba e khpul plār ta wukkhāyam, aw haghah ba darta wāyī, chi war sara tsa kawe.

The boy is lying uncovered and this person has two quilts, take one from him and throw it over him.

Halak baṛband prot dai, aw dah khatsa bṛastani dwe dī, yawa ti na wākhla, aw pre bāndi wāchawa.

128. SHORT PHRASES.

What is the matter with you?
Tā sara tsa shawai dai?

How is he?
Haghah tsa rang dai?

I am quite well.
Zah jak joṛ yam.

His is a slight ailment.	Da dah spuka nājoṛ-tiyā da.
She will be well in a few days.	Pa la-ago wradzo kkhke ba joṛa shī.
He will die, he is not (a case) for recovery.	Muṛ ba shī da raghedalu na dai.
Sit down here on this chair.	Dalta pa de kūrsī bāndi kkhkena.
Don't sit down. Let them not sit down.	Ma kkhkena. Haghah di na kkhkenī.
Won't you sit down? There is room.	Kkhke ba na na-ī? Dzāe shta.
She sat down with her own mother.	Hagha khpule mori khatsa kkhkenāstala.
He did not sit down with me.	Haghah rā tsakha kkhke na nāst.
We will sit down with these persons.	Mūng ba dwīo sara kkhkenū.
Get up. Won't you get up?	Pātsa. Na pātsa-ī?
If she won't get up I will get up.	Ki hagha na pātsī zah ba pātsam.
Why did they get up?	Hagha-ah tsala pātseḍal?
They have not got up.	Hagha-ah pātsedalī na dī.
Stand up. That will do. Don't move.	Wulāṛsha. Bas. Khwadzega ma.
Stand still. He stood still on the road.	Wudrega. Haghah pa lāri wudred.
What do you want? Nothing.	Tah tsa ghwāṛe? Hets.
I don't want anything.	Hets shai na ghwāṛam.
If I want anything I will tell you.	Ki zah tsa ghwāṛam ba darta wāyam.
He asked for five rupees.	Haghah pindza rūpa-ī ghokkhtali.
I have asked for even more.	Mā lā ziyāte ghokkhtali dī.
Don't ask for anything of me.	Rā na hets ma ghwāṛa.
Stay here till we return.	Dzamūnga tar jārwatalu pore dale pātai sha.
She stayed, but we came on.	Hagha pati sha, magar mūng rā rawān shwalū.
How many persons have stayed behind in the village? Not a man has stayed.	Wrusto pa kilī kkhke tso tana pātī dī? Yo saṛai na dai pātai.
Let them stay a few days with me.	Dwī di tso wradzo pore rā sara pātī shī.
We will stay with you for six days.	Tar shpago wradzo pore ba mūng tā sara pātī kegū.
Where dost thou dwell?	Tah charta ose?
Abide with us as long as you like.	Hombra chi zṛah di kegī, mūng sara osa.

He has dwelt many years in this city.	Der kāla pa de kkhahr kkhke osedalai dai.
When he arrives, will he live with you?	Haghah chi rāshi, ba e tā sara osī?
Whether he stays or not, he has the choice.	Ki osī yā na osī, wāk larī.
Who lives in this house?	Pa de kor kkhke tsok osī?
Show me the road to the city.	Da kkhahr lār rā ta wu kkhāya.
Come, I will show it to you.	Rādza, zah ba e darta wu kkhāyam.
He was showing me another road.	Haghah rāta bula lār kkhowula.
That man is blind, he could not show you the road.	Haghah saṛai ṛūnd dai, lār e darta kkhowuli na sha.
If I had not shown it to him, he would have lost the road.	Ki mā e warta kkhowuli na wai, lār ba e wruka kṛala.
He showed me my own father's house.	Da khpul plār mi kor, e rāta wu kkhowah.
He showed me his own father's house.	Da khpul dzān da plār kor, e rāta wu kkhowah.
Go on. Don't you go. Let them go.	Dza. Ma dza-ī. Hagha-ah di dzī.
Have they gone? They went this morning.	Hagha-ah tlalī dī? Ṣaḥār tlalī dī.
When did the men go away?	Saṛī kala lāṛal (*or* tlalī dī)?
Let me know when he comes.	Har wakht chi rādzī, mā khabar ka.
Don't come here. Let him come.	Dalta ma rādza. Rā di shī.
He has come. She has come.	Rāghai (*or* rāghlalai dai). Rāghlala (*or* rāghlali da).
Go out. Don't go out.	Ūza (*or* wuza). Ūza ma (*or* ma wuza).
They have gone out.	Bāhir ta (*or* warchane) watalī dī.
We will go out in the evening.	Mākkhām ba wuzū.
He came out of the house.	La kora bāhir wu wat.
He went into the house.	Pa kor kkhke nana wat.
Come in. I will come in by-and-bye.	Nana wuza. Pa drang ba nana wūzam.
The water was coming into the cistern.	Oba pa ḥauẓ kkhke nana watala.
Make haste. Be quick.	Talwār wu ka. Zir sha.
Follow them. Go quickly.	War pase sha. Pa gaṛandī dza.
Don't hurry. Be quiet	Talwār ma kawa. Pa qalār osa.
Stop. Take care. Be careful.	Wudrega. Khabar-dār. Pahm ka.
Don't you see? Surely you are not blind.	Na gore (*or* na wīne)? Ṛūnd kho ba na ye?
Do you see? How many are there?	Wīne (*or* gore)? Tso dī?

English	Pukkhto
Shut the door. Open it.	War pore kā. Liri kā.
Tie the cow's legs. Untie them.	Da ghwā pkkhe wu taṛa. Prā e nadza.
Undo this knot. It is tied firmly.	Dā ghūṭa wu spaṛa. Klaka taṛali da.
I can't undo it; do you try.	Zah e na sham spaṛdi, tah āzmekkht wu kā.
If the dog gets loose, you will not catch him again, for he uses his mouth.	Ki spai yalah shī, biyā ba e na nisa-ī, wale chi khula lagawī.
Don't fear. He will not get loose.	Werega ma. Haghah ba khalāṣ na shī.
Go to sleep. He is asleep.	Ūdah sha. Ūdah dai.
He is sleeping. He is lying down.	Khob kawī. Mlāst dai.
Lie down. Put the boy to bed.	Tsamla. Halak tsamlawa.
He is awake. Don't awake him.	Wīkkh dai. Ma e wīkkhawa.
Awake me early in the morning.	Wakhtī ṣaḥār mā wīkkh kā.
He has now risen from sleep.	Os la khoba pātsedalai dai.
Do you understand? Listen.	Pohege? Ghwag bāsa (*or* nisa).
He did not understand my meaning, but she understood.	Pa maṭlab me haghah wu na pohedah, magar da pohedala.
I have not understood it.	Pre poh na sham.
Do you explain to me. What does he say?	Tah mā poh kṛah. Haghah tsa wāyī?
I have not understood a single word.	Pa yawe khabare bāndi pohedalai na yam.
Say that again. I will not hear him.	Dā biyā wāya. Zah ba e wā na wram.
He has written the letter.	Haghah chīṭa-ī wukkhkali da (*or* līkali da).
I will write it on paper for you.	Stā dapāra ba e pa kaghaz bāndi wu kāgam.
What is he writing, and to whom?	Haghah tsa līkī (*or* kkhkī), aw chā ta?
What has he said in the letter?	Pa chīṭa-ī kkhke tsa e līkali (*or* kkhkalai) dai.
I don't know, he has not told me.	Khabar na yam, mā ta e na dai wayalai.
Look at me. Do you see me?	Mā ta gora. Mā wīne?
What is he looking at? I see nothing.	Haghah tsa ta gorī? Zah hets na wīnam.
Did you look at the mark? I saw it.	Nakkha di wu katala? Mā e wu līdala.
I was looking at the book.	Kitāb mi kot.
He had looked at it before.	Haghah e pa khwā katalai dai.
He did not see me, but I saw him.	Zah e na līdalam, lekin mā e wulīdah.
I am very fatigued, hungry, and thirsty.	Zah ḍer staṛai, ūgai aw tagai yam.
She is much hurt, but no bones are broken, and the doctor says she will be well in six or seven days.	Hagha ḍera khūga shiwi da, magar haḍūkī māt na dī, aw tabīb wāyī, chi shpag yā awwah wradzi pase ba joṛa shī.

Be silent. Hold your tongue.	Chup sha. Ĵiba di ma khwadzawa.
Don't say a word. Don't make a noise.	Yawa khabara ma wāya. Ghag ma kā.
Don't do that. Why do you speak?	Dā ma kawa. Tsala ĵiba khwadzawe?
Why I have not uttered even a sound.	Mā kho ghag hum na dai kaṛai.
I am not deaf, I can hear. He heard.	Kūnṛ na yam, āwredai sham. Haghah wāwred.
Hear my words. He does not hear.	Dzamā khabare wāwra. Haghah na āwrī.
I have heard that twice before.	Mā dwah dzala pakhwā dā āwredalai dai.
She did not hear, say it again.	Hagha wā na wredala, biyā e wāya.
I told her that he would not listen now.	Mā warta wu wi, chi haghah ba os na āwrī.
If I had heard your voice, I should have known you.	Mā ki āwāz di āwredalai wai, peĵandalai ba di wai.
Do you know me? Is that you?	Mā peĵane? Dā tah ye?
I don't know him, if he knows me.	Zah e na peĵanam, ki e mā peĵanī.
By what sign do you recognize it?	Tah e pa kūme nakkhe bāndi peĵane?
How do you know where he lives?	Tā ta tsa ranga ma'lūm dai, chi dah charta osī.
What do you know of this matter?	Da de khabare tā ta tsa ma'lūm dai (*or* tsa khabar ye)?
I know nothing.	Hets rā ta na dai ma'lūm (*or* hets khabar na yam).
He did not know the man when he was placed before him.	Saṛaí mukhā-mukh e chi wudrawulai wuh, haghah wu e na peĵāndah.
What is he searching for in the grass?	Pa wākkho kkhke tsa laṭawī.
It is not there, I have searched the whole house.	Halta nishta, ṭol kor me laṭawulai dai.
I can't search for it now, for I am not at leisure to-day. I won't leave you.	Os pre pase na sham girzedai, wale chi nan wuzgār na yam. Pre ba di na gdam.
He comes and goes every minute, and obstructs my work. Let me alone.	Sā'at pa sā'at dzī rādzī, aw kār me karyābawī. Mā pregda.
Not until she bit him did he let her go.	Hāla e prekkhodala, chi wrūnbi e wu chī chah.
Where have you left my stick?	Largai mi de charta ikkhai dai?
I placed it in the box with the gun.	Ṭopak sara pa ṣandūq kkhke me kkhekkhod.
Take it out, and see if this peg will fit in the box. It fits well into it.	Wu e bāsa, aw gora dā mogai ba pa ṣandūq kkhke dzāegī ki na. Pre kkhah dzāegī.

Put on your clothes.	Zaṛūkī di wāghūnda (*or* pa dzān ka).
Has he put on his uniform?	Jāme e āghūste dɪ.
I shall not wear this shirt.	Dā qamīṣ ba wā na ghūndam.
Take off your shoes. Put them on.	Panre di liri kā. Pa kkhpo e kā.
Tie on your turband.	Pagṛa-ɪ di wu taṛa.
Have you not a sword? Where is it?	Tūra na lare (*or* di nishta)? Charta da?
Who is that? It is not her.	Haghah tsok dai? Hagha na da.
Is your father at home?	Plār di kor dai?
He is gone to plough with his sons.	Dzāmano sara īwe la tlalai dai.
His trowsers are rent in the legs.	Paṛtāgah e pa pāentso kkhke shledalɪ dɪ.
Is there fire in the ashes?	Pa īro kkhke or shta.
There is not, they are cold.	Nishta, saṛe dɪ.
Light the fire, and put out the candle.	Or bal kā, aw dīwa mṛa kṛa (*or* kā).
Has he gone alone, or was anybody else with him?	Yawādzai tlalai dai, yā war khatsa bul tsok wuh?
What did he say to you?	Darta e tsa wi (*or* wayal).
What is your name?	Nūm di tsa dai?
Of which village are you?	Da kūm kilɪ ye?
Are you married?	Wādah di kaṛai dai?
Have you any sons? How many are there?	Dzāman di shta? Tso dɪ?
How old is the eldest?	Mashar ba da tso kālo wɪ?
The day is passed, it is late.	Wradz tera shwa nā-wakht dai.
Close the book.	Kitāb ṭap waha.

129. EASY DIALOGUES.

Where are you going?	Charta dze?
I am going home.	Kor ta dzam?
You go very fast, don't go so fast.	Ḍer gaṛandai dze, dombra pa gaṛandɪ ma dza.
Why do you make such haste?	Tsala dombra talwār kawe?
Come, let us cross the road.	Rādza, chi da lāri pore wūzū.
Whose house is this? Yours?	Dā da chā kor dai? Da stā?
And who dwells in it?	Aw osī pa kkhke tsók?
Do you know him? You don't?	Tah e pejane? Pe na jane?
Well, go on, let's get out of the village.	Kkhāh, dza-ɪ, la kilɪ na wūzū.
Walk slowly. That is good.	Ro ro dza. Dā kkhah dai.

Who is your companion?	Mal di tsok dai?
Where do you live? Is it very far?	Charta ose? Der liri dai?
I won't go there, I don't know any one, and nobody has invited me.	Halta na dzam, hets tsok na pejanam, aw chā sat na kṛalam.
Come with me, I invite you, I know the Khan, he is a friend of mine.	Rā sara lār sha, zah darta sat kawam, khān pejanam, āshnāe mi dai.
Then how shall I return to my own town?	Biyā ba tsa ranga jārwūzam khpul kilī ta?
The road is straight and easy, you will not lose it.	Lār sama da aw āsāna, wruka ba e na kṛe.
First you go straight forward, then turn to the right, and afterwards to the left; the road is unprotected, but there is no danger on it.	Wṛūnbe barābar makhā-makh lāṛshe, biyā kkhī lās ta girze, aw pas kīṇr ta; lār khūshi da, lekin yera pa kkhke nishta.
What's that? It's a man. He is walking towards us with a drawn sword in his hand. Tell him to stand still. Call out to him. Do you hear?	Dā tsa dai? Saṛai dai. Rā de khwā ta rādzī, rākkhkali tūra pa lās kkhke nīwuli. Warta wāya chi wudrega. Nāre waha warta. Āwre?
If he does not stop, I will take a shot at him, for I have no sword.	Ki haghah na wudregī zah ba pre bāndi guzār kawam, wale chi tūra rā khatsa nishta.

130. II.

Where shall we go to get some cotton cloth? I want the first quality.	Charta dzū chi tsa khāmtā ākhlū? Awwal kism ghwāṛam.
Let us go to Gangū, I always deal with him.	Gangū khatsa lāṛshū, hamesha war sara lāgī kawam.
Where is his shop? Is it far off?	Dūkān e charta dai? Liri dai?
No, it is close to us. Come along, I will show you the way.	Ya, rā khatsa nijde dai. Rādza, zah ba darta lār wu kkhīyam.
This is his shop, and there is Gangū.	Dā e dūkān dai, aw daghah dai gangū.
Have you any woollen cloth?	Tsa paṭṭū dar khatsa shta?
How do you sell it by the yard?	Da gaz pa ḥisāb, pa tsombra khartsawe?
It sells by the piece, I cannot sell it by the yard?	Pa ṭukī khartsegī, pa gaz e na sham khartsawulai.
I don't like the colour of this one; that is better; I like this one.	Dā dah rang mi khwakkh na dai; dā ghwarah dai; daghah dzamā khwakkh shah.
What do you want for this?	Da dah dapāra tsomra ghwāṛe.
It is too much; say your last price.	Ḍer dai; ākhir qīmat wāya.

I will tell you conscientiously, the price is one; I can't lie in such a matter.	Pa īmān ba darta wāyam, qīmat yo dai, pa dāse khabare darogh na sham wayalai.
Your conscience must be very easy, don't waste it on such trifles.	Īmān di ba ḍer arzān wī, pa dāhase spake khabare bāndi ma e wrukawa.
I will give you six rupees; here take them; it is not every day you get cash.	Shpag rūpa-ī ba dala darkam; hāyah wā e khla; hase na dai chi hara wradz rok mūmī.
I tell you truly, the price is twenty-four rupees, but give me twenty, and it is yours'.	Rikkhtiyā darta wāyam, baia da tsalor wisht rūpa-ī da, lekin shil rāka, aw māl stā dai.
I have told you the price. I will now go to another shop.	Mā darta qīmat wayalai dai. Os bul dūkān lara lāṛsham.
Here it is, take it, it is your property.	Hāyah dai, wā e khla, stā māl dai.
You get its full value, don't imagine you have given it me for nothing.	Pūrah qīmat e mūmī, hase ma ganra, chi e weṛiyā di rā kaṛai dai.
Shall I show you anything else?	Nor tsa darta wukkhāyam?
I don't want anything more.	Nor hets na ghwāṛam.

131. III.

You have come very late.	Deṛ nā wakht rāghlai ye.
It is yet early. Are you ready to start?	Lā wakhtī dai. Rawānedu ta tayār ye?
I will go as soon as I have put on my clothes.	Har wakht chi zaṛūkī mi āghūstī dī, rawān ba sham.
Do you go to school every day?	Hara wradz madrasse ta dze?
Which books are you reading, and how far have you read?	Kūm kūm kitāb lwale, aw tar kūma pore di lwustai dai.
He won't allow me to read.	Lwustalu ta rā ta na pregdī.
Yesterday, when I was reading my own book, he crept up behind me and threw dust upon me.	Pārūn, chi mā khpul kitāb wulwust, dah ghalai ghalai rā pase shah, aw khāwre rā bāndi wu lawastali.
He lets no one alone that he may read, for he is smearing something on some one or other all the day.	Hets chā ta na pregdī chi lwalī, wale chi drusta wradz tsa shai pa yo yā pa bul lawanī.
He is a very lazy idle boy, and is of no good.	Ḍer sust aw nā rāst halak dai, hets da kkhah na dai.
Have you learnt your lesson?	Sabaq di zdah dai (*or* kṛah).
Arise, stand still, repeat your lesson.	Pātsa, wudrega, sabaq di wāya.
You have not learnt it well.	Pa kkhah shān di zdah na kṛah.
Go, sit down, and read it again.	Dza, kkhkena, aw biyā e wu lwala.
As long as your lesson is unlearnt, I cannot let you go to your play.	Hombra chi sabaq di zdah na dai, lobe ta di na sham prekkhodai.

You read very quickly, one cannot either hear or understand it.	Ḍer zir lwale, tsok pre na āwṛedai na pohedai shī.
Speak slowly, and open your mouth.	Ro ro wāya, aw khula di wīta kā.
Don't be nervous, bring me the book; which is the place? Now read.	Wār khaṭā kega ma, kitāb lāla rāwṛa; dzāe kūm dai? Os wu lwala.
Who is your master?	Ustād di tsok dai?
How many schoolboys are there?	Tso dzanṛī dī?
I don't know his name, he is commonly called "master." He is an old man, and we are afraid of him.	Nūm e rāta ma'lūm na dai, akṣar pa mu'allim yādegī. Zoṛ saṛai dai, aw mūng tina yeregū.

132. IV.

How is the weather to-day?	Nan āsmān tsa rang dai?
It is fine. It is cloudy. It is windy.	Shīn dai. Waryadze dī. Bād dai.
The air is still, it is very hot.	Bād wulāṛ dai, der garm dai.
The fog is thick, and the haze is dense.	Laṛa ganṛa da, aw dūp drūnd dai.
When the sun rises it will scatter the fog. If the wind also blows, the clouds will be even more quickly dispersed.	Chi nwar khejī, laṛa ba e khwara kāndi. Ki bād hum ālwūzī, waryadze ba lā zir khware shī.
To travel in the noon-day heat, is not free from risk of death.	Pa takanre gharme kkhke lār wahal, khālī da yere da marg na dai.
Throw the blanket over yourself, the wind is very bleak, the cold will strike you.	Sharai pa dzān wāchawa, bād yakh dai, sāṛa ba di wahī.
At this season of the year the rain generally falls heavily.	Da kāl pa de mausim kkhke bārān akṣar ganr prewūzī.
In the winter snow falls, but only on the hill-tops.	Pa jamī kkhke wāwre prewūzī, magar ta-ash da ghrūno pa sar bāndi.
If it ever falls on the plain, it does not last, it soon melts.	Ki chare pa same prewate, pāti kegī na, zir wīlī shī.
This rain is very good for the crops, for it is heavy; that which is thin is of no use, the earth does not get moistened by it.	Dā bārān faṣl dapāra ḍer kkhah dai, wale chi ganr dai; haghah chi rangai wī hets da kkhah na dai, pre bāndi zmaka na lambdegī.
The heat is very great to-day, I never felt such heat before; one can hardly breathe; as for sleep it is altogether lost. I have heard that several people have died from the heat.	Nan garmī ḍera da, mā chare pakhwā da hase garmī na da līdali; wugaṛai pa mushkila sā ākhlī; har chi khob dai, dā kho amānī wruk dai. Mā āwredalai dai, chi yo tso kasān la garmī na mṛah dī.
From sunrise to noon the heat is very	La nwar khātah na tar ghārmah pore

great, but from noon forwards till sun-set it gradually lessens.	garmī ḍera da, magar la gharmah rāhis-tah tar nwar prewātah pore ro ro e kamegī.
It appears to me that it will rain to-day, for the clouds are dark and dense.	Rāṭa kkhkārī chi ba nan bārān oregī, wale chi waryadze tore aw ganre dī.
133.	**V.**
Did you clean my gun?	Bandūkh mi de pāk kṛah?
No, I have not yet cleaned it.	Ya, lā pāk kaṛai mi na dai.
Who has broken the stock?	Kundāgh chā māt kaṛai dai?
I don't know, he will know who brought it in from the sport?	Na yam khabar, haghah ba khabar wī chi e la kkhkāra rāwṛai dai.
I am very angry at this. Call Haidar Shah.	Zah pa de ḍer khapah yam. Haidar shāh rā wu bola.
Look at this. How is its stock broken?	Dā wu gora. Kundāgh e tsa ranga māt shah?
I am not to blame in this matter. I will tell you truly how it has happened.	Pa de khabare malāmat na yam, rikkhtiyā ba darta wāyam chi pa kūm shān sara shawai dai.
When we were coming home from the hill, the boy Umar told me he was very tired, and was not able to carry the gun.	Mūng chi la ghra na kor ta rātlalū, 'umar halak chi dai, rāta wu wi chi zah ḍer staṛai yam, aw dā bandūkh na sham wṛai.
I then shouted to the huntsman Piroh, and told him to take the gun from the boy, and to carry it, as it was his turn.	Nor mā kkhkārī pīroh ta nare wu wahali, aw warta mi wi chi la halak na bandūkh wākhla aw yosa, wale chi wār stā dai.
He took it at the time, but abused me, and said it was not his work.	Pa sā'at kkhke wā e khist, lekin zah e kkhkandzalam, aw rā ta e wi chi dā dza-mā kār na dai.
I became angry with him, and told him to hold his tongue, and not to make a noise.	Zah warta pa qahr shwalam, aw warta mi wi chi chup sha, ghag ma kawa.
He then dashed the gun upon the ground, and said, "There, take that;" and then went home alone by another road.	Pas de bandūkh pa zmake bāndi wu wīsht aw wi chi "dā, wā e khla;" aw biyā e yawādzai pa bule lāri kor ta lāṛ shah.
Call Piroh here. Here he is. He was standing behind you.	Pīroh dale rāwubola. Hāyah dai. Pase shā di wu lāṛ wuh.
What do you say to this? So-and-so	De ta tah tsa wāye? Palānkī, da dzamā

has accused you of breaking the stock of my gun.	bandūkh kundāgh mātawulu tuhmat, pa tā bāndi āchawulai dai.
He is lying, sir. I never threw your gun upon the ground; the boy, who is a favourite of Haidar Shah's, himself fell down with it.	Darogh wāyı, jı. Mā stā bandūkh pa zmake bāndi hets chare na dai ghwurzawulai; haghah halak chi da haidar shah yār e dai, pakhpula war sara prewatai dai.

134. VI.

How long is it that you are ill?	Tsomra mūda da chi nājoṛ ye?
To-day is the sixth day since I have fallen off from my work. What is the cause?	Nan shpagama wradz da chi la kāra prewatai yam. Sabab tsa dai?
Give me the hand. I wish to see the pulse.	Lās rākā. Nabẓ goram.
Look at me. Open the mouth; widen it.	Mā ta gora. Khula wāza kā; wıta e kā.
Put out the tongue; now take it in.	Jiba wubāsa; os e nan wubāsa.
Bow the head; turn the back to me.	Sar ṭıṭ kā; rā ta shā kā.
Turn the face towards me. Stand straight.	Rā ta makh ka. Sam ūdrega (*or* wudrega).
Stretch out the arms; open the fingers.	Lāsūna wu gazawa; gūte chınge kā.
Can't you draw a long breath?	Sāh pa porta rākkhkalai na she?
Run in that direction.	Haghe khwā ta (*or* ā khwa ta) manḍe waha.
Turn this way. Stand aside.	De khwā ta girza. Pa ḍaḍe wudrega.
Shut your right eye with the fingers; now the other. Shut both; open them.	Kkha-ı starga di puṭa ka pa gūto bāndı; os bula. Dwāre puṭe kā; wu e ghwaṛawa.
The sight of this eye is not very good, has it ever been injured?	Da de starge naẓar ḍer kkhah na dai, chare khūga shiwi da?
Yes, when I was boy I received a blow with a club on the eyeball; we were striking at each other in play.	Ho, chi zah halak wum da koṭak guzār pa starghālı bāndi me khwuṛalai wuh; pa lobe mūnga yo tar bula guzārūna kawalū.
Go over there and stand still.	Halta lāṛsha aw wudrega.
Why do you speak in a loud voice? don't you see I am trying whether he is deaf or not?	Tsala pa ūchat āwāz wāye? wıne na āzmekkht kawam chi de kūnr dai ka na.
Do you see that platform? well, run round it eight times, and then jump over this stick.	Hagha dunkācha wıne? kkhah, tre chāpera atah guzāra wuzghla, aw biyā de largı bāndi ṭop waha.

Your heart palpitates a great deal.	Zṛah di dṛazegī ḍer.
Why do you take breath in short catches?	Tsala sāh pa lanḍ lanḍ ākhle?
Which place hurts you?	Kūm dzāe de khūgegī?
When I press upon it does it prick?	Chi pre zor kawam tsiṛīke wahī?
Take this medicine and rub it over the place that is swollen.	Dā dawā wākhla, aw pa paṛsedalai dzāe bānde wu e maga.
You will be well in three days, please God.	Pa dreo wradzo kkhke ba joṛ she ka khudāe kṛī.

FAMILIAR CONVERSATIONS.

135. COUNTRY SQUIRE AND CIVIL OFFICER.

Sir, squire of —— village has come for an interview.	Ṣāḥiba,— khān da — kilī mulāqāt dapāra rāghlai dai.
Where is the squire? Is he here?	Khān charta dai? Dale dai?
Yes, he is here, he stands outside in the porch.	Ho, dalta dai, warchane pa manḍaw kkhke wulāṛ dai.
Has he come alone, or is anybody else with him?	Yawādzai rāghlai dai, yā war tsakha bul tsok shta?
He has left his own horse and three cavaliers outside on the road, and himself, accompanied by a young man, has come here on foot.	Khpul ās aw dre tana swārah e bāhir pa lāri prīkkhī dī, nor khān (*or* dah), aw war sara yo zalmai chi dai, dale pa kkhpo rāghlai dai.
Very well, take this chair and place it there in front of me; that will do; now go and tell him to come in.	Ḍer kkhah, dagha kursī wākhla aw halta dzamā pa makhā makh kkhkegda; bas; os wardza aw warta wāya chi rā di shī.
Good morning, sir.	Salām dai, ṣāḥib.
Good morning, squire, and welcome, you are well met.	Salām, khān, harkala rāgha harkala, pa khaira rāghlai ye.
May you prosper, sir, and flourish, and may God deal well with you.	Ma khwārega, ṣāḥib, loe sha, khudāe dar sara nekī wu kā.
Come, squire, let us sit down, you take that chair and I will sit on this one.	Rādza khān chi kkhkenū, tah hagha kursī wākhla aw zah ba pa de kkhkenam.
Are you well and flourishing?	Tah joṛ ye, kkhah joṛ, khūshhāl ye?
May you prosper, thanks. Are you well, sir?	Ma khwārega, shukr dai. Tah joṛ ye ṣāḥib?
How many days may it be since you left home?	Tso wradzi ba shiwi wī chi la kora rāwatalai ye?
This I think is the fifth day since we set out from our village.	Inshāllah, nan ba pindzama wradz wī chi mūng ia kilī na rā rawān shawī yū.

You must have made a long journey. How far is your village from this? How many miles may it be?

Loe pand (*or* mazal) ba di kaṛai wī. Stā kilai la de dzāya ba tsomra liri wī? Tso kroh ba wī?

Really, sir, I don't know about miles, but we have come here in three days, for we rested one day on the road, and this morning, which is our fifth day, we arrived at the city.

Yara, ṣāḥib, da krohūno pa ḥisāb na pohegam, magar mūng pa dreo wradzo kkhke rāghlalī yū, wale chi yawa wradz mū pa lāri tera kṛala, aw nan ṣahār, chi dzamūnga pindzama wradz kegī, pa kkhahr kkhke dākhil shwalū.

With whom are you lodging in the city?

Pa kkhahr kkhke chā tsakha ṭikāo ye?

A man, an acquaintance of mine, resides there in the Nurmalkhel division, and we are lodging with him.

Halta da nūrmal·khelo pa kandī kkhke yo saṛai dzamā pejandgalai osī, aw mūng haghah khatsa tikāo yū.

Have you ever come this way before?

Tah pakhwā chare de khwā ta rāghlai ye?

Yes, I have come, but I have not been here recently, and was not coming even now, but that a great urgency has occurred, and therefore I have transported myself to your presence that I might have an interview with you, and explain my own case to you.

Ho, rāghlai yam, wale pa dā zir mūde dalta kkhke na yam rāghlai, aw os hum na rātlalam, magar yo sakht ẓarūr rā ta pekkh shawai dai, aw dzaka mā khpul dzān stā khidmat lara rasawulai dai, chi dīdan dar sara wu kawam, aw khpul ḥāl darta kkhkārah kawam.

Why! It is well! what has happened?

Wale! Khair dai, tsa chal shawai dai?

I will tell you all the particulars, do you give ear and hear my words.

Hāl ba ṭol darta wāyam, tah ghwag kkhkegda aw dzamā khabare wāwra.

Well, I will listen, I will hear you a hundred times if you wish it; now, say on, but see, speak concisely, for I have not much leisure at present, and my other work becomes hindered whilst I am detained here.

Kkhah, wā ba wram, sil dzala ba wāwram chi tah e ghwāṛe; os wāya, aw gora, lanḍe khabare kawa, wale chi dā sā'at ḍer wuzgār na yam, aw zah chi dale nkkhatai yam nor kār mi karyābegī.

That cannot be, sir; my object will not be gained by short words. My business will only be done when you yourself hear every word, and sift the truth and falsehood from the midst. Do me this kindness, and then whatever order you may give I will obey it. It is accepted with all my heart (with both eyes).

Dā na kegī, ṣāḥib, pa lanḍo khabaro kkhke dzamā maṭlab ba pūrah na shī. Hāla ba dzamā kār wu shī chi tah pakhpula hare khabare ta ghwag kkhkegde, aw darogh aw rikkhtiyā pa kkhke laṭawe. Dā mihrbāngī rā bāndi wu ka, aw biyā har rang ḥukm chi farmāye ba e manam. Qabūl mi dai pa dwāṛo stargo.

Well, squire, I have heard all your words and also have well understood them. And now it appears to me that in such affairs no good will issue to you. If, however, you will accept my advice I will give you some counsel. You say that your enemies have gained the ascendancy over you and are hounding you, and you fear lest you may commit some rash act that will criminate you with the Government. Such is your meaning, is it not?

Kkhah, khān, stā khabare mā ṭole āwredali dī, aw hum pre pa kkhah shān sara poh sham. Aw os rā ta kkhkāregī chi pa dā hase mu'āmalo kkhke stā kkhegaṛa ba wu na khejī. Nor, ki dzamā pand ākhle, zah ba darta yo naṣīhat kawam. Tah wāye chi dukkhmanāno di dar bāndi ghalaba mūndali da, aw dar pase spī lagawulī dī, aw tah yerege chi mabādā stā da lāsa tsa khaṭā wu na shī aw pa sarkār kkhke gunāhgār na she. Maṭlab di pa daghah shān dai ka na?

Yes, sir, the case is exactly such as you state. Now I need your favour and require guidance. Do me the kindness to show me a road by which I may free myself from these calamities, and I will be your slave.

Ho, ṣāhib, laka chi tā wayal jukht pa daghah shān ḥāl dai. Os stā da mraste ḥājatman yam, aw kkhowuna ghwāṛam. Dā mihrbāngī rābāndi wu ka, lār rāta wu kkhāya chi la deo balāwo na dzān khalāṣawum, aw ba stā mraʼe sham zah.

My advice then is to this effect, viz., that you go back again to your own village, and, having written the substance of the related particulars on white paper, send it to me, that it may remain with me; and then at whatever time any business of yours may come before me I shall be acquainted with it. Another point is this, viz., when you arrive at the village, see that you do not take part in the factions and parties. All these discords arise from factions and parties. You must bear in mind that you are a great man, honourable, and reputable, and, moreover, the lord of a manor. The whole tribe, as well as the common people look up to you; but if a man of your respectability mixes himself up in such trifling matters, how can those

Dzamā maṣlaḥat biyā pa dā dai, y'ane, chi tah biyā pa biyarta jārwūze khpul kilī ta, aw da dagho bayān kiṛi khabaro maṭlab, pa spīn kaghaz bāndi wukkhkalai, rāwulege chi rā sara e prot wī; biyā har wakht chi stā tsa kār rā ta pekkh shī zah ba pre khabar sham. Bul dā dai, y'ane, har wakht chi kilī ta wu rasege, gora chi pa paro janbo kkhke gūṛa na khwadzawe. Dā pasātūna wāṛah la paro janbo na porta kegī. Yād laral boya chi tah loe saṛai ye, da 'izzat aw da i'tibār khāwind ye, nor, bul, da tape khān ye. Ṭol ulas sara da 'ammiyāno starge tā ta nīwuli dī, lekin ki stā pa shān i'tibārī saṛai pa dāhase khusho khabaro kkhke dzān gaḍawī, biyā kampāyah, adnā aw nādān ba tina (*or* trena) tsa ranga khālī shī. Na, chi khpul qadr aw 'izzat ta

of low degree, the vulgar and the ignorant, be free from them. No, if you look to your own worth and honour you will refrain from such useless acts.

gore tah ba la 'abaṣo khabaro na dzān sāte.

You have spoken very well, sir, your speech is appropriate, and highly agreeable to me, it is, as it were, law to me. I am sick and tired of past troubles, and have besides been beggared by them. If you will not be angry, sir, I will speak plainly, for I have suffered incalculable loss in these numerous lawsuits.

Ḍer kkhah di wu wi, ṣāḥib, stā wayai pa dzāe dai, aw ḍer mi khwakkh shah, ganre rā bāndi sanad dai. La ter shawī rabṛūno na staṛai stomān yam, aw hum pa e khwār shwalam. Chi khapah kege na, ṣāḥib, spīna khabara darta kawam, wale chi dzamā pa dagho ḍero muqaddamo kkhke be shāna loe tāwān shawai dai.

How? I don't understand your drift. Tell me the particulars.

Tsa ranga? Pa maṭlab di poh na sham. Ḥāl rā ta wu wāya.

Well, sir, since it is your order, I will explain the case to you. The real fact is this, viz., that your law is a great ocean; multitudes are drowned in it. For instance, whoever once falls into it and is not an expert swimmer can with difficulty get out of it, and if ever he should reach the opposite shore it is with so great an injury that the remainder of his life is without enjoyment. If you desire another simile I will put it in a different form. Know then that law is like a great glutton, it has without measure a great maw, it is not satisfied with much wealth, however much is cast into it so much the more it wants, it does not fill; continually shouting, it cries, Give, give!

Kkhah, ṣāḥīb, chi stā ḥukm shawai dai, pa ḥāl bāndi ba di poh kṛam. Aṣla ma'nā dagha da, ya'ne, chi da stāso 'adālat yo loe daryāb dai, makhlūq pa kkhke ḍūbegī. Pa miṣāl, kūm saṛai chi yo dzal pa kkhke prewat aw pa lānbo e maṛanai na wī, haghah ba pa mushkil sara tina wūzī, aw ki chare dzān e pore ghāṛe ta wu rasawulai, dombra pa tāwān sara wushī, chi da dah pātai jwandūn da khwand na wī. Ki bul miṣāl ghwāṛe, ba pa bul shān darta wāyam. Ganre chi 'adalat pa miṣāl da yo loe ghāṛī dai, be kacha loya geḍa larī, pa ḍere duniyā na maṛegī, har tsomra chi pa kkhke āchawuli shī hombra ziyāta ghwāṛī, ḍakegī na; pa nāro lagiyā rākā rākā wāyī.

I understand, squire, it appears that your allusion has reference to bribes. I will show you a remedy for both similes. Firstly, he that is not a good swimmer has no right to throw

Pohegam, khān, m'alūmegī chi isharat de ṛa baḍo pore dai. Da dwāṛo miṣālūno dapāra tadbīr darta wakkhāyam. Awwal, kūm saṛai chi lānbozan na wī, boya chi khpul dzān na pāyābo obo ta

himself into deep water. Secondly, the man who is wise does not invite a big-bellied glutton to dinner.

e na dangawī. Dwayam, saṛai chi e 'aql-man wī, gedawar gharī ta sat na kawī.

Bravo, sir, you have given me excellent advice, but it is not to my purpose; as the proverb says, "The pain is in the belly of the potter, and you give the purge to his donkey."

Shābāshi, ṣāhib, der kkhah pand di rāta wu kkhowah, magar dzamā pa sūl wu e na shah, laka chi matal wāyī, "dard da kulāl pa gede shah aw kāmbela āchawe khrah ta."

Well, squire, if you have not benefited by it, I can say no more. It is now late; we have had a pleasant meeting together. Go you and rest yourself, and I will return to my own work. Good day, squire.

Kkhah, khān, chi stā kkhegaṛa pa e wu na sha, zah nor tsa na sham wayalai. Os nā wakht dai; kkhāyastah majlis mū sara wu kṛah. Tah lāṛ shah, aw ārām wu kā, aw zah khpul kār ta biyā girzam. Salām, khān.

God bless you, sir, may he keep your steps on high, and grant you possession of exalted rank. Then I may go? Good day, sir, I have committed you to the protection of God.

Khudāe di wu bakkha, ṣāhib, pāya di pa porta sātī, aw da loye martabe khāwind di kawī. Bāre lāṛsham? Salām, ṣāhib, da khudāe pa amān mi spāṛalai ye.

136. VILLAGE CHIEF AND CIVIL SURGEON.

Well, khān, now that our greeting is well concluded, I will inform you of my object. I am come for the purpose of vaccinating, and require your assistance.

Kkhah, khān, os chi dzamūnga joṛ-tāzā pa khair sara wu sha, zah ba di khpul maṭlab bāndi poh kṛam. Rāghlai yam dapāra da rag wahalo, aw stā kumak ghwāṛam.

With all my heart (both eyes), sir, give the order.

Pa dwāṛo stargo, ṣāhib, hukm wu farmāya.

Well, do you be so kind as to send three or four of your own men to traverse the different quarters of the town, and give notice at the several houses of each, that I have come for the purpose of vaccinating, and am seated in your hostelry.

Joṛ, tah dā mihrbāngī wukā, dre yā tsalor tana da stā khpul saṛī wulega, chi dwī da kilī pa kandīo kkhke di wu girzī, aw da har yo pa biyal biyal kor kkhke di khabar wu kāndi, chi falānkai dapāra da rag wahalo rāghlai dai, aw da khān pa hujre kkhke nāst dai.

Here, Shahbaz! do you go to Malik Rustam and say that our "doctor" has arrived with a couple of vaccinators. Let him collect the boys and babes

Hīsta, shāhbāza! Tah wardza rustam malik ta wu wāya chi dzamūnga "dāktar ṣāhib," sara da dwah tana rag-wahūnkī, rāghlai dai. Pa talwār di halakān

quickly, and bring them here with himself. Then go to Haji and the other parish beadles, and give them information also.

aw mashūmān ṭolawī, aw dzān sara di dale rāwulī. Biyā tah ḥājī aw noro malikānāno khatsa lāṛsha aw hagho ta hum pre khabar kā.

If I may put you the question, sir, why do you trouble yourselves so in this work of vaccination? What advantage is there in it? What medicine is this applied to the tips of these pins? But this is not a pin, why, it is glass, and there is something like water stuck in the tube. What contrivance is this?

Ki tapos tina kawam, ṣāḥib, tāso tsala dā da rag·wahalo pa kār bāndi dombra dzān rabṛawa-ī? Tsa fā-ida da pa kkhke? Dā pa dagho stano bāndi tsa dawā pori kiṛi da? Dā kho stan na da, joṛ, kkhīkkha da, aw tsa da obo ghundi shai pa nal kkhke nkkhatai dai. Dā tsa chal dai?

Give it to me, you will be breaking it.

Mā la rākā, tah ba e mātawe.

Now, if you will keep quiet a little, I will show you the advantages of this art; for in such an uproar nobody will hear a word.

Os, ki tāso la-agkūṭī ghalī kega-ī zah ba da de ḥikmat fā-ide tāso lara kkhkārah·kawam, wale chi pa dāhase zwag·zwūg kkhke da chā ghwag ba khabar na ākhlī.

Be silent, men! Listen, and hear the gentleman's words.

Chup sha-ī, maṛo! Ghwag kkhkegda-ī, aw da ṣāḥib khabare wāwra-ī.

Formerly there used to be a great deal of this small-pox disease in my country. Sometimes it was spread over one district, sometimes over another, and occasionally throughout the whole country. It is a dreadful plague. If it once gets into a village, there is then no escape from it. It invades house by house, and prostrates both the suckling and the weanling, the young and the old. It leaves no one. Either in youth or old age it attacks and breaks upon them. It is, indeed, a fearful calamity. Multitudes have perished by it.

Pakhwā dzamā pa waṭan kkhke dā da nanako randz ba ḍer kedah. Kala ba pa yawe tape, kala ba pa bule, aw kala nā kala ba pa ṭol mulk kkhke khwarai shah. Ḍera bada wabā da. Ki e yo dzal pa kilī kkhke gaḍa sha biyā tina khalāṣī nishta. Kor pa kor kkhke nanwūzī aw hum tankai hum zāṛai, hum dzwān hum zoṛ e parzawī. Hets tsok e na pregdī. Yā pa dzwānī yā pa zoṛwālī pre wu nkkhlī ·pre wu khejī. Yara, bashpaṛa balā da. 'Ālam pre qatl shawī dī.

He speaks truly. Your speech is quite true, sir; we know the fact.

Rikkhtiyā wāyī. Stā khabara rikkhtīni da, ṣāḥib, mūng ta ḥāl m'alūm dai.

There is no doubt about it. Now I will return to my own story. Well, you will remember I said that multi-

Hets pa kkhke shakk nishta. Os zah biyā khpule qiṣṣe ta rā wāwṛam. Joṛ, mā, da stāso ba yād wī, wuṛai chi

tudes had met an early death through the small-pox disease; but, in truth, this is only half the fact.	makhlūq da nanako pa bīmārtiyā bāndi dzwānīmarg shawī dī, magar dā, pa rikkhtiyā, nīmgaṛi khabara da.
Behold him! What does he say? He brings a man to his death, and still says that the work is yet incomplete. I seek repentance of my God.	Gora-ī warta! De tsa wāyī? Saṛai khpul marg ta rasawī, aw hum wāyī chi khabara lā nimgaṛi pāti da. Dzamā da khudāe toba da.
Have patience, my lad! Allow me to finish my sentence. I say that those persons who do not meet their end by the small-pox disease, are not left free of its marks. Some become stone blind by it, of others, only one eye is destroyed, and in the faces of many others are left the pockpits. In fact, beauty and fairness are spoiled by pits and scars. If you do not credit my statements, look to yourselves. How many persons may there be in this assembly? Altogether there are eighteen persons present. Well, now examine them, and make an account. Look at that. The mind credits it not, but I have proved it before your eyes (faces). Amongst them, two persons are blind of one eye, in the eyes of six persons there are scars, and there are pock-pits on the faces of fourteen persons? Is this a small amount of damage?	Wār wu kā, halaka! Pregda chi khpule khabare sar ta rasawam. Wāyam, chi kūm kasān chi e da nanako randz khpul ajal ta na rasawī, haghah khālī da nakkhe da da na pātī kegī. Dzane pre tap ṛāndah shī, da dzano ta-ash yawa starga wrāna shī, aw da noro ḍero pa makh kkhke ḍoghalūna da nanako pātī kegī. Ganre kkhāyast-wālai aw paimakh-tob pa ta-apo aw pa gulūno habatah shī. Ki dzamā pa khabaro bāndi bāwar di na kegī, khpulo dzānūno ta gora-ī. Pa de majlis kkhke ba tso kasa wī? Ṭol-ṭāl atahlas tana ḥāẓir dī. Kkhah, os wu e laṭawa-ī, ḥisāb kawa-ī. Dā wu gora-ī. 'Aql e na manī, magar mā e stāso pa makhā-makh zbād kṛah. Pa mandz kkhke, dwah tana pa yawe starge ṛāndah dī, da shpago tano pa stargo kkhke gulūna dī, aw da tswārlaso tano pa makh kkhke da ta-apo ḍoghalūna dī. Dā tsa la-ag nūqsān dai?
Really, sir, you are a very wise man. Bravo! for your intelligence.	Yara, ṣāḥib, ḍer 'aqlman saṛai ye. Shāh-bāsh stā pa hokkhyār-tiyā bāndi.
Have a little patience, I am going to tell you something more. In what manner, think you, did this art of vaccination, that we practise, originate? Shall I tell you the particulars? Well, pay attention. Formerly, there lived in my country a very clever physician, named Jenner. He	La-agkūtī ṣabr kawa-ī, tsa bule khabare darta kawam. Dā da rag wahalo ḥikmat chi mūng chalawū, pa tsa shān sara pohega-ī chi e jārī shah? Ḥāl wāyam tāso ta? Kkhah, ghwag kkhkegda-ī. Pakhwā, dzamā pa waṭan kkhke yo ḍer hokkhyār ṭabīb, jenar nūmāndai, osedah. Ḍer e da nanako randz wu līdah, aor e

saw a great deal of the small-pox pest, and further, he learnt this, that the "aura" of this disease, for the most part, had no effect upon the milkmaids. Much astonished, he applied himself to enquiry and search. At length, he examined the hands of the milkmaids, and found two or three pimples on them. Next he examined the cows' udders, and pimples were apparent on them also. He considered a great deal, and concluded in his mind, that if one were inoculated with the matter of the cow's pimple, he also would remain protected from this disease. He vaccinated a few with it. On each person a single vesicle rose. And subsequently it became known that these persons, like the milkmaids, were free from the small-pox, for it had no effect upon them. Next, taking the crust from the arm of one, he vaccinated with it on the arm of another, and with him the same phenomenon occurred. At length, the advantages of this new system became known amongst the people, and now everybody adopts it. This is the account, I have told it to you very briefly.

dā m'alūm kaṛ, chi akṣar pa ghobano bāndi, "bād" da da maraẓ hets pāzah na kawī. Hakk hariyān pa tapos aw pa laṭawul wu laged. Ākhir, lāsūna da ghobano wu e katal, nanaka-ī dwe dre pre bāndi biyā e mūndali. Biyā e ghulāndze da ghwāwo wu katali, aw nanaka-ī pre hum kkhkāre shwali. Fikr e ḍer kāwah, aw pa zṛah dā khiyāl wu e tāṛah, chi ki da chā rag da ghwāwo da nanako pa māde wahalai wai, haghah hum la de randz na ba panāh osedalai wai. Da tso tano rag pre wu e wahal. Pa har yo bāndi yawa yawa tanrāka wu khatala. Nor wrusto ma'lūm shah, chi laka ghobane dwī hum la ganro nanako na khalāṣ dī, wale chi pre bāndi hets aṣar e na kāndi. Biyā e da yo da lāsa khīg ākhistai ba pre da bul pa lāsa rag wahal, haghah sara hum daghah yo shān chal wu shah. Nor ākhir, fā-ide da daghah nawī ḥikmat pa ulas mashhūre shwe, aw os har tsok pre 'amal kāndi. Dagha qiṣṣa da, ḍera lanḍa me darta wayali da.

But this seems a very simple affair. What fools we are. We understand nothing. Our monks and friars inoculate after a different fashion. They dig a hole, with pins, in the skin of the wrist, then they powder a small-pox crust, and rub it into the wound. After the eighth or tenth day ten or a dozen other pimples

Dā kho ḍer āsān kār kkhkārī. Mūng tsa nādānān yū. Hets na pohegū. Dzamūnga pīrān aw miyāgān rag pa bul shān wahī. Dwī da maṛwand pa tsarmani kkhke yo ghār pa stano kanī, biyā da nanako postakī oṛah kāndi, aw pre bāndi magī. Pas yā pa atame yā pa lasame wradzi chār chāpera tina las yā dwah-las dāne nore wūkhejī, aw wasara

crop up round about it, and there is also more or less fever. Sometimes more and sometimes fewer pimples rise, and, occasionally, it has even happened, that confluent small-pox has broken out over the whole body. Another point is this, as soon as one child is inoculated, soon afterwards the small-pox becomes rife in the village and spreads to others. Babes and infants never escape it. If it be one's fortune, he recovers, but most of them die. Occasionally it attacks old people. These don't recover. Truly, it is a great pestilence.

la-ag ziyāt taba hum wī. Kala ziyāt, kala la-ag dāne khejī, aw kala nā kala dā hase hum shawai dai chi ganre nanaka-ī pa drust ṣūrat bāndi rākhatali dī. Bula khabara dā da, har wakht chi da yo halak rag wahalai shah, nor zir pre pase nanaka-ī pa kilī kkhke gaḍe shī, aw pa noro bāndi lagī. Māshūmān aw hala-kān tina hets chare na khalāṣegī. Ki da chā nāṣīb wī haghah raghegī, magar akṣar pre mṛī. Kala kala pa zaṛo bāndi hum lagī. Dwī na joṛegī. Yara bada balā da.

Our plan, you will perceive, is free from these faults, there is no fear in it. If we vaccinate in one spot, that single vesicle rises, if we vaccinate in two places, those two vesicles rise, and, without vaccination, it never spreads from one to another. The great advantage of our system is this, that whilst it prevents the small-pox, it injures nobody. The great fault of your plan is, that it of itself disseminates confluent small-pox, and is injurious to everybody who may come under the influence of the "aura" of the disease.

Dzamūnga ḥikmat, tah ba pohegī, la dagho 'aibūno na khālī dai, hets pa kkhke yera nishta da. Ki pa yo dzāe kkhke rag wahū, hagha yawa tanrāka khejī, ki pa dwo dzāyo wahū, haghe dwe tanrāke khejī, aw be da wa alu da rag, la yo na pa bul bāndi hets chare na e lagī. Loya fā-ida da dzamūnga da ḥikmat dā da, chi pa man'a kawulu da ganro nanako bul chā ta ziyān na rasawī. Loe 'aib da stāso da ḥikmat dā dai, chi pakhpula ganre nanaka-ī e khwara-ī kawī, aw ziyān har chā ta rasawī chi lāndi da aṣar "da bād" da da randz rāshī.

Here he is, Malik Rustam has come. How many little ones have you brought?

Daghah dai, malik rustam rāghai. Tso tana wṛūkī di rāwustī dī?

These are the three. I could not catch any others, they have all hidden themselves. All the mothers are crying, and say they will not have their children vaccinated by the European. They have all run into their huts with their babes and young ones, and closed the doors.

Daghah dre dī. Nor me nīwulī na shwal, ṭol puṭ shawī dī. Mainde ṭole pa jaṛā lagiyā dī, aw wāyī chi māng da māshūmāno khpulo rag pa farangī na wahū. Ṭole, sara da tanko aw wṛūkīo khpul khpul kor kkhke nanawatali dī, aw warūna e pore taṛalī dī.

Oh, wretches! May God destroy you! They are a brutal people, sir. What can I say to you?	Ai kambakhtāno! Khudāe di mırāt kāndi! Ḍanga-ar khalq dı, ṣāḥib. Tsa darta wāyam?
No, no, khan! Be not angry. It will be all right. At present the mothers are frightened. I will leave this man of mine with you here. He is clever at vaccinating. Besides, he is a trustworthy person, and also a monk. He will go from house to house and vaccinate. I entrust him, then, to your care.	Na, na, khāna! Khapah kega mą. Khaır ba shı. Dā sā'at ba mainde yeredali wı. Dā dzamā saṛai ba dale stā khatsa pregdam. Pa rag wahalu hokkhyār dai, bul, i'tibārı saṛai aw pır hum dai. Kor pa kor ba e girzı aw rag wahı. Nor e pa tā me spāralai dai.
I will now go. Call to somebody to bring my horse. Here he is, standing behind you.	Bāre dzam. Chā ta ghag wu kā, chi dzamā ās di rāwulı. Hāyah, pa shā di wulāṛ dai.
Will you not drink some sherbet, sir? It is ready.	Tsa sharbat na tskkhe, ṣāḥib? Tayār dai.
I have had plenty, khan, and can take no more. I will mount. Let go the reins. That will do. You are in the protection of God, khan. Farewell.	Ḍer me tskkhalai dai, khān, nor na sham tskkhalai. Swaregam. Mlūne pregda. Bas. Da khudāe pa amān ye khān. Salām.
Farewell, sir. God be with you, and good betide you.	Salām, ṣāḥib. Khudāe dar sara mal sha, darsha nekı.

137. A TRAVELLER AND PEASANT.

Stop, my man, where are you running to? Come this way a little while, I wish to speak to you.	Wudrega, halaka, cherta drūme? La-agkūṭı rāhista sha, khabare kawam darsara.
What is it? I cannot stay. I am going to plough, and my oxen have gone on ahead unguarded. I fear lest they should trespass on some strange field, and the watchman take a fine from me.	Tsa dai? Pātai kedai na sham. Īwe la dzam, aw ghwāyah (*or* ghwāyān) mi khūshı pa wṛānde talı dı. Weregam chi dwı chare pa pradı paṭı kkhke ga-aḍ na shı, aw kakkhai rā na nāgha wā na khlı.
Well, if there is a loss before you, go, run, and guard your own property. I can obtain my wish from somebody else. Another man is coming this	Kkhęh, ki di pa makh kkhke tāwān wı, lārsha, wuzghla, khpul māl sambāl kā. Zaḷ la bul chā na khpul maṭlab pūrah kawam. Bul saṛai :ā di khwā ta rādzı,

way; here he is, he is come. Now you go, run!	daghah dai, rāghai. Os tah dza, manḍe waha.
Be not fatigued. I ask a question of you.	Staṛai ma sha. Pukkhtana tina kawam.
Peace be upon you. Be not poor. It is well.	Salām alaikum. Makhwārega. Khair dai.
And upon you. That hill is my object, by which road can I get to it? How far may it be? Can I ride there?	Wa alaikum. Niyat mi da haghah ghra dai, pa kūme lāri ba wardzam? Tsom-bra ba liri wī? Spor ba halta talai sham?
This is the road, it is a good mule track. It goes straight to the foot of the hill, then turns to the left, and winds up to the top. It is a long road, and fully a day's journey. If you start at once you will scarcely reach its summit by the evening. Why are you going to the hill?	Lār dagha da, kkhāyasta da bārgīr lār da. Sama da ghra wekh ta tili da, biyā e kīnr lās ta girzedali da, aw pa kālkūcho sar ta khatali da. Liri lār da, pūrah da wradzi mazal dai. Ki os pre rawān she hila ba mākkhām pore sar ta wu rasege. Tsala ghra ta dze?
I go for the sake of a ramble; I shall hunt after plants, examine stones, and inspect the rocks; and when I reach the summit, will take a view of the plain from some elevated spot.	Sail dapāra dzam, būṭī pase ba girzam, kānrī ba laṭawam, da gaṭo tīgo tamāsha ba kawam; nor sar ta chi wu khatalam la kūm ūchat hask dzāe na ba da same nandāra kawam.
What plants will you go after? The alchemy plant does not exist in these hills; hitherto nobody has met with it. Besides, you cannot go up the hill.	Pa kūmo būṭo pase ba girze? Da kimiyā būṭai pa deo ghrūno kkhke nishta; chā e tar osa pore mūndalai na dai. Nor tah ba ghra ta khatai na she.
Why can't I go up? Who will prevent me?	Wale na sham khatai? Tsok ba mi man'a kāndi?
There are many obstructors. Are you not aware that there is a feud between the Gaḍuns and Khodokhels. Both are seated on the boundary line, and engaged in making reprisals one against the other.	Man'a kawūnkī ḍer dī. Khabar na ye, chi da gaḍano aw da khodokhelo tar mandza patna da. Dwāṛah pa brīd nāst dī, aw lagiyā yo tar bula bota bramta kāndi.
I have now heard this intelligence from your mouth, I was not aware of it before. How many days' news is it? How did the feud arise? On what	Os stā da khule mi dā khabara āwredali da, pakhwā tre khabar na wum. Da tso wradzo khabara da? Patna pa tsa shān para porta shiwi da? Dwī pa tsa

are they involved? On what matter have they become estranged?

nkkhatī dī? Pa kūme khabare bāndi wrān shawī dī?

A woman is at the root of the mischief. Amongst the tribe the rumour is current to the effect that a certain Gaḍūn, being in love with some Khodokhel's wife, eloped with her. But the Khodokhels, not accepting the substitute, have girded their loins for strife.

Wekh da pasāt kkhadza da. Pa ulas kkhke khabara dāhase gaḍa da, chi kūm gaḍūn da chā khodokhel pa kkhadze bāndi mayan shawai, matīja e bīwuli wa. Nor khodokhelo swara qabūlā na kṛali, mlā pa patno taṛalī dī.

How long will these matters endure? Why don't they settle the business by councils? Cannot an umpire or mediator be found?

Dā mu'amale tar kūma pore ba pā-egī? Muqaddama pa jirgo wale na khalāṣawī? Mandzgarai yā gwākkh-grandai tar mandza na paidā kegī?

God knows. At first a settlement was practicable, but now the case has grown serious, it will not be easily settled, because blood has been shed on both sides, and there has moreover been death on one side. Had the case been otherwise there were some hope, greater or less, of a settlement, but now it appears that there is still greater mischief ahead.

Khudāe zdah dai. Wṛūnbe ba rogha joṛa kedala, magar os muqaddama grāna da, pa āsāntiyā sara ba faiṣala na shī, dzaka chī da dwāṛo lorīo wīne toye shiwi da, aw bul da yo palaw marg hum shawai dai. Ki ḥāl pa bul shān wai, biyā da pakhulā-tob tsa la-ag ziyāt umed ba paidā kedah, magar os ma'lūmegī chi pa makh kkhke lā ziyāta wrānī shta.

How many deaths have occurred, and on whose side?

Tso margūna shawī dī, aw da chā da ṭarfa?

Really, I have not been informed by any one of the exact state of the case, but I have heard that two Gaḍūns have been killed by the Khodokhels, and six others wounded.

Yara, pa jukht ḥāl bāndi chā khabar na kṛalam, lekin āwredalai mi dai chi dwah tana gaḍānah khodokhelo wajalī dī, aw shpag tana nor e jobal kaṛī dī.

Has there been no loss of the Khodokhels?

Da khodokhelo tsa tāwān na dai shawai?

Yes, their blood has also flowed. They say that the Gaḍūns shot three Khodokhels with guns. Nobody has made mention of any death, though one of them was hit hard and carried away by head and heels. Some people say that a Khodokhel woman was also wounded. She was

Ho, da hagho wīne hum bahedali da. Wāyī, chi gaḍano dre tana khodokhel pa ṭopako wīshtalī dī. Da tsa marg chā bayān na dai kaṛai, magar yo pa kkhke sakht lagedalai zam zambolai e bīwulai wuh. Dzani 'ālam wāyī, chi yawa khodokhela hum jobala shwa. Oba e yowṛala tsakkhtan lara, chi pa lāri teredala chā

carrying water to her husdand, and as she passed along the road some Gaḍūn took a shot at her. Some say that the bullet struck the jar and broke it; others say no, it passed over and missed, but the woman, terrified, stumbled against a stone in her flurry and fell. But God knows as to the truth or falsehood.

gaḍūn pre bāndi guzār wu kaṛ. Dzeni tsok wāyī chi mardaka pa mangī wa-lagedala māt e kaṛ; dzani nor wāyī chi na tre ter watala, khaṭā shwa, magar kkhadza yeredali pa wār khaṭā-ī kkhke tīndak e pa gaṭe wu khwāṛah aw pre-watala. Nor khudāe khabar pa rikkh-tiyā aw pa darogh.

Well, it appears to me that they are regularly involved in war with each other. Up to the present time how many fights have there been?

Joṛ, rāta kkhkārī chi dwī kkhāyastah pa jang lagedalī sara nkkhatī dī. Tar osa pore ba tso jangūna shawī wī?

I don't know the number; in fact, there is no reckoning. They are continually fighting, night and day. There was a hard fight in the robbers' glen the day before yesterday. The Gaḍūns, with banners flying and drums beating, seized a place on the gap. The Khodokhels in the glen below, having built a breastwork in the side of the cliff, waved their standards at them, and sounded their clarions. Then both commenced a yelling and shouting at each other. At length the Khodokhels, with drawn swords and singing of songs, issued from their breastwork and made an attack upon the gap. The Gaḍūns fired their matchlocks at them, and gave them several volleys. The Khodokhels were unable to mount the gap; they made a great effort, but their endeavour did not succeed. Finally, they retreated, and turned back to the shelter of their breastwork.

Pa shumār khabar na yam, haḍo ḥisāb e nishta. Shpa aw wradz lagiyā jang kawī. Waṛama wradz pa ghlo dare kkhke yo sakkht jang shawai dai. Gaḍano nakkhe yastali, aw ḍamāme wahali, dzāe pa kanḍaw bāndi wu nīwa. Khodokhelo kkhkata pa dare da kamar pa ja-ī sangar wahalai, toghūna wara tsanḍal, aw sarnāyah warta ghagawul. Nor dwāṛah yo tar bula pa nāro pa chigho wu lagedal. Ākhir khodokhelo tūre yastali, aw sandare wayeli, la san-gara rā e wuwatal, aw pa kanḍaw bāndi halla wu e kṛala. Gaḍano pre bāndi ṭopakūna khalāṣawul, tso tso baṛūna e pre chalawul. Khodokhel pa kanḍaw bāndi na shū khatal; zor e ḍer kāwah, wale was e wu na chaled. Dwī ākhir rā pastanah shwal, aw pa wrusto da khpul sangar panāh ta wu e jār watal.

Then the Gaḍūns won the victory? For the retiring of the Khodokhels is a sign of their defeat.

Biyā oarai gaḍano biyāmūnd? Wale chi biyarta kedana da khodokhelo nakkha da laṛwālī da.

No, the Gaḍūns did not win the victory, they did not defeat the Khodokhels, for the latter, having prepared and arranged everything in the darkness of night, carried a night assault against them. They made a surprise, beat the Gaḍūns, and, dispersing them, seized their position. In the morning succour arrived for the Gaḍūns, and they then set out for the gap. The Khodokhels could not withstand them, and descended to their own breastwork.

Na, gaḍano barai biyā na mūnd, da khodokhelo larai wu e na kṛ, wale chi dwī-o, da shpe, pa tyāro kkhke, har tsa sambāl sātalai, pre bāndi sho-khūn yowṛ. Chapāo e wukā, gaḍānah e māt kṛal, tār pa tār e khwarī kṛal, aw dzāe da dwīo wā e khist. Ṣahār da gaḍano happa rā wurasedala, aw dwī biyā kanḍaw ta rā rawān shwal. Khodokhel warta ṭīng na shwal, khpul sangar ta rā kūz shwal.

Why did not they stand firm against them? They gained no advantage by the night attack, they troubled themselves fruitlessly about it.

Wale warta ṭing na shwal? Hets da sho-khūn fā-ida wu e na gaṭala. 'Abaṣa dzān pre bāndi rabṛawulī dī.

The forces of the Gaḍūns greatly increased, but succour for the Khodokhels had not yet arrived, therefore they returned to their own entrenchment. Further, two Gaḍūns were lying wounded in the Gaḍūns position at the time that the Khodokhels took it from them. The Khodokhels cut them to pieces with knives and swords. Verily, the Afghans fight fiercely.

Da gaḍano lakkhkar ḍer wu shah, magar da khodokhelo komak lā na wu rasedalai, dzaka dwī khpul morche ta jārwatalī dī. Nor, da gaḍano pa dzāe kkhke, haghah wakht chi khodokhelo tina wā e khist, dwah tana gaḍānah joba-al prātah wū. Khodokhelo dwī pa chāṛo pa tūro ṭoṭe ṭoṭe kawul. Yara, pukkhtānah bad jang kawī.

Engaged in conversation we have walked a considerable distance. What village is that? I am hungry and thirsty. Is there any one in this village who will invite me?

Pa khabaro lagiyā mūnga ḍera lār wahali da. Dā kūm kilai dai? Wagai tagai yam. Tsok shta pa de kilī kkhke chi ba mā ta sat kāndi.

Come, an acquaintance of mine resides in this village; he will feed us.

Rādza, dzamā pa de kilī kkhke yo pejandgalai osī; haghah ba dzamūnga ḍoḍa-ī wu kṛī.

Can one go about on that side of the village?

Da kilī haghe khwā ta tsok girzedai shī?

No, no one can move about on that side; robberies occur on the road, and robbers tramp the highways.

Ya, ākhwā ta hets tsok na shī girzedai; pa lāri shūke kegī aw ghlah lār wahī.

Welcome, welcome! Come, sit down. The food is ready; what will you eat? There is plenty of buttermilk; batter cakes with sugar are ready.

Har kala, har kala. Rādza, kkhkena. Doḍa-ī tayāra da; tsa ba khwuṛe? Shomle ḍere dī; prāte sara da gūṛe tayāre dī.

God pardon thee. God enlarge thee.

Khudāe di wu bakkha. Khudāe di loe kā.

Enough. I am satiated. More is distasteful to me. Thanks, praise be to God! Oh Lord unto thee be the praise.

Bas. Moṛ sham. Nor me sekan kegī. Shukr, alḥamdu-lillah. Rabba ṣanā tā lara.

Take away the water, throw it away.

Oba liri kā, toya e ka.

Have you a pipe?

Chilam lare?

We must go, there is a long journey before us.

Dzū (*or* mūnga ta tlal dai), pa makh kkhke loe pand dai.

Well, you are master of your own will. God be with you.

Kkhah, da khpul wak khāwind ye. Khudāe dar sara mal sha.

Accepted be thy prayer. Peace be unto you. And unto your peace.

Du'ā di shī qabūla. Salām alaikum. Wa alaikum salām.

138. HOSPITAL VISITATION.

What is the state to-day? Are all the sick well? Has any new patient come?

Tsa ḥāl dai nan? Randzūrān ṭol joṛ dī? Tsok nawai marīẓ rāghlai dai?

All is well, sir. Eight new patients have come, amongst them is one woman.

Khair khairiyat dai ṣāḥib. Atah tana nawī rāghlalī dī, pa kkhke yawa kkhadza da.

Seat them all in the porch. We will first make enquiry of the in-door people, and will inspect them afterwards together with the out-door patients. Take the pen and inkstand with you, and the prescription book also.

Ṭol wāṛah pa manḍaw kkhke kkhkenawa. Wṛūnbi ba da danana-wālo tapos kawū, biyā wrusto ba da dwīo nandāra kawū sara da bāhir-wālo. Qalam mashwānṛa-ī dzān sara wākhla, aw da nūskho kitāb hum.

How are you, 'Umar? Is your wound well? Remove the plaister from it that I may look at it. It appears to me that there is some dead bone inside it. Bring the instrument tray this way. What has become of that long probe? Here it is. Don't be afraid.

Tsa rang ye, 'umara? Parhār di joṛ dai? Paha tina liri kā chi tamāsha e kawam. Rāta kkhkārī chi danana pa kkhke tsa mṛāw haḍūkai dai. Da kālo shkarai rāhista ka. Hagha ugda stan tsa sha? Hāya da. Werega ma, 'umara. Da stan pa parhār kkhke nana bāsam, aw

'Umar. I am going to introduce this probe into the wound, and move it about a little to examine the bone. I will not hurt you much. There, it is done. There is some dead bone in it. Give me the forceps. See, this piece has come out. There is yet another bit. It is caught in the flesh, and I cannot extract it without cutting. Well, if it is your wish, we will leave it for the present. But mark this well; the bone will not by itself be free for many days. I will take it out in a moment, and you will not even feel the pain. I told you so. Wash the blood from it, and cover the wound.

pa kkhke ba la-ag·kūṭɪ khwadzawam chi haḍūkai laṭawam. Ḍer ba di na khūg-awam. Bas, wu shah. Tsa mṛāw ha-ḍūkai shta pa kkhke. Nūtsɪ lā la rā'ka. Gora, dā yawa ṭoṭa rā wu watala. Lā bula ṭoṭa shta. Hagha pa gwakkhe nkkhati da, be da tsɪralu na e sham wu kkhkalai. Kkhah, ki stā khwakkh wɪ, ba e dā sā'at pregdū. Lekin dā kkhah pohega; haḍūkai ba pakhpula tar ḍero wradzo pore bel na shi. Zah e ba pa ṭakɪ wu bāsam, aw pa dard bāndi ba poh hum na she. Mā e darta wu wai. Wɪne tina wɪndza, aw parhār puṭ ka.

And what do you say, reverend sir? Have you observed any benefit from yesterday's medicine? Give me the hand. Your pulse is good; it is a little weak. And what is the state of the cough? Do you cough in the same manner as before? As yet I have noticed no benefit in myself. My cough is in the former state. My phlegm does not cut, it is hardened. When I take a breath, cracklings arise in my chest. I cannot remain lying down by reason of my breathing becoming oppressed. Write a prescription for the priest. That is one dose. Give it him three times a-day that he may take it, and point out to him the diet and regimen.

Aw tah tsa wāye, mullā ṣāḥib? Da haghe parūna-ɪ dawā bāndi stā tsa kkhegaṛa m'alūma shwa? Lās rāka. Nabẓ di joṛ dai; yo la-ag shān ta kamquwat dai. Aw da tūkhɪ tsa ḥāl dai? Laka pakhwā pa haghah shān tūkhege? Tar osa pore hets da kkhegaṛe pa dzān poh na sham. Tūkhai mi pa haghah pakh-wānɪ ḥāl dai. Balgham mi na ghwuts-egɪ, khiyam shah. Chi sāh ākhlam, pa sɪne mi shrangahār khejɪ. Mlāst na sham osedalai, da de la kabla chi sāh mi ḍūbegɪ. Mullā dapāra nuskha wu-lɪka (*or* wu kkhka). Dā yo khwurāk dai. Dre guzāra da wradzi wala warka, chi wu e di khwuṛɪ, aw pāl parhez warta wukkhāya.

How is he with the eye? Undo the bandage. Open the eye very gently. Look at me. Do you see me? How many fingers do I hold up to you?

Dā da starge khāwind tsa rang dai? Pa-ṭa-ɪ prānadza. Starga ḍer pa ro ro wrghwarawa. Māta gora. Wɪne me? Tso gūte mi darta nɪwuli dɪ? Biyā

Say again. How many are there? He has indeed got his sight. Close the eye. Tie it up again. Now see that you don't move, and don't even think of rising or talking. Remain lying straight on the back, like a corpse, for three days more. Shall I get my sight, sir? There is some hope, for there has been a slight improvement from the first state.	wāya. Tso dı? Da dah nazar kho wu shah. Starga puta ka. Biyā e wu tara. Aw gore chi wu na khwadze, aw da pātsedu yā da khabare kawulu khiyāl hum ma lara. Da murı pa shān, tār dreo wradzo pore stūnı-stagh prot osa. Nazar ba mi wu shı, ṣāhib? Tsa umed shta, wale chi la wrūnbanı hāl na tsa la-aga la-aga fā-ida shiwi da.
How goes it with you, Tūrān Shah? Has the purge of yesterday taken effect? Well. I have been to the closet six times. I have had three good watery stools, and three indifferent motions. I am somewhat better to-day, and have derived some ease. But that pain in my joints does not go. I have swallowed a deal of your physic, but have not got well upon it. It may not be my fate, hence. What more can I say to you? You have a little patience. This rheumatism is a very troublesome disease, and is not quickly got rid of. I will give you a liniment to-day; dip your fingers into it, and then rub the hand over the joints. In the evening, when you lie down to sleep, I will give you another medicine. Swallow it with a gulp of water, at bed time, and draw a quilt over yourself so as to perspire.	Tā sara tsa ranga teregı, tūrān shāh? Haghah parūnai jār pāzah karai dai? Kkhāyastah. Shpag guzāra chār-chobe ta talai yam. Dre kkhah da jullāb dastūna mi shawı dı, aw dre hera be khwanda nāst yam. Nan tsa la-ag shān jor yam, tsa āsāntiyā mi shiwi da. Wale dā da bandūno dard mi wrūkegı na. Stā dawā mā dera tskkhali da, magar pre jor shawai na yam. Naṣıb ba mi na wı, dzaka. Nor tsa wāyam darta? Tah la-ag-kūtı ṣabr wukā. Dā da bād bımārtiyā chi da, dera sakhta nājortiyā da, aw pa zir na liri kegı. Nan ba dala yo tel dar kawam; tah khpule gūte pa kkhke wu waha, aw biyā lās pa bandūno bāndi wu maga. Mākkhām chi khob ta tsamle, ba bula dawā dar kam. Mākhustan, pa gūt da obo sara ter e kā, aw brastan pa dzān rā wāchawa chi khwale she.
And what is your state, old man? Has the purging ceased? Have the gripes been stopped? Oh sir! I am dead. I have been sitting at stool the whole night. Blood and mucus pass from me mixed up together. I am burst with gripes, my bowels are lacerated.	Aw stā tsa hāl dai, spın-gıriya? Dastūna di wudredalı dı? Kānge di band shiwı dı? Ai ṣāhiba! mūr sham. Kara-ı shpa pa lāsto nāst yam. Wıne aw ra-ame gade wade rā na prewūzı. Pa kāngo wu chāwdalam, larmānah mi ghwuts shwal.

I am fallen from my guard, and have no more strength. My patience and endurance are both exhausted. For the sake of God pay attention to me. Really, I am dying; I cannot last. Don't give way, my good man. You will recover, please God. We will attend to you carefully, and for the rest our reliance is on God. Cheer up. Brace up.

La brama prewatalam, nor mi ṭāqat na kegī. Ṣabr zgham mi dwāṛah khalāṣ dī. Da khudāe da pāra dzamā ghaur wukā. Zah kho, rikkhtiyā, mṛam; pātai keʼdai na sham. Wār khaṭā kega ma kākā. Joṛ ba she, ki khudāe kṛī. Mūng ba stā kkhah khidmat kawū, nor bāqī tawakkul mū pa khudāe dai. Dzān ṭing ka. Takṛah shah.

How are you, Sanobar? Does your heart palpitate in the same way? Your complexion is very yellow (or sallow).

Tsa rang ye, sanobara? Zṛah di pa haghah shān pṛakegī? Rang di kho ḍer ziyaṛ dai.

I have observed no change. When I rise from a place, darkness comes over my eyes, and my head swims. I cannot go at all quickly, and when at any time I mount an ascent my heart flutters, I become nervous. My appetite is locked, I have no desire for food. If I eat a single mouthful, my belly at once swells, it does not digest. Moreover my face and feet are swollen.

Hets pa farq poh na sham. Chi la dzāya pātsam, tyārah pa stargo rādzī, aw sar mi girzī. Hets pa gaṛandī na sham talai, aw chi chare pa lwaṛa khejam zṛah mi dṛadzegī, wār khaṭā kegam. Ishtihā mi banda da, ḍoḍa-ī khwā ta mi na kegī. Ki yawa nwaṛa-ī wu khwuṛam, geḍa me pa haghah sā'at paṛsegī, haẓmegī na. Nor makh pkkhe mi paṛsedalī dī.

And do you say nothing of the spleen? Is it in the same state, large and heavy?

Aw da torī tsa khabar na kawe? Haghah shān dai, loe aw drūnd?

No, my spleen is somewhat better than the previous state. Some change has come in its weight and size; it is become somewhat lighter.

Na, torai mi la haghah pakhwānī ḥāl na tsa joṛ shān ta dai. Pa dranāwī aw pa ghat-wālī kkhke tsa farq rāghlai dai; tsa qadr spuk shawai dai.

We call your disease Anœmia. The salts of iron are very beneficial for it.

Stā maraz ta mū jolcha wāyū. Da dah pa ḥaqq kkhke da ospane jauha-ar ḍer fā-ida-man dī.

What man is this? When did he come?

Dā kūm saṛai dai? Kala rāghlai dai?

He came yesterday afternoon, and appears, as it were, demented.

Pārūn māzdīgar rāghai, aw saudā-ī ghondi kkhkārī.

Who are you, my lad? What is the matter with you?

Tsok ye halaka? Dar sara tsa shawai dai?

Look you at my pulse and tell me my state. I came yesterday, and have taken some medicine, but have felt no benefit.

Tah nabz wugora, aw ḥāl rāta wāya. Pārūn rāghlai yam, aw tsa dawā mi khwuṛali da, lekin hets pa kkhegaṛe poh na gham.

We are not diviners that we should recognize a disease simply by looking at one. Your disease can only be ascertained when you have explained the symptoms to us, etc.

Zbargān na yū chi ta-ash pa kātah da saṛī randz pejanū. Hāla ba stā maraz pejandai shī chi tah khpul ḥāl rāta bayānawe, etc.

Now come, let us inspect the out-door ones.

Os rādza chi da bāhir-wālo nandāra kawū.

Your head aches, and if you eat food or drink water you vomit? Show the tongue. Enough. Put it in. How are the bowels? His stomach is hard, he is costive. Give him a purge. I have asthma. Do you smoke? Did you ever smoke formerly? You require an emetic. Drink plenty of tepid water after it till vomiting come on. The phlegm will fall with the ejections, and your chest will be freed.

Sar di khūgegī, aw ki ḍoḍa-ī khwuṛe yā oba tskkhe jārbāse? Jiba wukkhāya. Bas. Nana-e-bāsa? Saḥrā ta tsa ranga kkhkene? Geḍa e klaka da, qabz kkhkenī. Jullāb warka. Sāh-lanḍī mi kegī. Chilam tskkhe? Pakhwā di chare tskkhāwah? Da jāryastalu dawā ghwāre. Pre pase taṛame obe ḍere wu tskkha chi qai darshī. Pa chālūno ba di balgham prewūzī, aw sīna ta di āzāda shī.

There is a scar in his right eye. It is exactly over the pupil, and is also dense. Close the other eye. He sees nothing. He is stone blind in that one eye. You cannot be cured at my hands.

Da dah pa kkhī starge kkhke gul dai. Jukht pa kasī bāndi dai, aw ghaṭ hum dai. Bula starga puṭa ka. Hets na wīnī. Ṭap ṛūnd dai pa daghe ṛawe starge. Stā 'ilāj dzamā da lāsa na kegī.

Why he also is afflicted in the eyes. Both are bleary. Here, come close to me. Your upper eyelids are inverted. The eyelashes are all laid against the eyeball. This can be cured. It requires cutting and stitching.

Joṛ de hum pa stargo randzūr dai. Dwāṛe lechane dī. Hista, rāta nijde sha. Portani zegme dí danana khwā ta aṛawuli dī. Bānre ṭole pa starghālī bāndi lagedalī dī. Da dah 'ilāj ba wushī. Prekawul aw ganḍal ghwāṛī.

My water scalds and dribbles from me drop by drop. These are symptoms of stone. Lie down on that cot, get straight on the back. Don't fear, I

Baul mi swadzi, aw tsātske tsātske rāna prewūzī. Dwī kho da gīṭa-ī 'alāme dī. Pa haghah kaṭ bāndi wu gazega, stūnī stagh sha. Werega ma, ḍer ba di na

won't hurt you much. Yes, th re is a stone. Do you hear? It sounds when I hit it with the sound. There is no fear. I will make you insensible with medicine, and you shall know nothing about it.	khūgawam. Ho, gīṭa-ī shta. Āwre? Chi sīkh pre waham, ghagegī. Hets yera nishta. Pa dawā ba di be-hokkh kawam, aw pre khabar ba hum na she.
I am weak and decrepid, and my sight also is very defective. Well, I will tell you more. You are deaf and white bearded also. Open the mouth. See, he is even toothless. These are all signs of old age. You are not ill, my good man; you are quite well. Don't suppose that you will again be a young man. Thank God you have lived so long, and repent of your past sins.	Kam quwat aw ṭap yam, naẓar mi hum ḍer kam dai. Kkhah, zah darta nor wāyam. Kūnr āw spīn-gīrai hum ye. Khula di wīta ka. Gora, kanḍās hum dai. Dwī wāṛe nakkhe da zoṛ-wālī dī. Randzūr na ye kākā; jik joṛ ye. Dā ma pohega chi biyā dubāra ba dzwān she. Khudāe ta shukr wu bāsa chi tar daghah 'umr pore pā-edalai ye, aw da ter shawī gunāhūno toba wubāsa.

139. SPORTING DIALOGUE.

Oh Mārifat Shah. Come here. Be quick.	Ai m'arifat shāh, dalta rāsha, zir sha.
Coming, sir. Here I am.	Dardzam, ṣāḥib, darāghlam.
Not to-morrow, but the day after, early in the morning, we shall go out for sport. We are three gentlemen; now you see to the sporting apparatus, and have everything prepared at the appointed time.	Sabā na, bul sabā, sahār wakhtī ba kkhkār la dzū. Dre tana ṣāḥibān yū; os tah da kkhkār kālo ta wu gora, aw har tsa sara pa neṭe pore taiyār sambāl sāta.
Very good, sir. In which direction will you go? After what game, and for how many days shall you go?	Ḍera kkha da, ṣāḥib. Kūme khwā ta ba lārsha-ī? Kūm kkhkār pase, aw da tso wradzo dapāra ba dza-ī?
We will first go to Paja hill after wild goat, and then when we have come down the hill we will shoot bartavelle, grey partridge, or quail, and will return home either on the sixth or seventh day. Take both my guns with you, and put four cans of powder, and twenty or twenty-five	Wṛunbe ba da paje ghar ta dzū ghartso pase, aw biyā chi la ghra na rā kūz shwalū da zarko, da tanzaro, yā da mṛazo kkhkār ba kawū, nor yā pa shpagame yā pa awwame wradzi ba biyā kor ta rā rawān shū. Dzamā dwāṛah ṭopakūna dzān sara yosa, aw tsalor kūpa-ī da dārū, aw yā shil yā

bullets for the rifle, and two or three bags of shot for the other guns, into the wallet. And tell the hawkmen that they must come after us.

pindzah-wısht dāne da mardako haghah rakhdār bandūkh dapāra, aw dwe yā dre taila-ī da charo haghah bul topak dapāra, pa dzola-ı kkhke kkhkegda. Aw bāzwānāno ta hum wāya, chi dwı li rāshı mūnga pase.

Very well, sir. Since you go out a sporting for a week I will take the large and small tents with me, and the pointer, and both horses with their gear; and the servants and attendants all collected together I will take also with me. And if so be the order I will take expenses for the road from the treasurer, and conceal it in the mule pannier with the clothes.

Ḍer kkhah dai, ṣāḥib. Nor chi tāsu ba da hafte pore kkhkār ta wūza-ı zai ba khaima aw dera dzān sara wṛam, aw khandai spai, aw dwāṛah asūna sara da asbāb, aw nokar chākar hum, tol yo dzāe malgarı kaṛı, ba dzān sara biyāyam. Aw ki ḥukm dāhase wı da lāri kharts ba la khizānchı na wākhlam, aw ba e pa yakh-dān kkhke puṭ kawam.

You have said it exactly, do so and start at noon to-morrow. And see, when you arrive at the village pitch the tents somewhere outside on clean bare ground, and be careful that you do no violence, or have no quarrelling or wrangling with the people of the village. Whatever you want of them, such as fowls, butter, fodder, or anything else, see that you take it for cash payment, and be careful not to trespass in the fields or gardens. Further, give my compliments to the chief malik of the village, tell him that I am coming, and shall require sixteen or twenty beaters of him, and let him understand that he must provide good experienced men.

Jukhta khabara di wu kṛala, daghah hase wu kā, aw sabā ghārmah rawān sha-ı. Aw gora, har kala chi kilı ta wurasa-ı dere chare pa spıne ḍāge bāndi wu drawa-ı, aw pahm kawa-ī chi tāsu da kilı khalq sara tsa zor ziyātı, yā tsa jagra steza wu na kawa-ı. Har tsa chi la dwıo na ghwāṛa-ı, laka chirgān, ghwaṛı, wākkhah, yā nor tsa, gora-ı chi pa rok wā e khla-ı, aw khabardār sha-ı chi pa paṭo yā pa bāghūno kkhke wı na girza-ı. Aw bul, da kilı mashar malik ta dzamā salām wāchawa, aw wāya warta chi falānkai rātlūnai dai, aw ba tina yā shpāṛas yā shil kasa kkhkāriyān ghwāṛı, nor tah e poh kṛah chi kkhah balad saṛı di paidā kāndi.

May you not be fatigued, sir. You are well come.

Staṛai ma sha, ṣāḥib. Pa, khaira ṛāghlai ye.

May you not be poor, oh Malik. Are you well? Where is our tent pitched? Show me the way to it.

Ma khwārega, malika. Joṛ ye? Dzamūnga dera kūm dzāe wudrawalī da? Lār e rāta wu kkhāya.

It is on that side of the village; go on,

Da kilı haghe khwā ta da; tah dza, dar-

I am with you. This is my hostelry, do the kindness, dismount here. Breakfast is ready, and the cots drawn out are placed outside.

sara yam. Dagha dzamā hujra da, mihrbāngī wukā, ḍale kūz sha. Ḍoḍa-ī taiyāra da, aw kaṭūna rāyastalī bāhir īkkhī dī.

Your kindness is great, Malik. We go to our own tents. Who is the chief of this village? You are? That is very good news. Have you collected the twenty beaters?

Stā mihrbāngī ḍera da, malika. Dzū khpulo ḍero ta. Da de kilī mashar tsok dai? Tah ye? Dā kho ḍera kkha khabara da. Haghah shil tana kkhkā-riyān di rā ṭol karī dī?

Long ago. They are all present, and seated there at the tents with your men.

Larghūne. Ṭol ḥāẓir dī, halta pa ḍero stā saṛīo khatsa nāst dī?

You have done very well. There they are, our tents are in sight. Now you stay behind, Malik, and after a while come to my tent, and we will have consultation together. Then it is agreed that, it being too late to-day, we cannot ascend the hill. We will start to-morrow at cock-crow, and if all is well will pass the night on the hill. This is the best plan. Oh men, do you go and cook your dinners, we will go up the hill in the morning.

Ḍer kkhah di wu kṛah. Haghe dī, dzamūnga dere rā kkhkāre shwe. Os tah pātai sha, malika, aw biyā drang sā'at pas dzamā dere lara rāsha, aw mū ba sara jirga wu kawū. Bāre maṣlaḥat pa dā dai, chi nan nā wakht shawai dai, ghra ta na shū khatalī. Sabā char-bāng ba mūng rawānegū, aw chi khair wī ba pa ghra ḥāndi shpa tera kṛū. Dagha ghwara da. Ai saṛīo, tāsu lāṛ-sha-ī, aw khpule khpule ḍoḍa-ī pakhe kṛa-ī, saḥār ba ghra ta khejū.

Come by this path. The ascent is difficult on that side; in fact, one cannot ascend by it. The reason of it is this, that the cliff on that side rises straight up to the sky, and there is no path. Even this road is not free from trouble, for there is the fear of snakes in that dense herbage, and in many places, by reason of the dry leaves, the ground is so slippery that many persons have fallen down on it. If one's foot were to slip on the edge of the cliff he is lost, for the ground slopes very suddenly, and then drops in a sheer precipice to a great deep

Pa de lāri rādza. Haghe khwā ta khātah grān dai; haḍo tsok pre na shī khatai. Sabab e dā dai, chi haghe khwā ta kamar negh khatalai dai āsmān ta, aw lār nishta. Dā lār hum khālī da wiswāsa na da, wale chi pa dagho ganro wākkho kkhke yera da mārān wī, aw dzāe pa dzāe da wucho pānro la kabla zmaka khwa-enāka dāhase da, chi ḍer saṛī pre khwa-edalī dī. Ki da chā pkkha pre da kamar da ĵa-ī khwā ta wu khwa-edala, haghah wruk shah, wale chi zmaka ḍer zir pa rewand tili da, aw biyā sama pa kkhkata yo loe star gaṛang ta prewati da. Har tsa chi

abyss below. Whatever slips on it falls into the abyss, and is broken, and becomes smashed to atoms; in fact, is utterly destroyed; its very dust is not perceived, so far down is the depth.

pre wu lwedah, garang ta prewūzī, aw māṭegī, ḍare ḍare shī; haḍo, fū fanā shī; da dah ḍūre hum na m'alūmegī dombra liri pa kkhkata jawar dai.

It must indeed be a stiff hill. It seems to me the ascent of it will be difficult. You go in front, I will keep behind you. Go slowly, I cannot mount so fast. My breath shortens and my calves have given way. Is that the top of the ridge? Well, let us rest a while, and take a little breath.

Dā kho ba be-shāna zig ghar wī. Rā ta kkhkārī chi khātah ba pre grān wī. Tah makh kkhke sha, zah ba darpase yam. Ro ro dza, dombra pa talwār na sham khatai. Sāh mi lanḍ lanḍ kegī, aw spīne mi wilī shwe. Dā da kamar sar dai? Kkhah, mūng ba yo sā'at pore ḍaḍa lagawū, aw la-ag-kūṭī dama kawū.

On which ridges do the wild goat usually wander? Do you see that peak, the one on the summit of which a stone is standing upright? Yes, I see it.

Ghartsa-ah akṣar pa kūmo kamaro bāndi girzī? Dā tsūka wīne, hagha chi pa sar e ṭīgr negha wulāṛa da? Ho, wī-nam e.

Tell the beaters to go along the brow side and ascend to that peak, and then, forming line, to come down towards us. We will lie here in wait, and when the wild goat pass along the road will have our shot at them.

Kkhkāriyāno ta wuwāya chi dwī pa daghe tselme ja-ī di dzī, aw haghah sar ta di wu khejī, biyā para taṛali pa kkhkata di rāwāwṛī. Mūng bā dale pasūnai nīwulai kkhkenū, aw har kala chi ghar-tsah pa lāri teregī ba pre guzār wu kawū.

Are the wild goat many or few on this hill? At this season there are not many, for the villagers, every day, roam over the hills in search of fuel and fodder, and some few also shoot over them, thus the wild goat, being frightened, depart and dwell in the higher ridges.

Ghartsa-ah pa daghah ghar bāndi ḍer yā kam wī? Pa daghe mūde kkhke ba ḍer na wī, wale chi da kilī khalq hara wradz pa ghruno bāndi bālanr aw wākkho pase girzī, aw dzane yo nīm pre bāndi kkhkār hum kawī, pas ghar-tsa-ah tre tarhedalī lwuṛī, aw pa uchato kamaro bāndi-osī.

Here he is, look, he comes, do you see? This side, here, to the left hand. Do you not see his antlers above that red bush? He is a large he-goat. Wait a little. He will come close to

Hāyah dai, wugora, rādzī, wīne? De khwā ta, dale, kīnr lās ta. Kkhkar e na wīne haghah sūr ḍakī da pāsa? Ghat wuz dai, La-ag-kūṭī wār wu kā. Os ba mūnge tā nījde shī. Pa wulī wu wula-

us presently. Aim at the shoulder. He is come, make haste, fire at him. Hit! well done! Give me a knife that I may cut his throat. He has very fine long and twisted horns, and see what a beautiful long beard this is.	Rāghai, zir shah, guzār pre wukā. Wulaged! shābāsh! Chāṛa lāla rāka chi ḥalāl e kawam. Ḍer kkhah ūgd kkhkarūna larɪ, aw gora tsa ranga kkhāyaṛta ūgda gīra e da.
L k out! another is coming. I saw him just now when he turned this way from that spur. Here, what is that under the white boulder? Gone! he is off! missed!	Pahm ka! bul rādzɪ. Os mā e wulɪdah chi la haghah kamara rā de khwā ta e girzedah. Hista, dā tsa dai lāndi tar haghe spīne gaṭe? Lāṛ! wu e lwukkht! khaṭā sha!
What men are those? They are coming this way in one mass. Sing out and ask them who they are.	Haghah kūm saṛɪ dɪ? Ganr rā de khwā ta drūmɪ. Nāre waha, aw pukkhtana ka chi tāsu tsok ya-ɪ?
It seems to me that they are our own beaters. Having come down the hill they have united together, and are now coming to join us. Without mistake it is them. I recognize them. They are come, see, they have arrived.	Rāta kkhkārɪ chi dzamūnga khpul kkhkāriyān dɪ. La ghra na rā kūz shawɪ, yo dzāe ṭol shawī dɪ, aw os rā rawān dɪ chi mūng khatsa di gaḍ shɪ. Bedū hagha-ah dagha-ah dɪ. Zah e pejanam. Raghlal, gorah, rā rasedalī dɪ.
Be ye not fatigued. How many persons are left behind?	Staṛɪ ma sha-ɪ. Tso tana wrusto pātī dɪ?
May you prosper. Nobody is left, all are here. Has any one a pipe? Here is one, take it. Don't you smoke? Will you smoke? It is very agreeable.	Loe sha. Hets tsok pātai na dai, ṭol dalta dɪ. Chā tsakha chilam shta? Hāyah dai, wā e khla. Chilam na tskkhe? Tah tskkhe? Ḍer khwand-nāk dai.
Arise, come, let us go. The descent is easy, we shall soon reach the tents; there is yet some sun. As long as there is sun there is light. Come forward two men. Tie this goat by the head and heels to a pole, and convey it down to the tents.	Pātsa-ɪ, rādza-ɪ chi dzū. Kūzedah āsān dai, zir ba dero ta wu rasegū; nwar lā shta. Hombra chi nwar wɪ ranrā wɪ? Wṛānde sha-ɪ dwah tana saṛɪ. Dā wuz zam zambolai pa largɪ bāndi wu taṛa-ɪ, aw kūz dero ta wu rasawa-ɪ.
It is a large goat, nay, huge, and monstrously heavy. Who shot him? The European? He is a good sportsman. Verily, the Europeans are all good sportsmen.	Ghaṭ wuz dai, wale nāpaṛ dai, aw be shāna drūnd. Chā e wɪshtalai dai? Farangɪ? Kkhah kkhkārɪ saṛai dai. Yara, farangiyān ṭol kkha-ah kkhkārɪ saṛɪ dɪ.

Be quiet, my lad. He is called the civil officer. Nobody calls them Europeans to their faces, because they dislike it.	Chup sha, halaka. Haghah pa mulki ṣāhib yādegī. Dwīo ta tsok pa makhā makh farangai na wāyī, wale chi bad e manī.
Speak of him as "master."	Pa "ṣāḥib" warta yādawa.
I am sorry for it. I was not aware. What do you think, will he be angry with me?	Dzamā pre toba da. Khabar na wum Tah tsa ganre, haghah ba rāta qa kāndi?
It is all right, lad, he also is unaware, for he does not understand Pukkhto.	Khair dai, halaka, haghah hum khabar na dai, wale chi pa pukkhto na pohegī.

THE END.